TEACHERS

By Catherine Collins and Douglas Frantz

SELLING OUT

By Douglas Frantz

FROM THE GROUND UP
LEVINE & CO.

TEACHERS

TALKING OUT OF SCHOOL

CATHERINE COLLINS AND
DOUGLAS FRANTZ

LITTLE, BROWN AND COMPANY

BOSTON   NEW YORK   TORONTO   LONDON

First Edition

Library of Congress Cataloging-in-Publication Data

Collins, Catherine.
    Teachers : talking out of school / Catherine Collins, Douglas
Frantz.—1st ed.
       p. cm.
    ISBN 0-316-29266-4
    1. Teachers—United States—Attitudes. 2. Teachers—United
States—Interviews. 3. Teaching. I. Frantz, Douglas. II. Title.
LB1775.2.C65 1993
371.1′00973—dc20   93-13487

10 9 8 7 6 5 4 3 2 1

RRD-VA

*Published simultaneously in Canada
by Little, Brown & Company (Canada) Limited*

Printed in the United States of America

To teachers everywhere
and in memory of
Frances G. Heaney

CONTENTS

TEACHERS

INTRODUCTION

THIS BOOK, in which America's teachers use their own words to describe the deep troubles and resilient hope that are realities in schools today, grew out of plans for the education of our two youngest children. We are believers in public education, and we were determined that they would attend public schools.

When we moved from Los Angeles to Alexandria, Virginia, a city of more than a hundred thousand across the Potomac River from Washington, D.C., we began to evaluate Alexandria's public schools. The city's mix of blacks, whites, and Hispanics offered a chance for integration to work, and its public high school, T. C. Williams, had an outstanding reputation. However, we also found problems. Test scores were low and dropping, and classrooms were crowded with disruptive students. The district's schools had been left to cope with more than their share of disadvantaged children because middle-class families, black and white, had abandoned them for the suburbs or private schools. At the cooperative preschool our children attended initially, many of the mostly white, affluent parents were shocked that we would even consider the city's public schools, given the well-publicized difficulties.

The nation's public schools — in the inner city and prosperous suburbs alike — are in deep trouble, trouble more serious than we realize. A decade after a presidential commission warned in the landmark report *A Nation at Risk* of a "rising tide of mediocrity" in education, the very fabric of the system that promised progress and hope for generations is unraveling quickly, perilously, and perhaps irrevocably. The explosion of drugs and violence on the streets has reverberated in the classrooms. Societal and economic changes have led to the highest number of dual-income families in our nation's history, which means the largest number of children being cared for outside the home and left unattended after school. Parents have less time to supervise homework and nurture and monitor academic progress. There are increasing multitudes of at-risk, turned-off, left-behind children. Indeed, our very future is at risk.

Yet we are also in the midst of a ferment of reform. The private sector is offering its own prescriptions for revitalizing education. Entrepreneur Chris Whittle and his Edison Project plan to create a private, for-profit school network for two million students on a thousand campuses, with the first schools scheduled for 1996. Whittle's ambitious and controversial program would educate children from birth to age eighteen, with high-tech desks and other radical plans.

Other for-profit companies, such as Education Alternatives, are operating schools from Maryland to Florida. In the fall of 1993, groups ranging from Outward Bound to the small Illinois town of Bensenville opened schools redesigned according to guidelines from the New American Schools Development Corporation, a nonprofit group affiliated with business and organized in 1991 at the urging of the administration of former president George Bush. Such plans offer models for wide-scale reform, although they are largely untested. For instance, the Outward Bound curriculum will be built on a series of expeditions by students and teachers.

Reform is alive on a smaller scale, too. Across the country, educators are trying to change schools one at a time. Detroit and Milwaukee have created Afrocentric schools designed to create self-esteem for a generation of black students on the brink of being lost. More than half the schools in Dade County, Florida, have redistributed power radically to give teachers and parents a genuine role in running the school, from making decisions on hiring to allocating budget resources.

Magnet schools, which offer specialized education programs to students across district boundaries, are available in almost every state in the nation. Implementation varies: Some districts accept students by lottery, while others require testing. The theory has been that by offering a single school where the curriculum emphasizes a single subject, such as science or the arts, public schools can retain the brightest students. A recent innovation on the concept was introduced in Cambridge, Massachusetts. Three special programs have been created to appeal to a cross section of the community: a computer-oriented school, an enrichment program for disadvantaged children, and a progressive elementary school.

Transforming abstract theories and model programs into a national renaissance in education means fighting a thousand battles and enlisting citizens, teachers, administrators, and policymakers in a long and bitter crusade. None of these innovations is without controversy and conflict. Placing education in the hands of profit-making enterprises is rightly viewed as a betrayal by public-school backers, who fear the drain on their already meager resources. Magnet schools and advanced courses for gifted students are under attack as elitist and even racist. Poorer, inner-city schools slip further behind as many innovations target richer, suburban districts. Abandoning the outdated, top-down system of governing schools that provides all the power to the administrators leaves some teachers and parents frightened and adrift.

Most of all, despite all the efforts in the 1980s to elevate the mission and standards of public education, fundamental flaws remain. Progress has been slow and halting in the best of schools and nonexistent in others. Some schools have even gone in the other direction, dropping further behind as test scores decline, the middle class continues its exodus, and some teachers all but give up.

Small wonder, then, that few of the other parents at our children's preschool were willing to take a chance on the city's public schools. Alexandria's education system suffers from many of the ills driving people away from public schools across the nation, particularly in larger cities.

Nationwide, enrollment in non-Catholic private schools is rising at the rate of 8 percent a year. The number of independent schools in the Washington, D.C., metropolitan area has grown from about 160 in 1972 to more than 270 in 1992. President Bill Clinton and his wife, Hillary, exposed the city's liberal secret when they decided to send daughter Chelsea to an elite private school where tuition tops ten thousand dollars a year. A generation that viewed itself as open-minded and socially committed suffered a humbling showdown with its own conscience when many of its members were revealed to have abandoned the same public schools that had educated them decades earlier.

When George Bush was in the White House just a few miles up the Potomac River from Alexandria, there seemed to be a nationwide fever to ditch the entire institution of public education, opting for a system of private enterprise that ran counter to democratic theory and threatened to leave those with the least hope even further behind. Bush's version of school choice was a radical one, proposing to give parents education vouchers that they could use in either private or public schools. Clinton advocates a more limited alternative, which would allow government-subsidized choice only within the public system. To do otherwise, he insists, would dangerously weaken the public schools. Yet Clinton sees a larger role for the federal government in helping to establish national standards for education and in promoting his form of choice. However, his administration has found the cupboard bare when it comes to providing the financing necessary to implement new programs.

Cities as diverse as Minneapolis and New York already offer a choice of public schools to students. But the system in Alexandria, as in most cities, is more rigid — under most circumstances, students are restricted to schools within the geographic boundaries of their home district unless they are bused to achieve racial balance.

As we examined the Alexandria schools, however, we discovered a single, overriding factor that convinced us our young children could thrive in the city's public schools: It was the teachers.

Talking to teachers and visiting their classrooms at various elementary schools, we discovered that they were dedicated, caring, passionate, and often troubled by their inability to work miracles. We listened and found that the stories they told us about their job were compelling, fascinating, funny, sad. Most of all, the stories gave us insights into the problems faced by the schools here and all across the country, and they gave us hope that those problems can be solved.

One of the first teachers we talked to was Celeste Lenzini, the teacher of a developmental, full-day kindergarten class at Maury Elementary School, in Alexandria. The developmental approach recognizes that children learn different skills at different speeds, depending upon their social, physical, and mental maturity.

Enrollment in Lenzini's class was by a lottery structured to divide the students evenly by race and sex. There was a wide range of abilities in the children. Some came to the first day of school knowing their numbers and letters, colors and shapes, ready for the next steps in their educational process, getting along in groups, learning to count and sort objects, learning to read. Some, however, came not knowing their full name and had a lot of catching up to do. Some children had been to preschool or Head Start, the highly successful government program designed to provide early childhood education for lower-income children. They came from families that read to them regularly and sent them to class fed and eager to learn. Other youngsters had never set foot in a school before, had never sat still to look at a book, and showed up chronically hungry and tense. Many met the definition of at-risk children, those who are chronically behind in reading skills and usually come from disadvantaged backgrounds.

The demands presented by twenty-five of these five-year-olds with such varied backgrounds were enormous, but Lenzini was not an elitist. She resisted pressures from some parents to group her children by ability or emphasize individual accomplishments. Instead, she followed a theory of blending, insisting that children with all ranges of ability work together in groups on projects.

"That's what happens in life, so why not start it in kindergarten?" she told us.

By the conclusion of our conversation, we knew that she was concerned about every student who came into her classroom, that she recognized the enormous challenges confronting teachers today and was equipped to cope with them. In the end, we were honored to be able to put our son in her care for his first year of school, and he and his younger sister remain in the city's public schools.

Our children have learned a lot in their first years of school here, and so have we. The classrooms are not as chock-full of computers and the latest learning tools as those of the private schools or wealthy suburbs. Despite those apparent disadvantages, our children are learning on a level with their counterparts in other schools. They also have something that cannot be measured on any standardized test — the advantage of going to school with children from all backgrounds and races. As parents, we have learned that putting children in public schools requires a tremendous investment on our part, not of dollars and cents, but of commitment and time.

Selecting a school for our teenage daughter was more complex. Middle schools are traditionally the most troublesome for teachers and students alike. These young adolescents test rules and push the limits of behavior. Such early stirrings of rebellion can translate into classroom disruption and a general atmosphere that detracts from learning. Largely as a result of that, our daughter enrolled in a private high school.

Her school is a world apart from that of her brother and sister, shiny and well equipped, with polite teachers and observant administrators. Classes are small and orderly. Learning is never a fight to hear the teacher over the din of laughter and scraping chairs. There are problems, of course. She misses the diverse student population of her public school days and sometimes complains about the elitism of students and teachers. We were appalled when one of her teachers mocked public schools, telling his students that if they wanted straight A's, they should go to the nearby public high school.

As we talked with teachers in Alexandria's public and private schools, we discovered that they shared similar concerns and attitudes. All were worried about how to reach the students at the bottom of their classes while sustaining the curiosity of the most advanced youngsters. They complained about low pay and tough working conditions, yet they exhibited an undiminished zeal for their job. They were worried about a trend in Alexandria to reduce the demands on students, because they believe the way out of the educational malaise is to raise expectations. They were frustrated by uninvolved parents and the administrative hierarchy. Yet without exception, they were committed to making a difference in the lives of their students.

How could education be in such a desperate state when it was in the hands of such caring professionals? We discovered part of the answer: *No one appeared to be listening to the teachers.*

This should not have come as a surprise. The American school is a nineteenth-century enterprise. It was created to provide workers for the nation's factories during the Industrial Revolution. Like those factories, the school was set up with a rigid hierarchy and was expected to produce workers for factory-level jobs. Orders came from the top, from school boards and administrators modeled after boards of directors and foremen. They were to be carried out by the workers at the lowest rung, the teachers. The debate over reforming education had raged throughout the 1980s, but it was a debate in which teachers were relegated to silence. They remained workers on the lowest rung, seen but not heard. This system ignores a simple truth: We cannot have good schools without good teachers. We cannot attract, nurture, and keep good teachers without giving them a voice.

Asking a teacher about his or her job is like poking a hole in a balloon: The stories come rushing out, almost breathlessly. Teachers are verbal by nature. They are observers by profession. They spend all day with the most important commodity in the world, our children. So their stories are not only entertaining and thoughtful, they are also vital to the future of our country.

The idea that no one was listening to them seemed impossible. We soon realized that it was true. It was no secret that schools were faltering, but the people offering advice for the rescue seemed out of touch with what was going on in the classrooms of America. Teachers certainly are aware that few people are willing to listen to them when it comes to the important matters of education. Teachers are consulted seldom about important school issues such as the budget, the hiring of new teachers, or the evaluation of peers.

Then we came across an essay by Ernest L. Boyer, the president of the Carnegie Foundation for the Advancement of Teaching. It summed up the sense we were developing. "With all the talk about better schools, I'm struck that teachers' voices are rarely heard," wrote Boyer. "There are pronouncements from governors, corporate leaders, academic experts, but what about those who spend their lives in schools and meet with children every day?"

The blunt message is that American education cannot be saved until we pay attention to the professionals who spend their days on the front lines of the battle, where they struggle with too little support to educate our children and ensure a better future.

The idea for this book grew out of those early conversations with teachers in Alexandria and out of the belief that they have something important about education to say to all of us — parents, policymakers, academic experts, and their own colleagues in America's classrooms.

For nearly two years, we traveled thousands of miles back and forth across the country to interview teachers about their job. While we visited with some in their homes, we met with most inside their classrooms or in a quiet spot in the school. We talked to teachers at schools in sections of New York where cabdrivers refused to venture, schools surrounded by high fences and burned-out buildings where students passed through metal detectors on the way into classes. At remote schools on lonely Indian reservations, teachers talked about melding modern education with ancient culture. At inner-city schools in Los Angeles and Chicago and New Orleans, teachers described the daily struggle to help their children just survive. At small schools in rural Indiana, where on the surface little seems to have changed in decades, teachers worried about the impact of broken homes and the influx of drugs. We interviewed teachers at strict religious schools and affluent private schools, teachers who worked behind bars at schools in juvenile prisons, and teachers at schools where the hallways were filled with the sounds of a dozen languages. In all, we talked with about 150 teachers at more than 70 schools. Their stories were inspiring, sad, charming, angry, funny, and dramatic. Each teacher opened a new window onto the state of education and provided a signpost on the road to revitalizing America's schools.

While the teachers who were interviewed came from a cross section of the profession, they were not chosen on a scientific basis. Some of them are recognized by their peers as outstanding teachers, educators of the year for their district, state, or the whole country. We thought it was important to get the views of those regarded as being at the top of the job. Others were found with the help of teachers' union representatives or, on occasion, school administrators. Many of the teachers we interviewed were discovered through word of mouth, by asking friends and friends of friends for the names of their favorite teachers.

Although we approached them as strangers who took much and gave little, our subjects were generous with their time and their wisdom. While our most obvious tool was the tape recorder, the real motivator to get them talking was simply our desire to listen. Some teachers bared their souls, breaking down in tears as they recalled special students, long-forgotten triumphs and hurtful failures, or simply very personal moments. Others spoke earnestly of their anxieties about the direction of their profession and of education itself. These are troubled times for teachers, all the more so because they care so deeply.

For each interview, the method of operation was virtually the same: Sit down with the teacher, turn on the tape recorder, and begin asking questions. Rarely did we need to prod; opinions and stories that had been dammed up for years came rushing out. The most vivid and gripping comments emerged from the experiences and hearts of the teachers themselves. The interviews became conversations: animated, opinionated conversations about dreams and frustrations.

Occasionally the discussions were with groups of teachers, which made for interesting and sometimes heated exchanges of views. A dozen teachers gathered in a portable office outside Miami Beach Senior High School to debate the issues of discipline and national standards. Three women ate a hurried lunch in a conference room at Miraleste Intermediate School, in Palos Verdes, California, while talking about school funding, teachers' salaries, and parental support. Through an entire day, teachers tracked us down in the lunchroom, various offices, and the parking lot to have their say at Van Buren Middle School, in Albuquerque, New Mexico. These discussions often illustrated the disparity in points of view, even among teachers themselves, and made us realize that there will be no single best solution that can be applied as a salve to the problems of all our schools. Instead, the solution will come from numerous approaches that suit the students, their communities, the parents, and teachers.

We wound up with hundreds of hours of tape recordings. Once transcribed, they amounted to more than seven hundred thousand words from the mouths of teachers on the state of education and their lives in it today. It was an easy decision to leave the stories in the words of the teachers themselves. There was no need to dilute the impact by trying to weave them into a narrative. Instead, the result is teachers describing life inside America's schools in their own words, with minimal intrusion from us.

Just as the choices of whom to interview were somewhat arbitrary, so was the selection of which teachers were to be included: Not all of the teachers interviewed appear in the book, and many teachers are heard from more than once. Some were able to articulate their views more effectively than others. Some simply had more to say. All contributed to our understanding. The process turned out to be something akin to prospecting, yielding a nugget here, a nugget there. In some teachers we found mother lodes.

The two years spent on this book divide neatly into two phases. The first was exploration and adventure. Just as anyone who has ever attended school has a general awareness of a teacher's job, so we began with many preconceptions. But with each visit to a classroom and each conversation with a teacher or group of teachers, the layers of myth and misunderstanding were peeled away. We learned that teaching the lowest grades is not the easiest task. We learned that entering a classroom as a teacher is an intellectual challenge, not just a test of patience. We began with the belief that arranging students in groups according to their ability, the process known as tracking, was elitist and discriminatory; we preferred a heterogeneous mixing of children of all achievement levels. Yet we wound up understanding that both systems can work if they are run correctly, and that neither is effective without a competent teacher.

During our hundreds of hours of conversation and visits to dozens of classrooms, teachers became our guides to the functional realities of their job. We found that a teacher's job lasts far beyond the bell ending the final period of the day, and that working conditions are far from ideal. Many teachers work in fear, and others suffer from the public's lack of respect. Yet few have given up. For every burned-out teacher, we found a dozen who remained passionately committed to their job. For every teacher defeated by the challenges, we found a dozen who were invigorated as they tackled each new day. Throughout our research, our underlying belief that teachers hold many of the keys to reforming education was repeatedly reinforced.

The second phase of our work on the book was distillation. The specifics of what we had heard from more than 150 teachers had to be coordinated to form a clear, compelling picture of the state of teaching today. Given the wonderful diversity and fluidity of American teachers, it was difficult to pin down their stories and opinions in simple groupings under specific chapter headings. These teachers would not be fenced in.

However, common themes did emerge, and to reflect this the chapters follow a fairly natural progression. Each chapter begins with an explanation of its central theme. In most cases, the opening contains information intended to provide a context in which to understand and judge the comments that follow from the teachers.

The stories that are told are as varied as the teachers themselves. There are bitterness, cynicism, and self-doubt, but also pride, commitment, hope, dignity, and devotion to making a difference in the lives of children. Most of the stories, however, demonstrate that our children are, by and large, in the hands of good people.

In the end, the book is a forum for a wide range of voices from the front lines. By listening to their stories, people will understand what educators — and American education — are up against. People will learn about the effects of low pay and uninvolved parents, of dictatorial administrators and disruptive children, of the triumphs, small and large, that bring teachers back to the classroom day after day, year after year. Out of that understanding can grow a new impetus for achieving the common goal of providing the best possible education for all of our children.

CHAPTER 1

WHY DO IT?

THE KIDS had finished doing their creative writing and I asked who would like to share what they had written. One boy, Louis, raised his hand and said, 'It's a rap, but I have to do it a cappella.' He started to sing the lyrics of the rap. 'Boys will be men' or 'Men will be boys.' I can't remember the exact title.

"Out of his mouth comes the voice of an angel. He starts to sing these words that deal with the difficulty of becoming a man, and while he is doing that the rest of the kids, just naturally, started beating out rhythms on the desks. It gave me goose bumps.

"That's why I teach. These kids are absolutely magnificent. It's incredible. The spontaneity, the beauty. Even though children nowadays don't have a lot of innocence in their lives anymore, they still come to us with childlike innocence, beauty, joy of life, the excitement of living. As a teacher, I get to share a little of it."

Nancy Brice, who tells that story, is a public school teacher in Miami, Florida. She is one of the 2.6 million men and women teaching in America's elementary and secondary schools today, the people entrusted with the future of our children and of our country.

For most of the teachers, their job is a love affair. They are passionate, devoted, demanding, and generous. Some became teachers because they didn't see any other options or because they wanted a career with summers off or a job that fit their children's schedules. Others could never imagine another profession so glorious and all-consuming.

Most professions are challenging, offering rewards and frustrations. But for teachers, the challenges can be more daunting and the rewards harder to find. Unlike other professionals, teachers have very limited control over their "product." Children are in class only an average of six hours a day. A teacher has no control over what happens to the children in the other eighteen hours of the day. Further, in a society where immediate gratification is the norm, teachers may never know whether they have succeeded in helping a child learn. Countless teachers mentioned in interviews the deep pleasure in having a former student return a decade later with a word of thanks. Unlike a doctor, lawyer, or banker, a teacher rarely sees the immediate results of his or her work.

John Schiff, who turned from the priesthood to teaching and now works at a private school in Santa Fe, New Mexico, was speaking for many of his colleagues during a thoughtful conversation one Saturday morning over breakfast: "I measure my successes with hope, like a gardener measures success in June."

Over time, some teachers become bitter and even hostile. They coarsen on the diet of unending challenges that are served up with little respect or appreciation. The definition of a teacher is changing. He is no longer just a dispenser of facts. A good teacher also must be a social worker and a parent, filling gaps left by the tears in society's fabric. Teachers are ordinary people who are asked to perform an extraordinary job, and most do so with persistence and optimism but with too little understanding from others.

The American education system is a national obsession these days. We are deluged with studies and documentaries testifying to the academic deficiencies of our children. There is plenty of blame to spread around. Money and other resources are scarce, raising doubts about the priority given to education by the public. Parents have abdicated responsibility to the schools, and administrators have dragged their feet at implementing the basic reforms necessary to modernize the education system. For instance, when the Los Angeles schools tried to grant teachers more power in running their schools, principals and other administrators formed a union to fight the move.

Still, when people gather to discuss the ills of education, whether at a cocktail party or an academic conference, the most frequent target is the teachers. The most logical reason is that teachers are the visible symbol of education, the point of contact with the system for the vast majority of us. However, they also are easy scapegoats for failed policies and calcified administrations because they are on the lowest rung of the education ladder. Parents blame teachers for the high failure rate of their children. Industry criticizes them for turning out illiterate, unskilled workers. And politicians saddle them with responsibility for the economic decline of the country.

Why would anyone become "just a teacher," much less remain in such a demanding, frustrating, low-paying job year after year? The average annual salary for teachers in 1992 was $34,213, an adjusted drop of $1,900 from 1972, according to the American Federation of Teachers.

Why do they do it? To hear a child sing about becoming a man, a cappella. To ignite and nurture the curiosity of a single child. To be surrounded by thinking, questioning minds rather than by mute computer screens. To make a difference in a life.

Studies over the past twenty years have found that nearly seven of every ten teachers decided to become a teacher because of a desire to work with young people, and it is the chief reason cited by six of every ten teachers for staying in the profession. They also are drawn to teaching because of its value to society, an interest in the subject matter they are teaching, job security, and, in a small percentage of cases, the prospect of a long summer vacation.

Many of us are trapped in careers too small for our spirits. We spend our working hours in a job. It's work. Teachers, however, spend their days at a mission. They hear the call in different ways, and respond to it by different means. In Pat Conroy's *Prince of Tides,* the character Tom was speaking for his real-life counterparts when he responded to his sister's admonishment that he could have been more than a teacher and a coach by saying: "Listen to me. There is no word in the language I revere more than teacher. None. My heart sings when a kid refers to me as his teacher and it always has."

So many of the teachers interviewed for this book still regard their profession with the same reverence. They are willing to work with low pay and too little respect because there is so much to savor in what they do. A seemingly hopeless child becomes an avid learner. A brilliant student goes on to more brilliant success. A speechless child breaks his or her silence. A troubled youngster pauses at the classroom door just long enough to mutter, "Thank you."

Carolyn Langston teaches third grade at a public school in a poor, predominantly black neighborhood of Newport News, Virginia, where she speaks eloquently of her devotion to her students. "They are our future and we are all responsible for our little part of it," she says. "They deserve the best part of us and what we have learned. They still love to know that there is somebody they can depend on, that there is somebody who is going to be fair, that somebody cares about them."

Satisfaction is measured in different ways, and so is the discontent. There is much of that, too, in teaching today. The constant criticism from the public takes a toll. So do the overcrowded classrooms, the violence of inner cities, the hungry and disadvantaged children, the unshakable hope-lessness that society is asking too much of its teachers while offering too little, the fear that a generation is being lost. Small wonder that some teachers would quit but for the pension they await.

Yet, despite all this, teachers are happier in their jobs today than they were just a few years ago. Half the teachers questioned in 1990 by the Carnegie Foundation for the Advancement of Teaching said they were more enthusiastic about their work now than when they started their ca-reers. Similar sentiments were found in a survey of more than thirteen hundred public school teachers in 1991 by the National Education Asso-ciation. The NEA found that six of every ten respondents would become teachers again if they were given a career choice. The figure is an increase from fewer than five in ten a decade earlier, reflecting the trend toward greater teacher participation in decision-making and a renewed emphasis on the value of education. However, the numbers are still discouraging: Thirty years ago, three of every four said they would have done it all over again.

The past three decades have taken a toll on teachers and on the teaching profession. The gap between poor children and affluent children has wid-ened, creating a sometimes unbridgeable gulf for teachers of the poor. There are children at every big-city school in America and many rural schools, too, who come to class without the basic necessities for learning. They are too hungry to concentrate, too unaccustomed to any intellectual stimulation but television to pay attention. Children in middle-class and wealthy com-munities are having more problems than ever before. Teachers feel the need increasingly to fill the voids often left by parents of those children who are too busy with their own lives to help their offspring. Drugs and crime, the scourges of inner-city neighborhoods, have made an impact on America's suburbs, too, creating new difficulties for teachers there.

Perhaps the best example, however, of the task teachers face today is the ever-increasing incidents of violence against teachers in the classroom. In New York City, there are at least two thousand physical assaults against the sixty thousand public school teachers each year. And although it is urban school districts in Chicago, Detroit, Philadelphia, Los Angeles, and Miami that we think of when discussing violence within the classroom, "rural students are twice as likely to carry handguns to class" than the national average, according to the *American School Board Journal*.

Most of us think we know everything about teachers and their jobs, but often our image is frozen in time from an earlier, far different period. We remember the fifth-grade teacher who gave us an A in spelling or the seventh-grade history teacher who sent us to the office for talking in class. When we say hello to the teacher as we drop our children off at class or attend a school picnic, that remains the vision of the job for many of us.

Few among us have the real information about what teachers do, and fewer still have much insight into what motivates the men and women who do it. We must listen to America's teachers talk about their jobs, their lives, their fears, and their hopes. They have something vital to tell all of us. As anthropologist Margaret Mead once said, "The solution of adult problems tomorrow depends upon the way our children grow up today."

Alfredo Lujan is a published short-story writer and poet, but his true vocation is teaching. Like a surprising number of teachers, he works at the school where he was educated. And like a large number of his colleagues across the nation, he was influenced in his choice of profession by his own teachers.

A stocky, blunt man, Lujan teaches English and writing at Pojoaque Middle School in Pojoaque, a dusty village in northern New Mexico. He also coaches basketball at a private school in Santa Fe. He is a demanding and an exacting teacher who will not allow excuses to stand in the way of excellence. Because two very different teachers showed him a path to success, Lujan is tough and determined when it comes to offering the same opportunity to the largely Hispanic and Indian students in his classes:

I never thought I'd be a teacher, especially a teacher of English. The prospect of perfect tense was too scary. Then I met José Lopez and Joan McGuire.

José was my ally and Joan was my rival. He was my junior varsity basketball coach and my biology teacher. He was from Springer, a small town in northern New Mexico, and his parents were farmers. She hated sports and was my U.S. history teacher. She was from Boston, a *gringa* whose father was a banker. When Joan stood next to José, she was Tinker Bell standing beside King Kong.

He cared about me. He didn't defend me when bullies picked on me and in that way he taught me to take care of myself, to be an individual. Yet he also taught me about being a team player and having confidence and leadership and generosity. José made me captain of the basketball team. Until then I'd only been a bench warmer.

One day José gave me the keys to his car and asked me to pick up a pair of his basketball shoes from the trunk on my way to practice. I was surprised when I had to dig through a pile of empty Coors cans to get to where his tennis shoes were. I never said anything about the beer cans because I knew that he had confidence in me. I also learned that he had faults.

Joan and I were on opposing teams. We argued often, and I had been ineligible to play for two games because of my grades and behavior in her class. She asked me one day what I thought of *La Bohème* in a class discussion. I told her it was a cheap wine and she laughed.

"Haven't you been to the Santa Fe Opera?" she asked.

"No," I said.

"It's only ten minutes away," she said.

"So are the waterfalls at Nambe Pueblo. Have you been there?"

I told her that all operas are tragic. And I said that La Bohème was the tragedy of Cheto's life. He was our hometown wino and he raked people's yards to earn enough to buy a pint of La Bohème Tokay.

"See," I told her in class that day, "it's like the French guy in that great book says, the most interesting thing about America is equality. You don't know La Bohème is a wine. I don't know it's an opera. See, we're equal in *ignorancia*." She cried in front of the class and I realized that she too had weaknesses.

One day she asked us to write down our future career plans. "The army," I wrote. The next day she took me aside and said I should go to college. I said my family didn't have the money and she said there are ways and sent me to the guidance counselor.

Many years later I was down in Albuquerque at a teachers' conference. I'd heard from a friend that José and Joan had gotten married and were living in Albuquerque. When she answered the phone, I asked for Mr. Lopez. She asked who was calling and she couldn't believe it was me.

"What have you done with yourself?" she asked.

"I'm an English teacher and a basketball coach," I replied. "I'm calling to thank you and José for what you taught me."

She laughed. "A teacher of English? I taught you? You hated me and you were the only student I had who could really get under my skin."

"But I learned stuff," I said. "I wouldn't have gone to school without both of you."

"What a nice thing to say," she said.

"Is José there?" I asked.

After a pause, she said, "Joe died last year."

I didn't know what to say.

It wasn't José's lessons on the basketball court or Joan's lessons on democracy or even her suggestion that I go to college that led me to a career in education. The most important lesson I learned about teaching was when I had to dig through José's car trunk and when I watched Joan cry in class. I learned that teachers are human.

Many teachers say they cannot imagine doing anything else. They believe they are born teachers and remember organizing friends and siblings into mock classes as youngsters. Often they worked as camp counselors or baby-sitters as they moved relentlessly toward the only job they ever wanted.

Joan Iversen is a quiet, soft-spoken woman who teaches first grade at St. Isaac Jogues, a Catholic school in Hinsdale, Illinois, an attractive, well-kept, and affluent suburb west of Chicago. Her inclination toward teaching began early:

Ever since I can remember, I wanted to be a teacher. I worked at camps in the summertime. By the time I was twelve, I was a junior counselor. I used to pretend to be a nun, actually. I went to a Catholic school where the teachers were nuns. We used to wear a pillowcase on the back of the head and rosary beads and I was always commanding the classroom. Somehow all my life I've wanted to do this. I never really thought of doing something else.

Jane Starner grew up in rural Indiana and has taught English there for thirty years. From the start, she brought a flair for drama to the job that engaged her students and provided a refreshing spark of life in the drab farm country. That flair also sustained her own interest. Now Starner heads the English Department at Warsaw High School in Warsaw, Indiana:

I never felt there was anything that I was barred from doing. In North Manchester, the small town near here where I grew up, we had a woman doctor and a woman attorney. There wasn't anything I didn't think I could do, but the thought of being an engineer or something never entered my mind. I just never considered it. When I am reincarnated I want to come back as a dancer. My vice principal says, "No, you will be a teacher."

John Scott teaches English at Hampton High School in the working-class community of Hampton, Virginia. He sees himself as a role model for his black students, particularly the boys. Scott left a life filled with far more glamour to become a teacher. He was a road manager for Miles Davis and set up European tours for American jazz musicians.

His school was one of the original "dual system" schools established in the South in the era before integration. Hampton High was paired with another school; Hampton was all-white, the other school all-black. Today Hampton High School is integrated; 65 percent of its students are African American. The school is perhaps best known for its football program, which has made it a major force in the state and sent several players on to top colleges and the National Football League. But Scott is determined to provide a fuller range of opportunities for his students:

I want to get more black males into nontraditional positions in schools. Just think about this: How many black male English teachers have you seen? Walk down the halls of this school and count them. There is a stigma associated with this. We're supposed to be weirdos.

There are large numbers of black men in physical education, in the trades, maybe a few in math or science. We have six physical education teachers here who are male, four of whom are black. We have four male English teachers, only one of whom is black, me. We have only one black science teacher.

I think black males are cut out of a lot of things right out of the box. You are told very early what you can't do. When you are told you can't do it, you don't try. I am trying to encourage more black males to major in English, without the final objective of becoming a writer in the newspaper. Unless we do something, we will put ourselves in a permanent bind. There are too many young men with skills that need to be refined. There are more black males in prison than in college, something like three to one. It is awful.

I am sick of hearing about Japan. I am sick of hearing about Germany. And I am sick of hearing about England. Because we are not Japan, Germany, or England. We don't cut people out of the system before they have had an ample opportunity to get in. Because if that were the case, I might be breaking into your house right now, stealing your TV. Understand what I am saying?

I am not saying that I was a bad kid. But if I was cut out before I had a chance to play, that is what could have happened. If I can't be influenced by positives, then I will be influenced by negatives.

Mary Bicouvaris teaches in Newport News, Virginia, not far from John Scott's school, as the crow flies. After spending twenty years working in public schools and becoming a national teacher of the year in 1989, Bi-couvaris took advantage of an early-retirement offer made to save the school district money by replacing older, higher-paid teachers. As a result, she now teaches in an upscale private school called Hampton Roads Academy.

A native of Greece, she became a teacher because her family was too poor to provide her with a dowry. Her mother decided that Mary would grow up smart, with a profession of her own in the event she never married. Eventually she came to the United States and became a teacher:

Over the years I have had my hard times, just like every teacher, and I had moments when I wanted to leave and I had moments when it was so hard that I didn't know that it was worth it.

I keep doing this because I believe that I make a difference. I believe teachers make a difference. I forgive the indiscretions and I keep telling them what I think is right and I hope that as I do I sow the seeds that they will need later on. They are better off for being with me than not being with me. I know that. And I can see the difference, even from month to month.

You see, I believe that education can fix everything, everything. What is it, AIDS? You tell me what else can fix AIDS. I tell my students, first education, and second research, both of which are based on education.

Mickey Weiner teaches fourth grade at South Pointe Elementary School in Miami Beach, Florida. South Pointe is a new public school, opened to accommodate a local population explosion due to immigration from the Caribbean and South and Central America. It is one of the slowly growing number of schools in this country being jointly managed by the local school board and a private, for-profit company.

The concept of for-profit companies managing schools grew out of a philosophy promulgated during the presidencies of Ronald Reagan and George Bush. They believed that the private sector could succeed in running enterprises where the public was deemed to have failed. As a result, a handful of the nation's 84,500 public schools turned over their management to private businesses. As far as most teachers are concerned, the idea will work only if it allows them to do their jobs better, and the verdict on that is still out. For now, Mickey Weiner goes on the same as she has for years:

The kids are balls of energy and information. They are what puts this job in a class by itself. If you sit down at the end of each day and jot down one or two comments, ideas, stories, or situations that happened, you would realize that you are the richest person in the world. I do not mean because of the paycheck, although that is improving, but teachers are rich all because of the students.

For instance, yesterday at the end of the day, we were sitting in a circle. We discussed the day, what they liked, what they didn't like, what was interesting. Usually they will say, "We like PE." But sometimes I throw out a phrase or a question. Yesterday I asked, "What is intelligence?"

"Intelligence is power. Knowledge is freedom," said one of the boys. To come up with a statement like that and for a fifth-grade student to be able to support it is worth a million dollars to me, and more.

Sandra Fernandez was teaching first grade at Santa Clara Elementary School in Miami's tough North End, but now works as a Chapter 1 resource teacher at the school, providing remedial assistance to children identified as needing special help in reading. She came to teaching after studying social work and psychology in college:

They say you're born to teach, and it must have been like that for me because I know education is the field where I belong. It's not just love of children, but it's hope for the future.

These children are the future of this community, and if these kids aren't taught and aren't able to get over prejudices and get over their own problems in the community, they are going to stay here and they're going to die here.

I know a lot of kids in my classes now aren't going to make it to be eighteen years old. There's a lot of shooting and things. But you just go on with the hope that you are making a difference. Maybe they'll remember one day that their first-grade teacher believed in them or smiled at them or gave them a hug once.

These children stay here. This community gets worse. Something needs to be done. These children need to be educated because it's their only hope.

A large number of teachers outside the parochial school system are former nuns or priests. At first glance, it may seem surprising. But teaching and religion have a similar grounding in service to others. In addition, the Catholic church has a long and honored tradition of teaching.

John Schiff was a teacher while a priest. When he decided to leave the priesthood, he saw no reason to abandon teaching, too. He now teaches at Santa Fe Preparatory School in Santa Fe, New Mexico:

There is some similarity between the vocation of the priesthood and being a teacher. They are both helping professions. But I found that I couldn't be a priest any longer. I used to come here with my parents when I was little. It was the only place that I knew that I could make it because my life was, without sounding overly dramatic, truly shattered over the decision to get out of the ministry. I came to Santa Fe and just started over.

I had been a teacher in the ministry, and I didn't see any reason to play like I didn't have a perfectly decent trade. And I love it. My grandfather taught medicine very successfully in Oklahoma. I have it in my blood, the ability to explain something to someone. When I was a theology student in Rome, part of our program was that you had to do something besides the heady theological stuff, an ongoing, everyday type of thing. You could do all kinds of things, hospitals, working with the poor. I chose working in a kind of posh international boys' school.

There were kids from all over the world, all kinds of languages. I liked it from the first time I set foot in the classroom, and they liked me. Plus, my inclinations personally are entirely intellectual. I'm one of those people who barely lives outside of his mind, and completely lives in it, with all the good and bad that comes with that.

Celeste Lenzini sent her three daughters to a private school in Alexandria, Virginia, yet she spent more than twenty years making a second family out of kindergarten students in the city's public schools. Her job was a family affair; she often brought her elderly mother to classes at Maury Elementary School, and she treasured each child as her own:

I had my own three children in four years. I just wanted to do something. I don't think I had any great motives at all, except for getting out of the house on a schedule that matched my girls' schedules. But somewhere along the way I got hooked. I began to be so fond of these kids. My children are raised. Every year my husband says, "Are you going back?" I say, "Of course. What else would I do?"

I have a little child in my class now with a very difficult home life. He lives with his grandmother, a very limited woman, and several siblings. He simply did not speak when he first came. I would say to him, "Oh, hello. How are you today?"

I never got a word out of him. He didn't speak for a couple of months. I just kept talking to him, chattering and chattering, but I never talked about the fact that he did not speak to me. Then one day he started singing.

That child owns my heart. He owns my heart because we go toe to toe, because he is rambunctious and comes from such an unstructured environment that he is likely to go bananas at any time. But I see such growth and I feel so good because I think I have made a difference for that child. He feels so secure. When he is sick and I take him to the nurse and she asks what is wrong, he will not say a word to her because he does not know her. But he will talk to me and he is beginning to talk to his friends.

Next year we can only hope that his self-confidence, his self-image, will improve enough that he knows that he can trust people. It is a tough world out there, more so for some children. You just try to do your best to try to make it as warm and comforting and structured as possible.

Michelle Kaufman teaches fifth grade at the Anna Howard Shaw Elementary School (Public School 61) on the Lower East Side of New York City. Often she finds herself in the role of social worker and counselor, too. For instance, when one of her students confessed that she just didn't want to live any longer, Kaufman pulled the child to her and kept her nearby for the entire day. She was letting her know that someone cared:

I always wanted to be a teacher. It is not a thankless job. At the end of the first year when I was teaching third grade, I asked one of the children to write down the most important thing she learned in third grade. She wrote, "The most important thing I learned in third grade was to respect people. It doesn't make a difference if they are rich or poor, if they are black or white, to have respect for all people, just like Miss Kaufman has respect for us." That puts it in a nutshell.

Dwight Brown grew up in a New Orleans public housing project called Desire. It took its name from the streetcar line that ended there, not from anybody's wish to live there. Brown was a rare success story. He escaped the cycle of poverty and crime in Desire, but then he decided to come back and found his place at Moton Elementary School.

Brown, a slender, handsome man, speaks intensely about the role that Moton plays in the community. When it was built to replace the decrepit school Brown attended, it was purposely situated on the edge of the community, a place where students could escape the harsh surroundings, at least for a few hours each day. Moton represents the desire to rise above those surroundings, and Dwight Brown is there to help his fifth graders:

I grew up in the Desire housing project. I spent twenty-five years here. I came back because I believe that is my role. There were not any positive black male role models here. That was something I had to do. It was always in my mind to come back and do something for the community.

I've had several jobs. I worked for the Postal Service for two years and the money was very good. I worked for the New Orleans Public Library for two years. I drove a garbage truck for about a year and a half and I owned my own time then. With those jobs, I wasn't motivated to get up in the morning to run out there and go to work. In this job, I'm ready for the challenge. I think I'm winning, too.

After I went back to school and got my degree, I got a plum job at a magnet school in a good neighborhood. It was 60 percent white and 40 percent black. At the end of the year I just told them I felt that I was needed in the Desire area, in my home community. That was eight years ago. This has brought a lot of personal satisfaction. I'm respected within my community. My family is very proud of what I'm doing. In my family, we have accountants and lawyers who are making nice money. But it seems like I'm the one they always put on a pedestal, saying, "Man, I don't know how you do it. How do you live down there anymore?" That makes me feel good, but I feel best when I see my children growing up and using the things that I've taught them to try to make their lives better.

At the magnet school, the job was easy. The kid were motivated and pre-pared to learn. Here it's a challenge. Nothing comes easy in this life. You defi-nitely have to be committed to work at Moton. Every year we have a high turnover rate. Teachers may be gone in two months because they say they can't deal with all this pressure and frustration. Kids are not learning and the teachers feel like they are not doing their job. They can't deal with these kids. They can't deal with the behavior. I have been able to stay here so long because I under-stand the problems of these children.

We're not just teaching here. We are saving lives. Moton is a safe haven. If a child stays home, he may get a stray bullet. A child can be molested. Being here could save their lives. That's basically it. More kids will be successful now because the school itself has brought a new sense of worth. More kids will leave this area and be successful.

Rita Logan works behind bars. Tucked into the bureaucratic sprawl of Miami's Juvenile Justice Center and hidden behind a blue metal door is a school for young criminals. Students march to her class in straight lines, under the watchful eye of armed guards.

For Logan, the best she can hope for is small victories. Sometimes she thinks it will take a miracle to reach just one of her students:

Ideally, I would love to break this cycle. I have this Jesus Christ complex, I'm the Messiah come again, but realistically I've been working with these kids for five years now and the damage is so severe that I know that we are sending them right back out there.

If I let a kid take something, a magazine, and he steps back into the room to say thank you, I count that as a victory. You know you've got a kid and you really think you've communicated with him, and he's gotten some insight, and he leaves this place to go back home and to school. Then he comes back a few months later. You see that as a failure. Somehow you want to do miracles, but these kids are hard-core criminals.

There is a lot of anger in these kids. They're full of rage. They hate the school system. It has done terrible damage to them, even beyond what their families have done to them. Their attitude is if you're not ready, tough. You're an idiot, stupid. Some kids just don't fit into the school system. It's no wonder these kids are so screwed up.

You've read about how the system is failing our black males? A student told me once about going to one of the Home Depot stores with his mother. He came out of the store and he'd left his lights on and his battery was dead. Another guy, older, a white guy, came and got into the car next to his. So the kid said, "Excuse me, but my battery is dead. Could you give me a jump?" And the guy said to him, "Don't talk to me, you fucking nigger." Later the kid said to me that the hardest thing for him was how could this man disrespect his mother like that? What should he do, as a seventeen-year-old kid?

Another boy described selling *The Miami Herald* door to door with a friend, who was white. They asked a woman for a glass of water. She gave a glass to the white boy and a paper cup to the black boy. This is a sixteen-year-old kid. This is not 1950 in Alabama.

What I am saying is that we can't write these kids off. A miracle might happen. I talk about how you shouldn't hit your girlfriend. My hope is that by showing a boy his faulty logic, that someday even if he doesn't change, he might hesitate before beating his girlfriend. We talk about everything: Is it all right to beat your kids? To make them kneel on a cheese grater? They say white people don't beat their kids enough. I say to them, "How many white people you see sitting here?"

Many people went into teaching to right the world's wrongs. One of them is Bill Walters, who teaches social studies at Camden High School in an impoverished area of Camden, New Jersey, which was featured in 1992 by *Time* magazine under the headline "The Other America: Who Could Live Here?":

I was born in Alabama in the thirties and was bused to school in the forties. I knew we passed all-black schools to get to the all-white schools. Many of my playmates were black, but here I was in this segregated society. Schools, restaurants, water fountains, bathrooms, theaters, buses. I could never understand that and I wanted to do something to help.

I saw teaching as a way of trying to help minority groups. I had seen what happened to black Americans living in the South and I was very sensitive to some of my friends whom I loved very dearly, who so often were not treated very well.

There is an appreciation for what I am doing here that keeps me teaching. I know that I am appreciated every single day. I think that in a wealthier suburban school, where the children have their needs met every day by supportive families, the appreciation would not be as great. My students here in Camden say thank you for staying that extra ten minutes with a genuineness that I will never forget. And they never forget.

You teach in Camden, and places like Camden, because there is a commitment. You've got to want to do it in order to go home sane every day. You have to know that when you come into this district there are going to be hungry children in your classroom. You're going to give kids money for lunch. You are going to pay for the occasional theater ticket. You are going to stay after school to provide that extra help. You do these things if you are going to be successful.

Darlene McCampbell, who teaches English to high school juniors and seniors at the University of Chicago's Laboratory School, has a dramatically different set of challenges and satisfactions from those faced by teachers like Bill Walters in Camden.

The Laboratory School is renowned throughout Chicago for its high academic standards, and it draws students from the racially mixed Hyde Park neighborhood surrounding the University of Chicago on the city's

South Side. A joke catches the attitude of the neighborhood: "You know the definition of Hyde Park? It's where blacks and whites stand shoulder to shoulder against the poor."

McCampbell gets her satisfaction by matching intellects with her bright young students. That is what keeps her going as a teacher:

We had an open house at school. I am now teaching the sister of a boy I taught a while ago. The mother came up to me and said something that, at least partly, I was deeply honored to hear. It was just direct and high praise. She said that I was the first person in school who had let her son believe that he had something worthwhile.

"If you went into teaching to change or influence people's lives, I want you to know that in at least this one case you were successful," she said.

"I've heard my colleagues speak lovingly and respectfully of your child," I told her.

"The child didn't know that," she shot back angrily.

With a little bit of embarrassment, I have to admit that that isn't why I went into teaching. I teach for very selfish reasons. I teach because I get my kicks out of it, because I love it, because I learn from it. I think my own love for it does help things happen for other people. I am not really doing it for other people, but because I get stuff out of it.

It is absolutely intellectually stimulating, but it is more than that. In the world of the classroom, when things are working right, there are twenty-some minds working together on the greatest literature that has ever been written. We are engaged with it and each other and ourselves. I feel truly alive when that is happening.

Chicago's North Side movers and shakers send their children to Francis Parker School in Lincoln Park, where Molly Donohue teaches third grade. Her philosophy runs counter to the conventional wisdom among teachers: Donohue doesn't particularly like children, but she doesn't think that has made her any less effective as a teacher, because she finds that the single most important thing is that a teacher respect children:

I wasn't born to be a teacher. I wanted to be a city planner. I am sure that if I were going to school today, I would end up in engineering or city planning. With what the world offers to women now I'm sure I wouldn't be a teacher. Why? Because

I didn't like children. I like teaching. I like to enable people to know things they didn't know before. I like problem-solving.

When I say that I don't like children, I mean that the only reason for me to be with children is to teach. It is not a maternal, nurturing instinct that drives me. I have a lot of respect for the students in my room. I recognize that they struggle and I admire their willingness to struggle. I think that is what comes across to them. I talk to children about a job we have to do. When you're grown up you will have a job. You have a job now.

I had a very hard time in school. I was an LD [learning disabled] kid. I couldn't read. I couldn't spell. So both receptive and expressive written language were extremely difficult for me. I didn't read until I was in the fifth grade. I never read a book by myself until I was in the eighth grade. I was always a very good math student, though. I loved numbers and building things and problem-solving.

The teachers were very supportive. They had no idea what the trouble was. They left me alone. It was wonderful. I can think of five or six teachers who made differences in my life, and that is probably why I ended up teaching. I was a different person when I left them than I was before. People who enabled me to believe in myself in very important ways. It isn't that I ended up being a teacher to emulate those people, it was those people who kept me liking school. If there is anything I want to do as a teacher, it is to help people like learning.

John Borsum teaches math at Beverly Hills High School, which has always catered to the wealthy and which became famous in recent years through a popular television series, *Beverly Hills, 90210*. There is an oil derrick in the parking lot, which is filled with BMWs and Corvettes.

Along with the children of the stars and the affluent, Borsum teaches the children of recent immigrants from a wide variety of countries. Still, his favorite story does involve a star:

I had met Jack Lemmon several years ago. When I was a kid, he was filming a movie near my house. I have a brother who has cerebral palsy and I pushed him over to the set in his wheelchair. One day, we were behind the ropes watching and Jack Lemmon walked over, held up the ropes, and said, "You guys come on in here." He let us sit up close.

Years later, I had his daughter in class. I said to her, "I know this sounds silly and I hate to sound star-struck," and then I told her the story and asked her to tell her father that my little brother still remembers. Every day she'd come back and I'd ask her if she had told her dad. She kept saying no.

So finally, it was back-to-school night and his wife came in. I told her the story and asked her to please tell him thank you for me.

"Why don't you tell him yourself? Just come over to the house and talk to him," she said.

For the next week or so, I thought it over. Friends said to do it. So I got up the nerve and called and was invited over. We sat down and talked about education and he turned out to be the greatest guy in the world. He is a wonderful man. We got to know each other a little bit.

"I have so much respect for teachers," he said to me one time. "I could never get up in front of a group of people like that."

"What are you talking about?" I said. "You're an actor. You've been on-stage, in front of hundreds of cameras."

"Yeah," he said with a shrug. "But never was it a bunch of adolescents."

"If you want to try it, let me know sometime," I said. "I'll prep you and you can come in to teach, in case you ever have a teaching role."

"No way," he said. "It is unbelievable that teachers can do that."

That is one of the reasons I stay in teaching. There are still people out there who have respect for you and what you're doing.

Marion Clermont is attractive and stylish. She would have been happy sending her child to Beverly Hills High because she grew up wanting to be an actress. She never made it to the stage or the screen, but she has fulfilled her dream by playing a different role in front of her students at Tilden High School in Brooklyn.

Yet, as with many of her colleagues, Clermont's years of teaching have been marked by a bitterness she can't escape. There is a price for this dream, too, she has found:

I was an avid reader and managed to get a degree in English. I started working as a per diem substitute teacher in order to make some money on the side because waiting on tables and going for auditions wasn't doing it. I was more or less corralled into teaching, but I really liked it once I got here. I found it to be a great outlet in terms of acting, performing five times a day, working with literature. I was really very happy with it. I ended up staying with teaching and giving up everything else. I do believe it is a noble profession. Going back to the Middle Ages, law, teaching, the priesthood, those were important jobs.

I try to show my students a genuine concern, that this isn't just a job, that I am not here just for the buck in the pocket. I am here because I really want to be here. I enjoy teaching and I want to help them avoid the mistakes I might have made. I listen, try to guide them along, help them make the right decisions. What do I want to give them ultimately? The skills that they need to be successful or just to get on with their lives. I'm there to teach them to read, write, and enjoy literature. I want them to leave my classroom competent in their communications skills and be able to talk about different things, to have an open mind about all sorts of things, to always want to better themselves. I want to give them values. Not necessarily my own, but something they can use to make this world a better place.

Right away, though, everyone wants to blame teachers. We really don't mean anything to anyone anymore. We are not considered a noble profession. I don't know what they want us to do.

Pat Maier has experienced some of that same bitterness. She teaches French at Palos Verdes Peninsula High School, an upscale community on the ocean outside Los Angeles where many of the students come from wealthy families. Parents are involved in the education of their children, ensuring that the school always finishes near the top in the state's academic rankings. But even here, Maier finds little satisfaction:

I am embarrassed that I am a teacher, because I am ashamed of the caliber of person in education. There are some real exceptions, but those people are so rare.

The system does not encourage excellence. It doesn't foster a collegial approach to problem-solving. And the system itself presumes that teachers are stupid. They are not supposed to create curriculum, tests. You are supposed to hand out a ditto and say do questions one through five at the back of the chapter. That is supposed to be teaching? Sorry, not in my book.

Margie Eriacho teaches in a place with far less in material terms. The Zuni Indian reservation on the lava plains of northwestern New Mexico is a poor, agrarian community where pickup trucks outnumber BMWs by a thousand to one. Yet Eriacho, herself a Zuni, has found deep satisfaction among her first-grade students at Dowa Yalanne Elementary School:

I lost my dad three weeks ago. It was a real hard time in my life. We were having a parent day at school, where we were all going to come and eat with our parents. Every parent was going to show up and I said to myself, "I really should be there." But I couldn't go to school.

When I go to school, my children usually come to hug me and I knew that I would just lose it. I would just break down. So I thought I would just hold off.

The next day, after the parent day, my assistant came to the house and she brought me these cards the kids had written to me and that gave me the energy. The next day I came back to school. When I sat among them, they were just so caring. They are six and seven years old and they are so caring. That's why I stay in teaching.

Mark Mattson always wanted to be a painter. While studying at the Art Institute of Chicago, he met a woman, fell in love, and figured that he had better find a way to pay the bills. He found himself drawing on his family's roots; his father was a minister and there were many teachers in his family. So there was some logic when he became an art teacher. He teaches now at Chicago's Francis Parker School:

Teaching is a way for me to celebrate what I know, and to explore it more. There is a self-empowerment there that is part of the process. For an art teacher a lot of what you do is creative in the sense that you are creating a situation in which other people create. And in doing that, something new gets created.

The payback? It sure ain't the money. Twenty-four years later, I am at the top of the salary scale. But there is the sense that you're an alive, questioning, searching being that is still capable of change.

There is something wonderful about seeing the students come back each fall. It doesn't matter if you're teaching all ages or the same age. When they come in it is a new beginning, a fresh start. It's a rebirth of the class for sure, but it is also a personal rebirth. You get to try it again, to be better at it. I get to do my favorite things all over again and do it fresh, with new faces in front of me. And new minds that are going to go "ah-ha." It is exciting.

Frank Tobin, a former priest, teaches teenage boys in the same city as Mattson but at a completely different kind of school, the Cook County Temporary Juvenile Detention Center. His students are hard cases, awaiting trial and sentencing for felony crimes:

Why do this? I think it has a lot to do with my background, my faith, my perspective on life and people. I think it is almost a calling. My faith gives me a special perspective. I know that these children are God's special children, His special concerns. I know He loves these children in a very special way. But we are still free and God isn't going to perform any damn miracles. Our freedom allows us to do such terrible deeds. He has created us as free creatures and He knows that we will make mistakes. I won't give up on these children; too many people have already.

I see what is wonderful inside of them, the innate beauty in a human being, a capacity to learn, a lovableness, a genuine goodness, a real appreciation, concern, and caring. A gratitude for things they receive, for the patience that you show them, and your effort to motivate them to learn. Sometimes it comes out in their art. Sometimes it comes out in their words. Sometimes it comes out in their writing.

I had a kid one time, just a skinny little black kid who was in for murder. He was educationally disadvantaged and, although he could read well, his writing skills were terrible. But he was very interested in poetry. He wanted to write. In fact, he wrote all over the place, although the spelling was terrible, the grammar was poor, he didn't have an extensive vocabulary, but he had soul. He could write about his experiences, about his mother, about life in the inner city, about gangs, about this place, about himself and how he felt — his despair and frustration.

He was very determined to keep writing, so I started working with him, trying to improve his skills. He read on his own and he kept writing and improving. Eventually he was convicted and sent to state prison. He appealed the conviction and while he waited he had two books of poems published. They were just little books, but being a published poet is a big achievement.

He won the appeal, got a retrial, and won his case. So after five years in the joint, he got out. While he was in prison he met a group of nuns working there. They sort of adopted him and he went to St. Louis to be with them. He got his GED, started studying photography, and he's still writing.

Leonard Mednick, a former teacher, is a guidance counselor at John Dewey High School in the Bensonhurst and Coney Island sections of New York City:

I can think of very few opportunities in life where you can selfishly protect yourself. I mean that if I do my job right, then I am going to have kids who care about themselves enough to care about other people. So I am not going to have to watch my back on the subway, so I won't have to fear for my life, or worry about my wife, or my own kids. I am going to have kids who want to give back for what they have gotten. There are so few opportunities for that to occur.

I also get a very real sense of what can be. You know, I don't get an opportunity to meet famous people. Except for this business. Three thousand kids a year come to this school. Think about that. I get to pick and choose the best and the brightest. They are my friends for life. One young woman is a reporter for *The Village Voice*. Another kid is a scientist. Another is on the medical staff at MIT. How the hell do I get to meet people like this? They are giants. How, otherwise, would they have known Len Mednick? Never. I would never have had the opportunity to meet them if I hadn't taught them.

Greencastle is a small Indiana town dominated by DePauw University, a small liberal arts college. The children of university professors go to school alongside children whose parents work in the town's factories and stores.

Linda Raines, whose husband teaches at DePauw, is a teacher at Jones Elementary School. After years of teaching children with learning disabilities, she was beaten down by the toughness of the job, so she got a second chance by moving to a regular second-grade class:

I kind of think teachers are born. There is some spark in there. You have to have enthusiasm. You have to love it. I know there are people who don't feel it, and I think how miserable it must be to go into that classroom every day if you aren't really wanting to be there. I think anybody would sense you are doing a poor job.

My husband and I laughed one day about what we would want on our tombstones. I said that I'd just like something like, "She made learning fun. She wanted to make children love learning."

Marilyn Givens taught for almost forty years before retiring. At the time of this interview she was teaching special education at Airbase Elementary School, in Homestead, Florida. She explained why she made the move from the regular classroom to special education:

I was teaching first grade and I noticed every year that there were one or two children I just couldn't reach. They just couldn't learn to read although I knew that they were smart children. I thought, why? I am varying my methods. I am doing everything you're supposed to do and still they can't learn.

For example, there was a little boy named Buster in my class. He could not spell. In first grade there was a formal list of words that we had to test every week. He made an F every single spelling test. So along about April, we had the color words for a spelling list. So I'd call out red and I could see Buster get his red crayon and he'd look at it and he'd write. I thought, at last he's going to get a good grade. At last he'll get a little self-esteem.

So I went very slowly and waited until he'd put each crayon away. Green, brown, blue. He'd take out each crayon and copy the word down. At last I announced, "Today I am going to grade Buster's paper first." Then I collected his paper and looked down at it and he had written "Crayola, Crayola, Crayola" eight times. He had such learning problems that he did not even get the concept that each word would look different. So I decided to go get my master's degree and find out how to help children like Buster.

And I have found teaching children with disabilities the most thrilling. So many of these children just don't fit in academically, socially, or emotionally. And to take them and change their lives is wonderful.

I had a boy named Eddie once. He was a very intelligent child but he had such severe learning disabilities that they affected him emotionally because he felt he was letting everyone down. By the time I got him he was in the fourth grade and he'd try to run out in front of cars to kill himself.

His mother volunteered in my class. After six months she'd seen this terrific change in him. He was being taught right, at his level, and he was succeeding. He just changed. She told me one day that her church group had started talking about miracles. They asked if anyone had ever experienced a miracle. She said, "Well, I have. It was the change in Eddie." To be told you are part of a miracle is wonderful.

CHAPTER 2

CHILDREN

CAROLYN EPPS JACKSON stands beside the smudged window of her classroom at Mary C. Terrell Elementary School. Beyond the glass are the bleak towers of Chicago's Robert Taylor Homes, one of the largest, poorest, and most violence-prone public housing projects in the country — and home to the children in her class.

"Walk the turf so you can see what the children actually experience," says Jackson. "You have no idea what it is like being in a housing project until you go to one. And even then, you have no idea what it is like living in one."

There is bitterness in her tone. It is understandable. The fact is that the lives of these children are nothing less than horrible. They are the next generation of what has become known as the permanent underclass.

Here are some of those facts, compiled by the Children's Defense Fund: One of every five children in the United States lives in poverty. Children are twice as likely as adults to be poor, and children grew poorer in the 1980s as the nation grew richer. Children are safer in Northern Ireland than in America. The nation's infant mortality rate is higher than that of Singapore. Twelve million children have no health insurance.

Few of the children raised in this environment have the power to change their lives, and for most, any hope at all of escaping the cycle of poverty and hopelessness must come from education. As Yale University professor Edward Zigler warns, "We are cannibalizing children. Children are dying in this system, never mind achieving optimum development."

Children of poverty are half of the fastest-growing segment of the American school population. The other half of the segment is composed of the children of minorities. By the year 2020, it is expected that half of all students in American elementary and secondary schools will be members of minority groups. California and Texas have reached that benchmark already. This population, too, brings its own set of problems to teachers.

Yet it is not just children from impoverished families or newly emigrated children who present difficult burdens to America's teachers. Children from middle-class and wealthy families arrive at school with little regard for the rules or respect for their teachers. Accustomed to watching television passively, they are ill prepared to concentrate on what a teacher is saying or what is before them in a workbook.

"I feel like I have to keep my lessons about thirty seconds long and move from spot to spot in front of the room just to keep their attention," says Linda Raines, who teaches second graders at an Indiana school.

Even children from functioning families and safe neighborhoods come to school unprepared to learn. They have been deprived of play time because they are required to fit into the hectic schedules of their parents. The periods of free play or simply of quiet times for reading or thinking have been vanquished by the assault of television and the demand for instant gratification. The gap between what children are capable of doing and what teachers believe they should be doing is widening, and the implications are frightening.

Jane M. Healy, a former teacher, calls attention to these changed children in her startling book *The Endangered Minds*. "Likable, fun to be with, intuitive, and often amazingly self-aware, they seemed, nonetheless, harder to teach, less attuned to verbal material, both spoken and written," she writes.

Many of these are children of the sixties generation, whose parents invented bell-bottom jeans, participated in the sexual revolution, and reveled in the abandonment of rules and disregard for institutions. Others have been termed part of the "latchkey generation" — children who leave school and find empty homes waiting. These are youngsters from families divided by divorce or changed dramatically by the economic pressures that require both parents to work. Theirs is a real social turmoil, too. Small wonder then that even teachers in the most affluent school districts in the country complain about disruptive students, drugs, crime, and a lack of motivation in their classes.

Numerous experts have described how the problems of society are washing over the schools, distracting and damaging children and reducing their motivation to learn. It is the teachers who see this daily, from the front lines. And it is the teachers who see the peril that confronts our future as a result.

Kindergarten teachers say a third of their children arrive at school unprepared to learn. By the third grade, teachers report seeing students relegated to lives of failure, defeated by abuse and neglect. Again, the proof is in the figures: Every eight seconds of the school day, an American child drops out. Every twenty-six seconds a child runs away from home, and every forty-seven seconds a child is abused or neglected. Every thirty-six minutes a child is killed or injured by a gun, and every two and a half hours a child dies because of poverty.

The roots of these problems are found in the problems besetting society at large, such as the lack of universal health care, the absence of organized day care for the children of working parents, the failure to provide early childhood education for children and parents through programs such as Head Start, and the lack of career and vocational training programs in secondary schools. A single statistic tells much of the story about the nation's priorities: America spends a smaller percentage of its gross national income on elementary and secondary education than any other major industrial country, including its direct competitors — Japan, Germany, England, and France.

For teachers, these are not just statistics and theories. It is the reality they must face every day in the struggle to help children succeed — or at least survive. Simply put, the kids are changing, and those changes place a whole new set of demands on their teachers. Finding a spark to kindle inside these minds is a challenge met one child at a time, day in and day out, year after year.

Many of these problems confront Leonard Mednick every day when he goes to work at John Dewey High School, which serves three thousand students in a neighborhood that straddles the neat single-family homes of Bensonhurst and the housing projects of Coney Island. The school, named for an educator who advocated "learning by doing" as the basic principle of the classroom, stresses independent study. It also is a groundbreaker in another sense. John Dewey High was the first school in New York City to hand out condoms to its students.

Mednick, a former teacher, is a guidance counselor who tries to help his students overcome the problems of the outside world when they come to school for its distinctive eight-hour day:

I tell my kids, "Imagine you put your troubles in a bag and leave it on the steps of the building. Who is going to steal it? Nobody wants your garbage. Everybody's got his own. So you can feel real comfortable if you take your troubles, put them in a sack, and leave it out there. For eight hours, you think of nothing but what you have to do for your future, the subjects you have to do, and the homework you have to do. Troubles aren't going to go away. They'll be out there."

But I tell them, too, that the people who get hurt out there are the ones who are vulnerable. They cannot hurt someone who is strong and independent. "You make yourself strong and independent and use the school to do that and you'll have a great life," I tell them. "But the first step is to get your little butt to class."

Once they get here, you see them laughing all day long. You watch them on the train and they have to put on a train face. You cannot look at another kid on the train. If you make eye contact, it's a signal. At the same time, if you disengage, you may be soft and easily victimized.

We tell kids that they cannot carry a weapon in school, but they got to go home. Stuff happens. There is turf carved out all over. This is Coney Island. At night over there are hookers. There is a lot of crack. This is a part of life you and I have never dealt with. I wouldn't want to be a kid today.

Barbara Ruggles teaches third grade at Black Hawk Elementary School, in Park Forest, Illinois, a racially mixed suburb of Chicago. A liberal, outspoken single parent herself, Ruggles sees children coping with more responsibility and domestic crises than ever before in her twenty years in the classroom:

We had this one little girl, Latasha. There were six kids in her family. Her mom had been paying rent every month, but the landlord had been buying drugs with the money. Latasha's mother was evicted. She couldn't read. She had had a job but lost it. Our principal went over to the house and in there they had a couch and an unplugged refrigerator with piles of rice and potatoes in it and a pile of blankets and clothes where the kids slept. That's all there was. When the mother went to lay the baby on the floor, first she had to sweep away the roaches.

This little girl came to school and she wouldn't talk. Yet I knew she was bright when I read her stories. I could see her sparkle and that she caught on before lots of other kids caught on. It was really hard to get her to talk. We thought we were finally making progress when the family had to leave.

They found a room in the Heights. The mom was terrified to go shopping because she couldn't afford cab fare. She'd keep the kids at home, lock the doors and windows. One day she walked to the Jewel grocery and she came back and found that the baby had crawled into the bathroom, where there was a leak, and drowned. So the state came and took all of her remaining five kids because she was an unfit mother. She was hysterical and came to the school and asked us to help her.

Suddenly the whole family disappeared. She hid. We don't know where she is. If you're rich, you can get yourself out of a jam and pretty much work everything out. If you've got nothing, you've got nothing.

We went to the Field Museum of Natural History one time and a little boy, Derek, was looking at one of the dioramas. I said, "Time to go," and he turned around and started to cry. "I could stay forever," he sobbed. You know, thank heavens we brought him.

Art Murnan is a religion teacher and guidance counselor at Providence-St. Mel, an inner-city, independent school in Chicago with a nationwide reputation for giving black students an opportunity to succeed. It is a tough school with high standards, both in terms of academics and student behavior, set in the midst of Chicago's tough West Side. Murnan has been there for more than twenty years:

There is probably no school like this in the whole country. I have seen so much hope in this school. The kids are different. I had a couple of freshmen this year. The first couple weeks I thought, "Oh, God. These kids' skills are so low; they've had such negative educational experience. They don't even want to be here. They were sent." They were saying, "This is too hard, too demanding." Then sometimes something happens. It doesn't happen to all kids. We lose some. But you see them begin to believe in themselves and their expectations rise.

They are real frightened to make the leap because it is easier for a kid to say, "I failed because I didn't do it" than to say, "I tried and I didn't make it." You have to give them a lot of support, rebuilding. You can't be afraid to let them fail. I use the example of learning to walk. I act it out. I fall. The baby, when he falls, doesn't say, "Well, damn, I'm not going to do that again." He get up and tries again. Of course he's going to fall again. How many times? Lots. But eventually he'll walk. And then when he walks, he runs, he climbs, he keeps expanding.

I remember, maybe ten years ago, when I recruited a kid for the track team who had just finished his freshman year and had not been able to participate in sports because of his grades. I worked with him during the summer in track and he really got into it. He saw track as his vehicle to take him someplace, and he really started to work academically, too.

I remember the second semester of his junior year. We were going to a basketball game and he was on the student bus with me. The assistant principal was on the bus, too. She said to me, "Oh, by the way, Rodney's cumulative average just reached 2.0." I called Rodney to the front of the bus and told him. He turned and ran down the aisle, yelling, excited. Just to know that, wow, here's a kid who, on paper, should have dropped out, who shouldn't have made it. But because someone somewhere was able to give him something to allow him to believe in himself and then because he struggled and struggled, he was going to make it. Rodney went on to go to college and to graduate.

There are lots of kids like that. What makes me so excited is to go into the grocery store and hear some kid call out, "Mr. Murnan," and you get a big hug and a kiss in the middle of Dominick's. Especially when it is a male. Everyone wonders what is going on, but he's just happy to see you because he is making it in life and he feels good. They aren't the president of IBM, but they are doing something and they are happy and you were the one who inspired them. That is a tremendous shot in the arm.

We had an affair last night at the Harold Washington Library. It was a celebration of our SOUL program. It stands for Summer Opportunity of a Lifetime. We had 155 kids last summer who were at the University of Paris, Oxford, working in Singapore, going to Exeter, wilderness experiences, working for big corporations all over the United States.

There were five hundred people at the program. It was emceed by a senior. There were five or six speeches, starting with a fifth grader, going up to a senior, talking about their experiences. Tears were coming down my cheeks, thinking that I had been connected with each one of these kids in one way or another. The confidence, the spunk they had. Don't ask me what they said, but you had to be so impressed with these kids. Here they were in front of five hundred people, real power people, and they spoke with such unbelievable confidence, right from the heart. That kind of thing gives you the adrenaline to keep going.

Yeah, there are down moments, times you're frustrated, you know you've worked hard with a kid, but you just want to scream. I have a resurrection philosophy. There's death and dying, but you know it will rise again. I have a poster at home. It says, "I believe in the sun, even when it doesn't shine."

Teachers whose students come from the most disadvantaged backgrounds must count their victories in small increments, deriving satisfaction one child at a time. Ron Cooper is young, a former athlete and tennis coach who ignored a business career and chose teaching. As a teacher at Van Buren Middle School in Albuquerque, New Mexico, he confronts children with such limited horizons that he broke down and cried as he recalled the story of one:

David was one distraught little kid. I knew there was a lot going on in this little kid's life so I went on a home visit. I have to understand what is going on at home so I can understand what is going on in school.

It was kind of shocking. There were three kids in the family. His mother was a landlord and a prostitute. The apartment was foul. I began to see why David was so frustrated because he wasn't receiving the attention he needed. He just needed someone in his life who thought he was worthwhile. He was predestined to a life of pain because his mother didn't know any better. David was caught between his mother and society, just trying to survive.

I look out at this community and I think, "Shit, these kids are being sacrificed and no one is doing a fucking thing." I am resentful as hell because there is no goddamn money to spend here, to help these kids, our kids.

I look at David and I think, "This kid deserves a fucking medal just for being where he is today." It's taken a long time. Some days I have to pick him up, take him outside the class, and say, "Hey, man, relax. It's okay." David knows he counts now.

I measure success one day at a time and in very, very small increments — for me, as a teacher; for a kid, as a student. Today Shane wrote a sentence, or Louis showed interest in what we were trying to teach. I have one kid who doesn't get enough sleep. Hey, it's a success if Samantha is here today, she smells good, she's well fed, and she slept.

From special children come special joys, as Celeste Lenzini, a kindergarten teacher at Maury Elementary School in Alexandria, Virginia, discovered:

I get bored at cocktail parties with adults. It is rare that I get bored in the classroom, because with twenty-two children around, someone is always doing something witty or insightful and charming the pants off of you at any given moment.

I had a wonderful lesson in the second or third year I taught, from a little boy. He was severely handicapped and he used crutches. He came in and had very little control of his legs. One would be here. One would be there. And I thought, "Oh, my God. How will we manage here in this classroom?"

Well, we managed very well. These crutches would land on everyone. They'd say, "Get your crutch off my foot." Five-year-olds are a glorious age. His mother was dynamite. She was determined that he would have all the same experiences as other kids. When we went to the library on the second floor, he and I would leave early and we would walk up and the rest of the class would join us. When we walked to get a pumpkin, he went. All the things we did, he did. It was a lesson in courage.

At the end of the year, we took a trip from the school up to the Baskin-Robbins ice cream shop at the top of the hill, a very long walk. Earlier in the year, I had pulled him in a wagon. At the end of the year, he held my hand and we walked. I was so overwhelmed by the courage of that child. I learned so many lessons about what five-year-olds are, how kind they are, how normally they treated him.

When he graduated from high school three years ago, his mother called me and said he had asked for three teachers he loved to come. I was so moved. This is what teaching is to me. I had helped a child, but in turn he had helped me and all of us, immensely, much more.

You see, teaching is a two-way process. That is what education courses don't convey. They say it is teacher to child, and it is not. You are learning from the children. I have had a fortunate life, but I learn from children who have not. And by teaching their young mothers, I hope I have become more sensitive and developed a sense of empathy for how hard it is for some people just to get through life. They really don't get very many breaks. The sun does not shine too often on them, so one learns to have understanding. I would have been much more brittle if I had not had the opportunity to see people and understand how hard it can be.

Frank Tobin's pupils range in age from fourteen to seventeen. These students are inmates in the Cook County Temporary Juvenile Detention Center in Chicago, awaiting sentencing for murder, armed robbery, or drug dealing:

From my experience with these kids, I recognize that there is something very beautiful and very good about each one of them. They don't know it. I have them five days a week, all day long, for an average of ten months. They can't hide it that long. Ultimately it comes out. Their defenses break down after a period of time. It has been my experience that underneath all this rough, gruff exterior there are just a lot of little boys looking for a father.

These kids have two big needs. One is to improve their self-esteem. It is terrible. If, through what I do in the classroom, I can help a kid get a little self-respect and awareness of his own dignity and worth, he will better himself. Then, if they are going away to the joint, which most of them do, I try to get them ready for that by showing them how important it is to take control of their lives and not let circumstances control them. I want them to have some self-respect and not be destroyed by the system.

The most destructive thing schools do is not respecting them for the human beings that they are. A lot of teachers, especially with these kids in the inner city, will just chalk them off as lost causes. It's dehumanizing. It is saying it is not worth all the trouble it would take to do something for you. The system doesn't have the money or resources.

I say that we have two kinds of teachers. Strong, sensitive teachers and strong, insensitive teachers. You have got to be strong one way or another just to survive. The strong and insensitive survive because they just don't give a damn and they are strong enough to put up with all the garbage and they don't care about the kids. They keep the peace and pick up their paychecks. The strong and sensitive are tuned in to the needs of the kids. They try to work with them and do what they can.

I had a kid, a Puerto Rican kid who had been in here over a year waiting to go to trial. Sometimes kids wait two years. It is terrible because sometimes they just might be innocent. They have to do the time because they can't afford bail.

I had a hard time with this kid. We respected each other, but he was very resistant and he had a hostile attitude. He was always sent upstairs for fighting. He was a big-time gang banger. The other day he sat down next to me and I tried to get him to talk. He said, "I just don't care what happens to me. I don't care." And that's the way he acts. It's his despair. He's been here so long. He has no hope for the future. It is easy for a kid to get a hopeless attitude. He hasn't had the chance for role models in his community to give him hope. His life is all gangs and violence and drugs.

Their worlds are just that small. They don't have any perspective about the real world. You ask a kid like him how many people live in Chicago, and he might answer three thousand. We try to broaden them a little bit. They have no idea how big Chicago is. Some don't even know about Lake Michigan or the Chicago River. Some have never been off their damn block. They are very involved in only the life on their block and it takes up all their life and strength.

Michelle Kaufman teaches fifth grade at Anna Howard Shaw Elementary School (Public School 61) on New York City's Lower East Side:

I had a child tell me that he wanted to be a drug dealer when he grew up. I asked why and he said because you get respect, you get to drive around in a beautiful car, and you can take care of your family. He had no idea that that was something negative. That it was illegal. He had no idea that there were other ways to get those things.

These kids come to school with such deficiencies. We are losing some children. What is at stake? The future of America. The future of our country. I keep on telling my kids that they are the key. Their parents haven't done such a wonderful job in terms of caring for the world and it's up to them to make the difference.

Cary Tyler was a precocious eight-year-old when he moved with his family to Albuquerque, New Mexico. In Chicago, he had failed the first grade and was already disenchanted with school. But in his new school, a teacher took an interest in Tyler and he excelled.

When he graduated from college years later, Tyler went to work for the *Albuquerque Tribune*. Covering the police and education beats, he got a close look at the troubles confronting the city's youngsters. It didn't take long for him to decide that he wanted to do more for them. Taking advantage of a New Mexico program that licenses teachers without an education degree, he took a five-hundred-dollar-a-month pay cut to become an English and writing teacher at Van Buren Middle School, the same school where Ron Cooper teaches:

I think a lot of first-year teachers come in thinking, "I am going to save the classroom. All my kids are going to make it. They are so cute." No, not all these kids are cute. There are going to be discipline problems. There are some who just don't care no matter what you do. They are not going to click.

I covered this area when I worked at the newspaper, in both education and crime beats. I know about the juveniles arrested for murder and armed robbery. So I know what these kids are like. And their attitudes. So I wasn't surprised when I had a gang member in class. I wasn't surprised when a kid who looked like he was going to make it suddenly dropped out.

As a teacher, you can only do the best you can. If you think you are going to win over all these kids, you'll go home disappointed and you will start stumbling and eventually you won't care any more. That is why we lose so many first-year teachers; they honestly came in thinking they could change the world.

But I can handle this. I am going to give these kids exactly what they need and maybe, just maybe, they will escape, by being able to read and write and think.

After twenty-four years of teaching and chemistry, Joel Kaplan has learned that you can't change the world. But over those years, he has discovered that he can change the lives of individual children. Yet Kaplan, who now teaches at T. C. Williams High School in Alexandria, Virginia, finds little joy in today's students:

I've always played counselor, friend, et cetera, particularly in New York. I used to spend 50 percent of my time teaching chemistry. The rest of the time was doing other things. The things the kids really cared about. With all this, my students always performed at the very highest levels in the school. The other teachers were always amazed. "He's never doing chemistry. How do they do so well?" We used to talk about other things. Then I'd say, "All right, now we have to get to the chemistry and you have to give me your undivided attention. You must really concentrate."

There are kids alive today because of these little chats in class. But they took a lot out of me. I spent too much time with those kids and not enough time with my own children. So I don't do it anymore. So, if any of these kids need that help now, I refer them to our school shrink.

One of my ex-students, a kid I had helped to stay alive, was getting married. This was after she graduated. She used to bring her boyfriends out to the house. A lot of my students and ex-students used to do that. It was really neat. The day she was getting married was a Sunday, and there was this hall in New York where it was taking place. For a teacher, money is always tight. The bus coming up from Washington was late. We ran into traffic somewhere. We were about forty-five minutes late and we had to go to another former student's house to change into our wedding clothes.

So we go through the big double doors of the hall, and here is this little girl in this full, magnificent wedding gown, running back up the aisle. When she gets to me, she jumps on me, wraps her legs around me.

"Is it all over?" I asked.

"How could I get married without Mr. Kaplan?" she replied, shaking her head no.

Nobody knew why they were holding up the wedding. I heard people asking, "Who is this guy?"

"He is her ex–chemistry teacher," someone said.

That was very nice. I have appreciated that throughout the years. She had had problems, serious problems. She couldn't put things together. I couldn't do that for her. But I could help her survive, to solve her self-esteem problems.

This is the first year I can tell you that I have been bored and it is all because of the nature of my students. They are changing. I do labs today that would have made their older brothers and sisters say, "Wow." They don't get turned on the way they used to.

A lot of what I do in class is not directly related to chemistry. I will relate chemistry to politics, to business. The kids used to really get into it, doing this real world stuff. But these kids today just don't care. They say leave me alone to do what I have to do to get by. They are nice kids. They are bright, no less bright than their older siblings. They just don't care. There is no inner drive, no natural curiosity.

Cities across the country have set up magnet schools to offer specialized programs and compete with the private and suburban schools. They usually offer open enrollment to all children living in the district, sometimes by lottery and sometimes by testing. Some magnet schools emphasize the arts or science. The Disney Magnet School on Chicago's lakefront is a school without walls, where teams of teachers operate minischools within the building.

The philosophy at Disney is to stimulate the whole class by mixing the brightest students with those who are behind academically. But Tom Starnicky, a large man who moves around the science laboratory on a chair with wheels, has found that even the brightest students are deficient:

The kids we have today, everything is hand-fed to them. They are not challenged in looking for what would be new. They all have tape recorders. They don't know what a printed circuit is, they don't know what a chip is, and yet it's entirely part of their lives. They don't know how a laser disc works. When they check the food out at the grocery counter, they don't understand that simple light mechanism. I think that's where we are missing and that's where I want to go. Because so many things are a part of their lives and they just accept them. They don't seem to care. They don't make the extension and application to real life.

When they go out the school door, it's like a wall drops. This is what they learn in school, but it isn't part of their lives. There is no analytical thinking. They should be challenging everything. When they understand how something works, they might understand why it goes wrong. We're trying to show them that what they are doing in school is relevant to their lives and their future.

Some of these kids are ten or twelve years old, they turn on a TV and see cars that fly and they believe it. They don't make the judgment that this flying car is the result of someone's imagination. If they don't like it they just push a button and change the channel. Someday they will run out of buttons.

More than sixty languages are spoken by the children who attend Miami Beach Senior High School, a wonderful melting pot of traditions and cultures that reflects Miami as a whole. Paul Hirko was teaching math at Miami Beach Senior High School at the time of his interview. He has since become assistant principal of Westview Middle School, also in Miami:

One of my favorite things about this job is when you see true creativity from children, either academic or social. This is one of my favorite all-time stories.

I was teaching in another school. When I am in a classroom, it is mine. Kids don't come in unless it is their time or they have a pass. I had been in the school long enough for the word to get out. Kids just didn't bother to come into my room to visit with friends.

One day I had a knock at my door and the terror of the school appeared. This gal was just awesome. I was afraid of her. She was a real street tough. She came to the door and said, "I want to see so-and-so." I asked if she had a pass and why she wanted to see this girl. She said she had the pass and she needed to see her friend because she had her shoes. I looked down at her feet, and sure enough: no shoes. So, of course, I let her in and they chatted. When they were done this kid pranced down the hall, went to an unlocked locker, reached in and took out her shoes, and away she went. I appreciated her creativity.

Faye Williams has taught cosmetology for nineteen years at Carver High School, which is near a huge landfill in a bleak section of Chicago's South Side:

Currently there is a young lady who lives in a local housing development and who is from a very low-income family. She came to me as a freshman and had a baby that same year. We fought like dogs. She was really so belligerent and incorrigible. I would have to go get a dictionary to describe how difficult she was as a freshman.

I can't tell you why I kept trying, except that I must have been totally crazy. I try to focus on those kids who want to learn, and not put a lot of energy into the have-nots. But I have not been very successful at it. I still tend to reach out to the kid who needs me.

The second year she was a little easier. Then this spring, her junior year, she was able to compete for state office in the vocational-professional organization. The morning of the election, I asked her to write out her speech. She was intimidated because she was black and she figured all these white kids would be sharper. She felt she did not have a snowball's chance in hell.

"Let me suggest something to you," I said. "Just write your story. Write how difficult your life has been. Write what vocational education means to you, how you've learned to interact with groups. Life at home is not a bed of roses, but you have learned to give it a shot."

So she wrote it, and I helped her a little to shape it. She was shaking as she had to give that speech, but she got up there and she had the officers and advisers in tears. She is now the state vice president. I just hope that she sticks with it because she is still in the housing projects.

Although Jeff Jackson began his career at Merrill Lynch in Atlanta, he knew that something was missing. Growing up, he had worked with kids and missed them. At the time of this interview he was a third-grade teacher at Maury Elementary School in Alexandria, Virginia, but he has since returned to Georgia to teach at Minor Elementary School in Lilburn:

First-year teachers, they all go through this. I did last year. They come in thinking that you are going to do miracles. Save the world in your first year of teaching. I had a rude awakening. I learned I have no control over where these kids go every day when they leave here. The only thing I can control is my classroom. That was hard for me to accept — that I am limited in what I can do.

I had this one child last year, who on the third day of school, called me a name. Something I won't repeat now. That was the kind of year I had with this child. It was constant. Every day. Of course, he was screaming out for help. He wanted discipline, authority, attention. But he rebelled against it also. After a whole year of this, I didn't think I had any impact on this child at all.

This year, he's in a different school because his family moved. I got a letter from him. He was asking about my class this year. He wanted to know if they were being nice to me. He talked about last year and how much he enjoyed being in this classroom. Well, it was the reading teacher in his new school who got him to write me, she said, because all he would talk about was "Mr. Jackson, this. Mr. Jackson, that." That let me know that I did have some influence. He knew I cared.

Kids know. You can't fool them. We teach the basic facts, but teachers do much more than that. With a kid like that, if he can always look back on his third-grade year and get some kind of feeling of security or warmth, then I guess I have succeeded with him.

Ray Devenney, who teaches in the English as a Second Language program at Bell Multicultural School in Washington, D.C., does not worry about what cannot be changed but tries to deal with the reality faced by his students:

What are kids like today? I have no idea. I never see them. It is something we joke about. If you see a fifteen-year-old walk in with a real family and no economic pressures, he or she is an anomaly.

It was interesting. We had a group of Japanese teachers visit the school last year. We heard a lot of them saying, "American students don't study very hard. We go to school 250 days a year." To that, I say, "Yeah, but my kids work till 2:00 A.M." Every kid in my class is working. Over half of them at full-time jobs. You could see their faces drop. What do you mean, the kid is the sole support of the family? What do you mean that you have an economic system where kids have to go out and support their families?

Our students are wonderful students. They could be brilliant students. They could be great. But the reality of the situation is that the pressure on people to live is so great, so overwhelming, that it becomes a battle to convince them that education will pay off. You'll get something from it. Your family is going to be better off. You're going to be better off.

This is not a country that takes a long-term view. There's an economy in trouble, but there is always someone out there with a bad job for you. There is always someone out there willing to exploit you. There is always a large building to be cleaned, and if something falls on you or you get sick, there is always someone else to take that job.

These are the realities of life for a lot of people. I think that separating this kind of system from educational goals is preposterous. My goals when I come to school every day are to get involved and make a difference and try to show the students that in the long run the things that I am saying are beneficial, that it does give them control, and that it does give them power. And that what they get now is not power, they get exploited, they get used, they get to be paid minimal amounts of money with no protection and no future.

Carolyn Langston teaches third grade at Dunbar Erwin Elementary School, a public school in a poor, predominantly black neighborhood in Newport

News, Virginia. She grew up there. The neighborhood hasn't changed much, she says, just the color of the skin of the people living there. Everyone is still poor. She is guided by her own difficult childhood in dealing with her students today:

These children are different from children of years past in some small ways. But not a lot. They still love to know that there is somebody they can depend on. That there is somebody who is going to be fair. That somebody cares about them. Those things never change, and they never will, ever. Certainly these children today have a wider knowledge of worldly things. They have seen a lot of unlovely things. But you know, I did, too. I was born in this neighborhood. People think it has changed, but it hasn't. Only its color has changed, not its economics. But when I was a child, we just didn't talk about it. My mother said, "Close those curtains and lock the door and we are not going to talk about it." That is the way I was raised. My father drank and beat up on us. Today you say that you can help the children if they tell. But you can't always. Sometimes you just have to give them the tools to live with what their life is like.

If a child comes in and smells because his mother is on drugs or drunk and is not going to bathe him, it's okay to call her on the phone all you want. But let's teach that child how to bathe himself. Just call him aside and say to him, up front, point-blank, you don't smell good. And the other children don't want to sit next to you. Now I know that you don't like that, that it doesn't make you feel good. But let me tell you what you need to do.

It's simple; why make a big, complicated case out of it? Children can handle that. If a child can handle living with a druggie for a mother or a daddy, he can certainly handle bathing himself. Certainly. We don't give children enough credit for the things they can do. Nobody wants a child to live in these circumstances, but many do.

The school I worked in before was very affluent. There was a guidance counselor there who is a wonderful person, but she was also very affluent. A member of the country club. That is all she knows. I can remember distinctly hearing her advice to a child one day. Obviously the child had told her something in confidence about a parent drinking and some kind of abuse. I heard her say to the child, "Have you tried talking to her?"

I thought that only tells me that you've never lived like that. You don't talk to a drunk. What you learn down here is that you don't call a parent on Friday night. Wait till Monday. I knew that a long time ago. That's when my daddy got drunk. I also know that when you have worked in a factory or picked crabs or whatever you have to do to live, you don't feel like reading to your children at night.

I think every teacher should have to teach at both ends of the city. These children are wonderful. I see their low scores and their low performance as being lack of vocabulary and experience. It is not a lack of intelligence, but that there is so little they've been exposed to. This four-block area is their lives.

But they are our future and we all are responsible for our little part of it. They deserve the best part of us and what we have learned. They still love to know that there is somebody they can depend on, that there is somebody who is going to be fair, that somebody cares about them.

Marion Hamilton grew up in Waco, Texas, a small town where he had the option of becoming a preacher or a teacher. He chose the latter and moved to California because he thought it would be less racist. Now he teaches fifth grade at Wadsworth Avenue Elementary School, which is in a high-crime area of Los Angeles, near the scene of the race rioting in the spring of 1992:

Some of our children come in motivated to learn. But some of ours haven't had breakfast. Maybe the night before they didn't sleep. Or if they did, you don't know where they slept. You don't know if they were at home by themselves. You just don't know. You have a certain feeling about these kids, that you can just about tell what some of them are going through. I had a student once, a little kid, very gifted orally. He could talk so beautifully. Couldn't read. Couldn't write. But could hold his own in a conversation with adults.

I asked myself, "What is with this kid? Why is he not learning? Why can't he read, write, do column addition, subtraction?" So I asked around. Other teachers told me, "You know the conditions he lives in? The mother and father do drugs." Finally they had a raid on his apartment and the child took off to his aunt's house. It was the best thing that ever happened to him. He can do things now. You have to be aware of these things. He had so much going on in his life that he just couldn't concentrate.

About twenty miles and a world away, Pat Maier teaches French at Palos Verdes Peninsula High School, in an upper-middle-class area overlooking the Pacific Ocean:

Teaching, I love it and I hate it. I love the kids. I get angry with them. Every kid who walks through my door is my kid. My kid.

I don't think we expect enough of kids today. I know a lot of people who say a kid has a right to fail. By God, a kid does not have a right to fail. For starters, he isn't old enough to make that decision. It infuriates me. You do not have a right to fail. Not in my classroom. We just do not expect enough of children today.

Father Wilbur Atwood has taught high school boys for thirty years at St. Augustine High School in New Orleans. It is a school where young men are addressed as "Mister" to build their self-esteem and respect for others, and it has established a sterling record for sending young black men on to the nation's best colleges:

I don't find students that much different than those that were here when I first came thirty years ago. They are still trying to find any weakness in your armor in order to slip one through so they can score one. That is part of the challenge of teaching, to stay on your feet and sharp enough so that you can mentally and intellectually do battle with them each day.

Perhaps it's the location. Perhaps it's the teacher. But John Schiff has found substantial changes in students over the years. He teaches at Santa Fe Preparatory School, a progressive, well-regarded private school in the capital of New Mexico. His students tend to be bright and hardworking, but Schiff echoes the concerns of many teachers who worry that they are not making the critical difference in students' lives by making them good learners and not just "grade grubbers":

Kids are very different today than when I started. I find kids are much, much more grade-conscious, and that produces in them a kind of desire to quantify and objectify learning in a way they can draw within their easily achievable grasp. They don't want to learn how to think, they want to learn how to score high on standardized tests. They don't want to learn what is important about the French Revolution. They don't want to learn about Locke, Hobbes, and Rousseau. They don't want to learn anything about political theory, but what they want to learn is how can you get a high grade on the test.

For many years Dren Geer was principal of the prestigious and expensive Francis Parker School in Chicago. When he retired, Geer was far from done with education. He signed on as the development director at Providence-

St. Mel, an all-black high school on the city's West Side. He also teaches an advanced placement English class, and there he continues to be astounded and renewed by his students:

I'm in this class teaching *Othello.* I've probably taught *Othello* eight times through the years. I remember the first time I read *Othello.* It was in high school and I thought I was a hotshot because I got one of my first really good grades.

When I was teaching *Othello* this last time, with a spectacular kid, we were looking at the relationship between Othello and Iago in Act 1. And in two forty-minute periods I was in another dimension of the play. I mean I was probing, exploring, and seeing things I'd never seen before.

This kid said to me, "Now, I'm black and Othello is black. Othello wouldn't last ten minutes on the street in my neighborhood. But Iago, he's the man. Iago is an inner-city black. He knows how to put on a different face. Othello is just a pompous ass. He was white, but in terms of real character, Iago is the real black man."

This kid was calling Othello an oreo. He was brilliant. Marvelous. What do you have to do to get this? Show me a lawyer who experiences this kind of thing and people like this day in and day out.

Much has been written about how today's busy parents program the lives of their children, maintaining appointment calendars for children to play together, and generally imposing an excessive amount of structure on these young lives. Molly Donohue, who teaches third grade at Chicago's Francis Parker School, has seen the effects of this regimentation:

Kids of today are different. The biggest change I've noticed is that the women's movement might as well never have happened. My girls are so feminized now that they are all wearing dresses. They are emulating what they see — the dangly earrings, heels, nylons, makeup, hair. They're concerned about their weight. I feel the girls I am educating now are more fearful, physically more fearful. They have less of a sense of physical competence. They don't want to play in gym.

In fact, I think parents right now are very fearful of the world and are very protective of their children. They won't let them go out and experiment. They are afraid something is going to happen to them. I think they are more fearful for their daughters than their sons, because society expects boys to go out and do more dangerous things.

Parents say to me that they cannot let their child go out and ride a bike on the city streets. Well, my brother had three bikes stolen from him. I was taught as a very young child which people to watch. I wasn't allowed to ride my bike unless I had somebody with me, but I was never told not to ride the bike. I was told to go find someone to go riding with. I was told always that although the world had dangers I could and should be able to find my way in it.

That, to me, is what the women's movement was about. Yes, it is tough out there, but these are the options. You can and should expect yourself to be able to do these things. I think children are hearing, "Oh, don't do that yet."

Think of all the after-school athletic programs there are. Our children go to eight specific play groups and athletic programs. We don't see third graders playing football with sixth and eighth graders. But that's how you learn the game, by playing with people of different ages. That's how you learn to cooperate, to make exceptions for each other. When I played baseball, I was the youngest player and my brother had to pitch to me on his knees.

They don't see themselves growing. Every goddamn day they're out there playing against the same kids.

Mary Bicouvaris, who teaches at Hampton Roads Academy in Newport News, Virginia, has seen changes in today's students, and she fights to avoid letting them change her:

I could have done something that some teachers do for survival — leave half the people behind and keep going with the other half. But I've never been able to do that. I struggle and struggle and sometimes I get slapped right and left by the same people I am trying to help: the students.

There is a growing level of indifference among students. The attitude is often, "Leave me alone. Get off my case. I don't care about this. I lost my book. I don't care if you give me a zero. I don't care if you give me 100."

In the 1960s, when I first started teaching, I recall the things for which we used to punish children. I can't believe it. We punished children for chewing gum. I remember my school suspended a student for riding his bike down the corridor.

The problems we had then were so different. The children were basically more obedient and their parents more supportive of the teacher. There was less anger and more compatibility in the classroom. There were some kids who were lost souls in the 1960s, but they were more idealistic. In a way it was exciting because they wanted answers to questions.

In the seventies and eighties, the idealism was lost. The children became cynics. They became more materialistic and less respectful of teachers. Slowly they came to look at their teachers as the failures they were for not meeting the materialistic aspirations that either some of the parents or the people they admired had.

Their attitude was, So what if you don't like it? You make only twenty-five thousand dollars a year, so what's the big deal?

During the last decade I have told my students many times how much I miss some of the students I taught in the late sixties and early seventies who would argue for hours about ideas when I wanted them to stop so we could move on to the next thing. That doesn't happen much anymore. They come in with their minds made up today and it is very difficult for teachers to change their minds. For example, this generation I am teaching right now has made up its mind about civil rights, affirmative action, and all the big issues.

I keep divorcing my feelings from what the students do as much as I can and I do the same thing I do with my own two children at home. I forgive the indiscretions, but I keep telling them what I think is right. I hope, as I do with my own children, that I am sowing the seeds that they will need later on. They are better off for having been with me — I know that.

It hurts me. I came with stars in my eyes. What I see now upsets me. We've dropped the ball here, we've dropped the ball there, we've dropped the ball everywhere. I think the American people will rally and they'll understand that the other people's children are everybody's children. It has to happen.

CHAPTER 3

PARENTS

ANGRY PARENTS. Pushy parents. Proud parents. Worried parents. Absent parents. Teachers deal with all kinds. They can be a teacher's closest ally, ensuring that a child comes to school fed and clean and prepared to learn, urging a child to do his or her homework at the end of the day. They can be a teacher's worst enemy, destroying the self-esteem of their own children and blocking educators at every turn. One thing is certain: They are a constant in the life of every teacher.

The most common complaint about parents from teachers is that mothers and fathers no longer set aside time to work with their children. Too many parents are drained at the end of their own workday, left with too little energy and not enough time to make sure the homework gets done. Others simply have no interest in the education of their children, preferring to leave all responsibility with the schools. The result is twofold: Specific work does not get done and children fall behind, and the lack of parental involvement diminishes the value of education in general in the eyes of children.

The wall of a kindergarten classroom in Washington, D.C., was graphic evidence of uninvolved parents. A chart listed the name of each student and recorded who had brought in his or her completed homework. It was the simplest type of work, circling the right number of ducks in a drawing or finding the item that doesn't belong in a group. However, someone had to read the instructions to the child when he or she took the work home, and the chart was a daily reminder that no one at home was taking the time to help. Some of the names were followed by a string of blanks across the chart; they had not returned a single piece of completed homework all year. At five and six years of age, these children were already falling behind, starting a spiral that too often ends in failure, because their parents were either unable or unwilling to help them build the scaffold of learning.

"The biggest problem I face in teaching is not having parents who really care," says Jeffrey Raab, a social studies teacher at Reelsville Elementary School in rural Reelsville, Indiana. "They say they care and they are good people, but they just don't want to spend the time it takes to show their children the importance of education. The teachers are being blamed for it, but I really believe the parents are the key that is missing."

Other teachers tell harrowing stories. "We have a kid here who brought a gun to school and his parents came over and wanted to defend it," says John Scott, an English teacher in Hampton, a southern Virginia community with a small-town quality that would seem to preclude such activity. "The parents talked about taking the issue to court. What kind of message did that send to the kid? When parents support kids when they are dead wrong, when parents send kids signals that doing the wrong thing is okay, what then can we, as teachers, be expected to do? I don't live with the ninety-six kids in my classes."

The forces at play are well known, even if their impact on a generation of children remains largely ignored. Poverty and violence have become constant companions of more children. Anyone in authority is an adversary. Economic pressures mean parents have less income and less time as they juggle work and family.

No matter how much excellent teaching a child receives at school, studies show that long-term outcomes are much better when families are also involved. Yet demographic changes in the past decade have made it harder for parents to find the time. During the 1980s, the number of two-income families rose dramatically, as did the percentage of single-parent homes. Two working parents or one absent parent does not translate directly into less concern for children or even less time for them, but it often means that children are coming to school less prepared. Once there, teachers find that these children are less able to take advantage of the opportunities offered them.

Another complaint from teachers centers on what some call "fast-track parents." Compared with parents who neglect their children or justify taking a gun to school, the demands of parents who want too much for their youngsters seem minor. However, those pressures can have a negative effect on children, too, causing them to measure their worth by grades alone, inhibiting curiosity, removing a child's right to learn from failure, and fostering elitism.

At the annual parents' meeting in the fall of 1992 at the exclusive St. Stephen's and St. Agnes School in Alexandria, Virginia, the head of the school, Joan Ogilvy Holden, stressed to parents that they must not measure their child's education by grades alone, but also by the degree to which their children learn to think for themselves and become lifelong learners.

There is a deepening perception among teachers that parents view them as adversaries, that parents have joined the remainder of the public in blaming educators for the problems in education. Every five years for the past three decades, the National Education Association has asked teachers to rank the hindrances they face in doing their jobs. The negative attitudes of parents and the public showed up as a concern among teachers for the first time in 1986. Nearly one teacher in ten said his or her job was harder because of poor parental and public attitudes, a ratio that has held steady since.

A survey of American teachers for the Metropolitan Life Insurance Company in 1991 found that seven of every ten respondents agreed with the statement "Too many parents today treat their children's schools and teachers as adversaries."

Teachers are an easy target. They are vulnerable to criticism because they are the human side of an education system in which people are losing faith. Some parents have expressed their dissatisfaction by withdrawing their children from the traditional school setting. The number of students educated at home by their parents has soared, from ten thousand in 1970 to three hundred thousand today, and the increase shows no signs of abating. A majority of these home schoolers still are conservative Christians, but a rising number are parents who value education and are fed up with the opportunities and hazards offered in public schools.

Countless studies have concluded that getting parents involved is the most important element in the educational success of a student. This is particularly true when the students are poor, hungry, and raised in an environment where education is not a priority.

Teachers and parents must work as cooperative partners for the benefit of the child, and often they do. Mark H. Mullin, the headmaster at Washington, D.C.'s exclusive St. Albans School, offered the following advice to parents: "Most people become teachers despite the low pay because they care about young people. Parents should keep this in mind when they meet with teachers."

Parents make the difference in whether children succeed or fail, said Laura Maners, a math teacher at Miraleste Intermediate School in Palos Verdes, California:

This school uses the California Assessment Program as a measuring tool. Every year, the Palos Verdes district scores about 95 percent. Then they have the Golden State Algebra Test. About 16 percent of the state's students score in the honors category and about 6 percent score in the high honors category; about 22 percent of the kids in this state score in those two categories. But of the students in Palos Verdes, 98 percent score in those two categories. What makes the difference? Motivation in the homes.

Kids come to school in this district ready to learn. Pressed, pushed. And if they don't get it in school, they get outside help, tutors.

We have a very large percentage of Asian students in our school, and their parents push. They still want to know what more a child can do when the child is already getting straight A's. One of my mothers is calling about her eleven-year-old in my class. She asks what she can do so the child will score well on the SAT's. The pressure is there.

Parents of many students at Beverly Hills High School are important people, and they expect their children to be important people, too, despite the many demands on the schools, as teacher John Borsum discovered one day:

I got a phone call from the school operator, saying, "Call Mr. So-and-so at this number. Urgent." The area code was 212: New York. On our phones we can't call long distance without getting permission, so I got permission and I called and he answered.

"This is John Borsum at Beverly Hills High School," I said. "What can I do for you?"

"Well, how has my daughter been doing?" he asked.

"She is not doing well," I said, "but before we get into that, what is the emergency?"

"There is no emergency," he said.

"I was given a message and I was told it was urgent," I said.

"Yes, it's important that I find out how my daughter is doing," he said.

Ten years ago I wouldn't have questioned the man because I was very passive. The parent is always right. I have learned over the years that you really shouldn't let these people get away with this kind of thing.

"Sir, I am very busy," I said to him. "You could have called me sometime after school when I was free or when you were in Los Angeles. Do you live in New York?"

"I live in Beverly Hills," he replied. "I'll be back tomorrow."

"Couldn't this have waited?" I asked.

"I suppose it could have," he said.

"Sir, I want to let you know something," I said. "Our school district has very few funds left and you've asked me to call long distance to New York. Maybe I'm being a little picky about money, but I think having to make this call is a little inappropriate."

He said, "If you ever have to call me again in New York, call collect."

I did talk to him briefly about his daughter. I guess it was his nerve that really bothered me. The school operator later told me that he made her take messages for every single one of his daughter's teachers.

Carolyn Barlow, a second-grade teacher at Maurice Hawk Elementary School in Princeton Junction, New Jersey, talked about the pressure some parents place on their children today:

I had one parent who was a professor at an Ivy League school. His child was having trouble with handwriting. The father came in, told me he was a graduate of a big-name school, that he was a Rhodes scholar. I told him that was very nice but we were there to talk about the child. He said that because he went to the big-name school he expected his child to go there also, and because he did well his child must do well. I couldn't believe it. The child was seven years old.

When you come to an area like West Windsor, you find everybody does well in West Windsor. I find that it's more "keep up with the Joneses." You should take your child for what he is, see what he can do well. There's too much competition. It's unbelievable in a district like this. Little kids give you a sign when they're ready for something. Especially the primary grades. But everyone wants his kid to do as well as another kid right away, instead of accepting him for where he is right now. He will be there, maybe in three months, but right now he's not there. Parents are so worried about what their neighbor will say, or think of their child.

Then parents are always there at the kid's every whim, every command. If a kid forgets his ice cream money, the parents pop in the door with it. Let him forget it one day. He won't forget it the next. Kids don't learn about life. Parents need lessons on how to parent.

Sinai Akiba Academy is a conservative Jewish day school in Los Angeles that offers both Hebrew and traditional curricula. It is very family-oriented, requiring parents to volunteer for work at the school, from preparing earthquake kits to presenting special programs in classes. Kathleen O'Neill recognizes the importance of keeping the lines of communication open with the families of her first and seventh graders:

This school is very high pressure. This year, most of my parents are pretty low-key. They're right on top of everything, though. Parent communication is very important, and I send letters home once a week. I write comments about each student and it goes in the Friday folder.

Sometimes parents can drive you crazy, and sometimes they can be very supportive. I don't know where I'd be without them. The support and the encouragement are key. I try to call parents once a month. They have a lot of questions, so I like to try to keep in touch so concerns don't grow.

Sometimes I think parents don't trust teachers as much as they trust their doctor or their lawyer. That's difficult to deal with sometimes. Teachers are busting their butts to give children a great education, and you have parents who are questioning their ability and decisions. They don't see the whole picture.

Dwight Brown would love to have Kathleen O'Neill's problem with the occasional overbearing parent. At Moton Elementary School in the Desire housing project of New Orleans, he has almost no communication with the parents of his fifth-grade students, although he used to run the same streets with them. So of necessity he has become, like many teachers, a parent too:

The kids that I work with are not often in a loving environment. Their mother doesn't have time to hug them. So they respond to my affection. I really think that is my main contribution. If I was at another school, I wouldn't have to do that, but in this school here, I have to tell my kids that I love them.

My students are the children of my peers when I grew up here. I see them locked in this environment. The parent is locked in and so are most of the kids. Most of my friends are at Angola in the state penitentiary or on the corner drinking wine. I have very few friends who went on to be professionals. I think they look at me as being a person to show their kids how to get out. Even though they still live in the nightmare, the dream can still come true. They look at me in that way.

We went to an eleven-month school year here at Moton. This is one of two schools in the city with this program. What we had found was that, in a nine-month school year, you would have to go back and reteach what they learned at the end of the previous year for the first two months of the new year. In this community, kids do not have the chance to drive to Atlanta or California or Disney World and be stimulated over summer vacation. So now they come back sooner and their retention level is much higher.

The testing results are not that great. They haven't gone up much, if at all. But you have to look at it this way: You are not dealing with everyday children. Ninety-nine percent of our kids are at risk. Ninety-nine percent. So your gains are not going to be seen immediately.

I don't think it would make much difference to the parents if the test scores started going up. Most of these parents can't read. Most of my parents do not know the value of education. They don't see that education is the key to prosperity. They can't see that, so they don't value education the way the average person does or the way I do. They don't see the benefit because they haven't benefited.

They just think that you go to school and that's it. As long as you are there, that's enough. Some of them look at us as baby-sitters. Their kids come every day without supplies, come every day with no homework done, come every day without a parent coming to pick up the report card during conference. I don't think they would say "hooray" over higher test scores.

We need parental involvement. It should be a three-way street among the student, teacher, and parent. Parents do not come to meetings. The parents are not really involved. It's not that they don't care. They are just not involved. In this area, there is a lot of frustration and very little hope. They just feel like they have been left out.

Art Murnan, a guidance counselor and religion teacher at Providence-St. Mel in Chicago, remembers a different relationship with his own parents:

I was talking to my mother on the phone last week about all my nieces and nephews. She said, "Do you remember how you all used to sit around the table and I would sit there with you while you did your homework and when you were done I would drill you?" She was very involved in our education. We saw our parents as an integral part of our education. Today I think a lot of parents, they will ask the kids if they did their homework, but they need to be more involved. What my mother did was the right thing. Parents have to sit there, especially when the children are young, you know, so that you can see that the kid is handling the situation. And even if they are handling it, you need to provide that constant reinforcement.

Neither one of my parents was college-educated. So it wasn't that I was dealing with grown-ups who were really into education from their own experience. My father, I'm sure, graduated from high school in a miracle. Somehow it was very important to them that their kids got a good education. Somehow they learned along the line that they had to be involved.

There was an accountability. You were accountable to your teachers and to your parents. The one thing you did not want to happen, you did not want your teacher to call your parent and say you did not do something. My father made it very clear to me that if my teacher called from school, there was no question about who was right and who was wrong. The teacher was right.

Things have changed today. One of the problems I deal with is a lot of parents who were poor growing up and are now middle class. There is a real desire to give their kids what they did not have. It is real important for their kids to have their own room. Privacy is given to kids. Privacy is important, but when it comes to education, parents have to check more carefully.

Pojoaque, New Mexico, a small village north of Santa Fe, is not far off the main road to Taos. The majority of the residents are either Native Americans or Hispanics. The community is not poor. Many of the people who live there work at Los Alamos National Laboratory, a few miles to the west. Vera Trujillo-Ortiz and Alfredo Lujan teach at the junior high school in Pojoaque. They share a common concern about the relationships among students, parents, and teachers. Lujan:

I think parents have the responsibility of raising their children. The teacher is responsible for whatever skills the class is about. The parents are part of the educational process directly, but they're not professional educators. They need to have books at home and all of that, but I'm the professional educator and I feel like I know what's best for each child inside the classroom. If I have too many hands, well, I don't find it necessary.

Trujillo-Ortiz:

Parents as a whole haven't taken on or not wanted to accept that the children are their responsibility. They raise them. They feed them. They send them off to school and say, "You've got them eight hours a day. You deal with them." It's not okay to send them to school and say that we are going to solve the problems because we can't solve all the problems. There are just too many kids with too many needs. We are responsible for teaching them.

Lujan:

Once again, I think my job is primarily to come in and teach. I guess I'm fortunate because, in teaching writing skills, I don't find any parents arguing that their kid doesn't have to learn that. It's a literacy skill and they need to learn it. I encourage the students to share whatever writing they want with their parents, and some parents edit their writing. Sometimes when I get a paper that's been edited by a parent, well, it's pretty obvious because of the mistakes. Parents need to trust teachers.

Eve Stark teaches a class for talented and gifted fifth graders at Tzoua-nakis Intermediate School in Greencastle, Indiana. She is a veteran teacher who went back to school and learned how to work with gifted students. Most of her students come from homes where parents are eager partners in the education of their children, providing the sort of textbook support that teachers yearn for. Stark's problems with parents spring from another source — the jealous parents of students who are not in her class:

It's heaven. It's wonderful. They are the students who are most in need of a differentiated curriculum among the five fifth-grade sections here. They are children who have good IQs, above 125. They are children who predominantly score above 90 or 95 on the California Achievement Test. They are students who predominantly have straight A's.

In this community, you have a lot of backlash toward having an accelerated class. They feel that all kids should be treated equally and these kids shouldn't get special treatment. They don't realize that these children are the ones who drop out of high school and have a high suicide rate because they are bored to tears. The parents have the misconception that these gifted and talented children will survive on their own. They will survive on their own only if they have a very supportive and nurturing family. Some of the children with these talents do not come from that background, and these kids are lost if we don't work with them and their abilities.

There is a lot of envy. If their child is not in this class, the parents perceive that their child is not getting as good an education. A lot of parents want their child to be in here so they can brag about it. It's a designer-jean kind of labeling. If parents were intelligent enough to realize that their child is where the child needs to be and not put a label on it, then everyone would be better off.

Right now there is a question about whether we will have a self-contained gifted and talented program next year. We have a broad-based committee that is studying it. The parents are very covert about their opposition in some ways. You have one very powerful teacher who, because she does not want to lose these children from her classroom, is spearheading a very strong group to stop it. She has not taken any training in gifted and talented, but she is convincing all these other people that there is a better way of doing it. It's in the board's hands right now.

It would be a tragedy if the program were not continued. The parents evaluate the program at the end of every year, but I have the children do written evaluations in January. One child wrote, "I have learned more this year than in the previous five years." Another says, "I love being able to work at my own pace." They all can say that they are learning more. Isn't that what education is all about?

Sometimes children are raising children themselves. Teen pregnancy has become an enormous problem, particularly in inner cities. Some schools have responded with workshops to teach parenting skills to these young parents. But it doesn't always work, as Cynthia Puckerin, a guidance counselor at the Community School (Public School 59) in the Bronx in New York City, has discovered:

I don't think there is anything more important than parent participation. If parents come into the school and let teachers know they're there, and they say, "You're going to teach my child. My child is going to get an education, and I'm going to know what he is doing. I'm going to be on top of everything."

But that doesn't happen often. So I can understand teachers who say, "These parents aren't coming in here. We can get away with anything we want to get away with. We don't have anybody looking over our shoulders." Sure they feel that way.

Over the years, we've had parent-teacher nights and about eight parents would show up. Maybe on a good night twenty parents in a school with eight hundred kids. When I first came, we had parents' meetings with a social worker from an agency here in the building, an on-site mental health agency. The social worker and I got together and said, "Let's run parent workshops, have people come in and talk to parents, doctors, et cetera." We wanted to give the parents some training.

Well, we did it and it didn't work because we couldn't get the parents interested. My principal suggested that we do something to get the parents to come, so we raffled off a prize each week. Well, when the people came in the first time, they drew the prize winner and they left. The second time, we did the drawing at the end of the meeting. Not that many people came in that time. One parent won the prize. They talked about it, and they said it was cheap. The next meeting we decided the prize was not worth the trouble, so the number of parents attending dwindled. We tried writing them a strong letter: Did they care about their child's education and future? If they did, come to these meetings. That didn't work either.

Meltras Ammons has taught for fourteen years in the Chicago area, at private and public schools, in the suburbs and the inner city. Often she has seen the effects of lack of parental involvement. But now that she teaches at Mary C. Terrell Elementary School, it has become her biggest problem as she deals with children who live in the Robert Taylor Homes housing project on the city's South Side:

The lack of parent help at home is my biggest hurdle. Kids are sent to school unprepared. It is hard to control a child who hasn't had a good night's rest or a child who comes to school hungry or a child who comes in so late that he isn't relaxed. Our school offers a subsidized breakfast program, so if the parents can just get the children out of the house on time, they can eat, and that helps.

I tell my parents about counting from one to one hundred. I want them to help me at home, but they don't know how to teach it. I tell them when the elevators are out to count the stairs as they walk. Have them count the doors on the porch. Make them see that numbers are not just inside the classroom, but everywhere. For the ones who care enough to help, I get good results. The problem is that most don't care enough to come in and talk to me about it, to see and ask questions. There are so many parents you never see, even at report-card time.

They are like silent partners in a business. They give you the child as their investment. But they don't do anything to see how their investment is growing.

Rita Gilbert wanted to be a doctor but found that she was too squeamish. Then she turned to social work with juvenile delinquents, but eventually left and turned to teaching because she hoped to apply similar skills in a preventive situation. Now she is a sixth-grade teacher at South Pointe Elementary School in Miami Beach. While she can get at problems earlier now, she finds that parents are sometimes the hurdles in this job:

We are in the business of building the children up and making them feel good about themselves. We spend a lot of time doing that in our classroom.

Parents are supposed to come in for a conference. Finally, I got this one parent to come in after two or three months of trying. The child was really feeling good about herself. Her confidence was blooming. She was speaking in the morning meeting, reading stories aloud, visiting other classrooms to read to little children. The parent sat there and said, "There may be times I have to pick up my daughter early from school because I have her in a modeling program."

"That's good, very good for her," I said.

"Yes," she said, "because I know she will never make it past twelfth grade, if she gets there, because she has nothing up here [pointing to her head]. I don't expect her to make it. At least she has a pretty face. I want to get her involved in a career that can use it."

I wanted to tell her off. But all I said was, "Can you do me a favor? Can you not tell her that she isn't going to make it? I think she is. I think she will make it."

Here's where we are. We get the children to feel good about themselves, and there is plenty of evidence that they do. And when they go home, they hear, "You're nothing."

You can be defeated, but you have to keep working at building them up, even if they get knocked down every day. I see kids come back totally different the next day, and I know they have seen something at home, a fight or abuse. Something happened between 3:00 P.M. and 8:20 A.M. If the parent doesn't feel the child is going to make it, it is a big hurdle that you're up against.

Andrea Waters teaches remedial reading with Sandra Fernandez at Santa Clara Elementary School in an impoverished neighborhood on Miami's North Side. Almost all the children in the school receive either federally subsidized or free meals, depending on the income level of their families. The poverty is so deep that parents had to be barred from the cafeteria because they were stealing their children's meals. In the face of that brand of parenting, Waters finds herself assuming responsibilities beyond teaching:

We do as much parenting as we do teaching. Sandra and I eat lunch with our children. We aren't required to, but we think it is important. So many of them are like little savages, brought here straight from the jungle. At the beginning of the year, you help them with their food tray and they just put their faces down in it and eat like little animals. You tell them to use a fork and spoon. They say, "What is that?"

Sometimes parents become scapegoats, as Gary Smith, formerly a physical education teacher at Roberto Clemente School (Intermediate School 166), in the South Bronx in New York City, observed:

Teachers blame parents. Teachers turn around and say, "Look at you. I contact you and you don't really care when I tell you your kid isn't really functioning." Teachers blame parents all the time. It's probably the biggest out teachers have. I hate to say it.

Teachers say, "The parent doesn't care. What can I do?" And I say that, as a teacher, you are wrong. I can give you fifty other things you can do. If the kid was living in the street, I could give you fifty other things you could do to make the kid a better student. But a lot of teachers use the parent as an excuse.

Haugan Elementary School serves an ethnically and racially mixed community on the Far North Side of Chicago, where the signs on the storefronts are in Korean or Spanish but seldom in English. Ruth Prale teaches special education at the school, and she has learned something about parents and their own fears:

My first open house, I was shocked. A man came into the kindergarten to talk about his child. He had taken a shot before he walked in. I could smell the booze. "Wait a minute," I thought. "He needed that shot just to walk through the door."

He's not a drinker. He's not an alcoholic. Many of these parents were not successful in school. Coming into school itself is a traumatic experience. I don't want to say they aren't capable, but their experience in school has not been so positive.

Sometimes I think our children reflect how we feel. My children loved school because I loved school. My grandson loves to go to my school. School is a very big part of his life. This is very important to us.

I've always felt that you tell parents the positive things about their children, and even negative things can be told in a positive way. I remember one mother came and she had twins. I had one twin, and the teacher across the hall had the other. I'm sure they were both the same.

The other teacher said negative things about her twin, and then the mother came across to me.

"Robert is doing very nicely," I told her. "He's a typical six-year-old boy. He has a few problems sitting in his seat, but he's learning."

I tell you, my student graduated eighth grade on time and the other twin did not leave until a year later. Robert and his mother had a different view of Robert than of the other twin.

Whereas Ruth Prale strives to find positive things to say to parents about her students, parents who can afford to send their children to expensive private schools often demand positive results. Sherley Keith, who teaches English at St. Stephen's and St. Agnes Middle School, a private Episcopal school in Alexandria, Virginia, finds that parents sometimes think nine thousand dollars a year buys good grades, too:

These kids will say things like, "I want to go to law school and make a lot of money." They are at the age where they see the big house, the BMW in the driveway, the fancy vacations as an index of success. We keep hearing that there is a new spirit of liberalism, of doing things for people, of making the world a better place. I am seeing it in some students. I have some who talk about getting jobs working with the environment, but they still want to be things like environmental lawyers.

Parents are very much affected by the consumer mentality, and that is a problem at a school like this: "We are spending nine thousand dollars a year," one mother said to me. "I am not interested in C's."

They think they want them to learn, but many are just looking for success. It is telling the child that he never has the right to fall down or to take risks, that he must follow the narrow path toward success. It doesn't allow for any independent thinking or the normal developmental pitfalls that are essential for learning. No one can learn because someone else makes him or her learn. You learn because you make a decision to learn, because you have life experiences that make you want to learn. You learn from failures, too.

One of the toughest things we have to do is to educate parents that nine thousand dollars doesn't guarantee instant success. You pay the tuition because you want your child in this atmosphere, because you believe this is where your child ought to be, and these are the teachers you want teaching your child. But it does not guarantee a string of A's. You cannot buy those.

Private schools do not have a monopoly on parents whose expectations are not always tempered by the kind of values education is supposed to impart. Pat Maier, a teacher of French at Palos Verdes Peninsula High School, in an upper-class neighborhood bordering the Pacific Ocean outside Los Angeles, discovered that in trying to discipline students caught cheating:

I had a terrible cheating incident two years ago at Miraleste, a nearby high school. I had gone away to a conference up north. I had left a verb test for the kids to take with the sub. I have to do that because generally speaking there are no subs who really speak a foreign language. So if you don't want a baby-sitting situation, you have to come up with an activity that will be constructive in which the teacher doesn't have to do anything.

These kids had no reason to cheat. If they did not do well, there would have been another test in two weeks where they could have made up the score. And this was a really brilliant class. One kid wrote on the test, "Madam, wholesale cheating took place." The sub said, "There was talking going on during the test. I couldn't control it."

When I walked into the class the next day, I said, "I want to know who didn't cheat in this class. I already know that most of you did. Is there anyone who wants to maintain that they did not cheat?"

Two kids said they did not. But the answers were being called out during the test, so I asked, "Did you hear those answers? Did you verify or change any of your answers as a result of hearing those answers?"

"Yes."

"Then you cheated."

I was crushed. These were my kids. I had taken them to Europe. I had them for three years. So I wrote a letter, which the kids had to take home to parents to sign. In the letter, I told the parents that every kid would receive a U in citizenship for the semester for cheating, and they would receive an F on the test. If I caught them cheating again, they would get an F in the class and that would be it.

I had innumerable parents who were very upset that I was willing to give them a U in citizenship because it might affect their future. I said, "Well, what do you want me to do?" They said, "It's your fault. You weren't there."

We had a long discussion about ethics in class. I had one kid who is now at UCLA who told me point-blank that his responsibility was to get an A in every class so that he could get into the school of his choice, and his parents had made it very clear to him that it didn't matter how he got those A's, just as long as he got them.

"It isn't just average kids," he said, "but those getting the straight A's."

The same group of kids got caught cheating in the advanced placement physics class.

Teachers often say the dynamics of their classes vary dramatically from year to year. The same holds true for parents, according to Kathy Johnson, who teaches kindergarten at Katherine and Jacob Greenfield Elementary School of Arthur and Anna Goldstein Hebrew Academy, a large, beautifully landscaped complex in pastel shades in Miami:

I really lucked out this year. I see the interaction of my students and their parents, the hugs and kisses and the nurturing. Of course, there are mistakes here and there, but overall these children feel loved, and that's what counts.

Last year, I had so many kids with emotional problems. Forget learning. That was out the window. It was impossible to get through to them. And the parents — divorces, separations, parents working all the time. Those kids didn't have one person in their lives whom they knew accepted and trusted them no matter what.

The parents don't mean to be like that. I don't think they know any better. I think many parents, if they understood the effect of what they are doing on their children, would change. It takes exceptionally strong people to put the child first.

Lyn Smith, who teaches third grade at Hilton Elementary School in Newport News, Virginia, has seen a gradual change in parents during eighteen years on the job:

You don't have the support from parents that you used to have when I first started teaching. I wasn't expected to be a caretaker of children. I was expected to be their educator.

I had a parent come in just the other day for a conference because the child is having some difficulty academically. The parent expects me to teach him the academics, morality, values, and all this kind of thing that I thought he should be dealing with at home.

I deal with parents a little differently than other teachers. I sort of hit them between the eyes with what is going on. I don't soft-soap anything. I tell them if a child is having trouble with reading. I don't say their child is doing wonderfully in this area, but I'd like him to work a little harder on reading.

In a way, I am resentful of parents. That may be a harsh term, but I had a conference the other day with a parent. The mother comes in and sits on the chair, pulls her legs up crosslegged, and she is almost asleep talking to me because she has been up half the night. The child has been tardy to school numerous times, coming in at ten-thirty because he overslept at home. The mother works a late shift and doesn't get the kids from her mother's until eleven o'clock. I am certain the child is not getting proper nutrition. The mother just got the water and electricity turned back on. How can the child be expected to come in and learn when the mother is not providing any better situation?

I do feel resentful of parents like that. It is not the children's fault, but they are the ones suffering.

At the other end of the scale, you have parents who do have electricity, water, and all the financial means. They provide their child with TV in their bedroom, stereo, Nintendo, and it goes on and on. Yet they don't spend any quality time with their children. They take them to see Santa Claus and be seen doing all the right things, but not to sit down on the floor and play a game with them, to talk. Those kinds of things are not happening.

I do resent what parents are doing to their kids. It is happening in the upper class, the middle class, the poor. It is the full spectrum of different ways of not providing for the basic needs of children.

CHAPTER 4

A NEW JOB DESCRIPTION

TEACHERS have always had a responsibility beyond educating. We have depended on our schools to reinforce the values taught at home — manners, responsibility, respect, and discipline, to name but a few. Traditionally, it has been a partnership. However, as we have seen, changes in the contemporary family and society at large have forced more of the burden of these tasks onto the teachers. All too often parents are either unable or unwilling to shoulder their share of the partnership's responsibilities. As a result, teachers have been forced to assume much of the role of parenting as well as educating.

"You can't just walk into a classroom and unload material anymore," says Bill Walters, a slightly built veteran of thirty-three years in the profession, who now teaches at Camden High School in Camden, New Jersey. "Society has thrust upon us a new role, and it keeps growing and growing and growing."

Fulfilling this expanding new role, particularly when confronted by today's children, means more than helping a child with "please" and "thank you." It means teaching them about sex, helping them learn to choose the safest type of condom. It means warning children as young as first grade about the dangers of drugs, the perils of picking up dirty hypodermic needles on the playground, gun awareness, and traffic safety. It means trying to find a way to instill values and respect so that we can live together as a community.

In many places, schools are the only functioning organizations left. Homes are broken. Parents are missing. Community centers are boarded up. Church is no longer the center of people's lives. Schools are, as Dwight Brown described Moton Elementary School in New Orleans, a safe haven for children seeking refuge from poverty, drugs, violence, and the other perils that we tragically allow to confront the most defenseless segment of our population.

Our sense of community has been fractured; in some places, it has been shattered. More and more, it is the schools that seem to unite us as a repository for community values and as a center for community instruction. Schools are no substitute for a safe and nurturing environment and an intact family. However, for increasing numbers of children, schools are all they have. For their teachers, the fight to educate is often relegated to second place. They have found that they cannot begin to teach each morning until all their children are fed, warm, and secure. To that end, many teachers keep a box of Cheerios and cartons of orange juice on their shelves, next to the math workbooks and art supplies.

This is one of the issues that divides teachers most clearly. Society has redefined their job, and some fear that the new definition means further dilution of their role as educators. They decry the time drained away from teaching and worry that the system focuses less and less on education.

Twin Buttes High School sits on a dusty patch of land on the Zuni reservation in the desolate Indian country of northwestern New Mexico. It has only about fifty students, many of whom have had problems adjusting to school elsewhere. "The school, in trying to do everything, ends up doing nothing well," warns Richard Brough, who teaches social studies and world history at Twin Buttes. "The schools should focus on getting the kids to use their minds, getting them to learn how to think. The rest will follow."

Others worry that, in feeding, housing, and providing moral instruction to an increasingly large percentage of youngsters, the schools risk letting marginally involved parents think they are superfluous and can leave everything to the schools.

However, most teachers accept the new demands, believing that they have little choice even as they bemoan the lost time for instruction and the risks of further distancing parents from their proper responsibilities for children. The philosophy of these teachers has a common theme: If we don't do it, no one will.

"What other choice do you have?" asks John Cook, who left a university teaching post to become a high school teacher in Princeton Junction, New Jersey. "Where else are young people going to learn that, almost in the blink of an eye, they are going to be making some very serious decisions about their lives?"

Anthony Jackson teaches fifth grade at the Ninety-ninth Street Accelerated School, a public school in the Watts neighborhood of South-

Central Los Angeles. A former bus driver and salesman, he turned to teaching after seeing how much his wife enjoyed her job as a teacher. He was recently selected as one of the nation's outstanding teachers by the Walt Disney Company:

America has changed. Teaching has changed. You can't deal with new problems with old solutions. You can't just teach. Teachers have to accept that they have to do more. You have to be a friend, and everything else to a child.

There are two Americas. In one country, the values that are put forth all the time as being the right values don't mean shit, excuse my French, in front of that other America. To parents in this other America, how a child is doing in school is not the most pressing concern because they are just trying to survive. They can't even see how their child is doing in school relates to his survival later on. It is just a different set of values.

You, as a teacher, can't judge which set of values is right because that puts you in the position of being moralistic. I think you have to take a neutral position because people are taking on values that work for them in their lot in life in a given time. It is not for me to say someone is a bad parent. They might be doing the best job they can, although it is not the way I was raised.

So if that is the case, I have to make up the difference for that child. That is the bottom line. I cannot, as a teacher, just lay it all on the parents. I have to accept that I can't count on some parents. I can go to the parent, but they might not get themselves together in the ten months the child is going to be in my class. I talk to the parents because I know no one loves that child more than they do, but that has nothing to do with whether or not they are doing the right or the best thing for that child all the time. If not, I try to step in and make sure it gets done.

After sixteen years of teaching English, Marion Clermont at Brooklyn's Tilden High School finds more demands than ever:

I struggle to find the sociological reasons behind all this falling apart, but I don't want to generalize and oversimplify. The overall climate at Tilden is absolutely horrendous. The principal is trying. The supervisors are trying. The teachers don't want to open their doors and help people move along. They just don't want to get involved. They are afraid, and you can understand why. When the door is open, you are vulnerable to anything.

My child goes to a Catholic school. I won't send her to the local public school. The kids are out of control and the teachers can't handle it. Her best friend goes to a public school. Her mother couldn't handle the tuition at the Catholic school. Within a month, the kid sounds like a — well, I won't repeat the language.

It is a struggle in every single class, from beginning to end. Out of a forty-minute period, a lot of time is spent just trying to get them to settle down. And you get responses like "Fuck you" or "You wait a minute" or "When I'm ready."

I was educated and trained, but not to deal with this. My education courses in college had nothing to do with what I am trying to manage here.

You can no longer just teach. I've become used to doing five things at once: José, get off the windowsill. Maureen, leave the lights alone. You get out of the closet. You step out of the hall.

I am working on getting out of Brooklyn before my daughter is a teenager. To head up to the mountains. The school systems aren't perfect up there, but she won't be exposed to the tremendous amount of violence and peer pressure that are prevalent here. There is no escape here. Where can she play? Where can she go? There is no beauty around us. It is dirt, soot, buses, crowds. At least up in the mountains you can smell the flowers and look at the stars. You don't have to deal with all the other little things that chip away at the quality of your life here. I've got to get her out of here.

Sherrill Neale arrives long before the students in her reading classes at Patrick Henry Elementary School in a neighborhood of Alexandria, Virginia, where families come and go, rarely staying long enough for them or their children to put down roots. A serious woman in her forties, Neale is very discouraged about the changes that have engulfed her profession in recent years:

My first year of teaching, a boy came at me with a heavy-link chain in my fifth-grade classroom. He did that to see who would back down. I don't think he ever would have taken a step to hurt me with it. I asked him for it and he gave it to me. I wasn't frightened. This kid had a history of that kind of thing. He slept in a car. His mother and father were never around. There was no home. Why shouldn't he come at me with a chain? I wanted to take him home all the time. But we would kill ourselves if we got emotionally involved with every kid whose life was so rotten.

We have two boys here right now whose parents have died from drug overdoses, and one of them wants love so bad. You've never seen a kid who wants someone to care for him so bad. No one does. So he brings a knife to school. He torments the other kids. He torments us. He does everything he possibly can to get attention. Can you blame him?

That is the kind of kid we don't want in the classroom because it's upsetting everyone else. All the other kids start acting out, too. Yet you know if he leaves you, he's not necessarily going to a better situation.

You have to put limits on yourself. You have to write some off, do what's best for the group. I write children off all the time, in the sense that I have done everything that I can think of and I'm getting nowhere. If I tried it with another kid, I'd make a lot of progress. Where can I go? You have to be a realist. You have to go where you can do some good.

You never stop worrying about the others, but there's nothing you can change. I can call social services, but they're completely overwhelmed. The police will come when you call them, but they'll tell you the same thing: It's your problem. All you want is someone to care for this kid.

Yes, they fall through the cracks and they're the ones out there in the prisons. But we should be concentrating on academics. We shouldn't be taking on more and more the role of the parent. They want us to. They want us to feed them breakfast. They want us to keep them after school until they can come and get them. They want us to protect them and they want us to take care of them. When does the parent start taking responsibility for the child?

Hilton Elementary School is a lovely, small school situated along the James River in Newport News, Virginia. It serves neighborhood families and also draws children from across the city because its traditional curriculum emphasizes basic educational skills. Still, Lyn Smith, a committed teacher in her forties, worries that some children are falling through the cracks:

There is too much, "This is not your fault. You are not to blame because your mother knifed her boyfriend last night. You couldn't do your homework because of whatever." The excuses become limitations.

We have a lot of "at risk" children across the nation, but we are spending so much time dealing with them and their problems that I think the children who are not "at risk" are getting slighted.

Across the nation, it is the middle kids who are getting nothing. Yet those are the kids who are going to get through school, get jobs. They are the glue that keeps our society stuck together. They get along.

When she was interviewed, Nancy Brice was on a nine-week sabbatical studying how students can be taught to solve their differences without fighting. Her research was sponsored as part of a special continuing education program for teachers in Dade County, Florida, called Dade Academy for Teaching Arts (DATA). A social studies teacher at South Miami Middle School in Miami, Brice speaks bluntly about the increasing demands placed on teachers:

The schools are given responsibility to correct all the social ills. We are the front line. They use schools to socialize, Americanize, institutionalize. Yet there are so many areas over which we have no control: the breakdown of the family, the recession we are dealing with now, the fact that the entire medical industry is such that, unless you are wealthy, you cannot get medical treatment.

A young boy helped me with a project, a videotape on conflict mediation. He was always looking depressed — down and out. We were sitting in there working on the computer and I said to him, "What's happening?" He had been living on the streets for about four or five months and he was arrested and brought back to a shelter. He is in the eighth grade, a thirteen-year-old boy. He was arrested because he was caught going into a warehouse to steal food. He had been abandoned at infancy, adopted by another family, and that family turned out to be abusive, with beatings and God knows what else. He ran away from home and he is now at a home for wayward children, living there until he doesn't know when.

He doesn't know where he is going to live each day. Nobody wants him. Nobody loves him. He has to go to class each day and function, and they are saying that the schools are responsible. There is no one answer, not in the schools or anywhere else.

Ruby Wanland, a social studies teacher at Miami Beach Senior High School in Miami Beach, experiences the same sorts of extra demands as Brice. But Wanland, who was participating in the same continuing education program, embraces the additional responsibilities because she believes no one else will do it if teachers don't. Like many teachers, she dips into her own pocket to provide supplies and special material for her students:

I don't think I resent being their mother or their father. I think many of the students who come through the classroom look at their teachers as mothers and fathers. We become that for them. We teach values — putting on makeup, combing your hair so it looks attractive, how to behave — plus world history, language arts, math. Unless those needs are met, we can't do our jobs.

Just a couple of weeks ago, I had a kid who couldn't see the board. Even putting him in the front row didn't help. Nothing helped. If I want to wait for the proper channels, I might get lucky and get glasses next year. He would have lost a whole year in the meantime. I got permission from his parents and I hauled him up to my eye doctor, and I bought him glasses. Now he can sit wherever he wants in the room and see the board. Already I can see a change in his grades.

Do I resent this? No, not at all.

Dwight Brown's students come to Moton Elementary School in the Desire housing project in New Orleans to escape the squalor and violence surrounding them. Sitting in the living room of his small, neat home not far from the school, Brown is almost evangelical in describing his mission:

Three years ago, we had a fourth grader at our school who was killed by two drug dealers. He was shot in the head because he was selling drugs and he owed money to the big dealers. They made an example out of him. He was a Moton student, but he was shot inside a crack house.

It wasn't too much of a shock to the teachers because the child was a behavior problem and his parents were drug addicts. The kids weren't even too surprised. There weren't any questions from the kids about it because they were giving me answers. They knew he was selling drugs. They used to see him out late at night. They see guys in broad daylight selling drugs on the corner. This wasn't anything new to these kids.

But inside the school they escape all that. The school is the jewel of the community. It is something new for everybody in the community to come and see and come to. There's nothing new and bright in this neighborhood at all except the school. It's like heaven. You are saving lives here. Moton is a safe haven and I am more than the teacher of these kids. I am their guardian, at least while they are here.

Georgia Epaloose now teaches the enrichment program for gifted students at Zuni Middle School, on the Zuni reservation in New Mexico. For a while, she taught in Albuquerque:

In Albuquerque, I worked with teachers in what we termed "war-zone areas," places where there are a lot of social problems and so school was a refuge for students. It wasn't a place to go learn, you know, academically or learn about the larger society or learn about math. It was a place to go where you knew you would be safe for six or seven hours.

This one family had five of the kids at school, at every grade level. The kids came to school very dirty, smelly. That is what prompted three teachers to get together to make a home visit to find out about their physical environment.

There was no furniture in the apartment. There were bedrolls, blankets, and stuff that the kids slept on in the living room. I don't think the sink worked in the kitchen. They had only cold water; no hot water because they weren't paying the gas bill. It was so cold. This was after Thanksgiving and there was no heat, no hot water, no food in the refrigerator.

Two of the teachers said, "This isn't the role we should play. We really shouldn't be providing clothing for the kids, and we shouldn't provide showers. But if we don't do it, who else will?"

So they took it to the PTA and the school nurse and made sure the kids got showers and clothing. The two older ones, who were in fourth and fifth grade, they took them into the nurse's room and showed them how they could put a glass of water on the window to warm it up in sunlight. That kind of thing, survival skills. We taught them that they should want to be clean, mainly so that you don't feel bad about yourself. But what happens next year? What if these kids move to another school district and don't have this kind of care?

The staff at this school was really torn about the position they found themselves in, playing the role of parent. They would go back and forth. If we don't do it, who will? These kids shouldn't be penalized for something the parents are not able to provide.

———————————————————

Alfredo Lujan worries that education is diluted by the amount of school time students spend outside his English and writing classes in the junior high at Pojoaque Middle School in Pojoaque, New Mexico:

I resent very much having to parent kids. I think the schools are for education. They are not social welfare agencies. I don't resent counseling students because that's part of the job. I do resent having an overload of counselors and having AIDS and alcohol awareness and that sort of thing. It is important, but kids are pulled from class for group therapy for this and for that, so the instruction time is interrupted too often.

Those types of problems are home problems. I know, I know. The school is responsible in part for bringing up the kids, but I don't think it can replace math or English skills with counseling.

I teach a class called "Writing Across the Curriculum." It's a writing-skills class in a computer lab. It is affected directly by three interruptions a week. If you have a kid with problems at home and the kid is pulled out of a class where he is learning literacy skills or communicating skills or math skills, the problems are perpetuated because the kid is missing skills he should be getting in the first place. They are getting counseled about what is going on at home and they are falling behind in class.

I don't think schools are responsible for raising children. They are responsible for providing certain kinds of competencies. We need to concentrate on what they are in school for. More and more every year, they are taken out of class for other matters. Sex education. Drug education. AIDS education. Now they have group therapy sessions for troubled kids. We all grew up with some problems. We all had to deal with them. We all had to get educated. What good does it do to have a student come out of the eighth grade with a lot of counseling and reading at a third-grade level?

Across the country at Hilton Elementary School, a traditional public school in Newport News, Virginia, Gail Davis agrees:

Every government official, everyone who makes a decision that has anything to do with children, automatically thinks it has to be carried out in the schools because children are required by law to come to school. We have to teach everything. That is wrong. That is one of the reasons test scores are dropping in some areas, because we are spending too much time doing all these other things.

I don't agree with it. I feel resentful. I can only stay up so late and work so hard. I take home work every night. I am here every morning at seven-thirty. I work on weekends. I am still behind. I don't do things I want to do with my husband many nights because of the job.

Mary Bicouvaris, who has taught in both public and private schools in Newport News, is characteristically to the point:

Sex education should be done by a doctor in a white robe and a stethoscope around his neck and a beeper at his waist. Not by a teacher. We're doing it all wrong. A physical education teacher who took one course in health will teach students sex education? No! The authorities are the medical people — the doctors and the nurses. They can do it without blushing. They can say it the way it is supposed to be said, not out of a book.

Mary Horton, who is known to her students as "Reverend Horton" because of a tendency to lecture them about values, teaches history at Richmond Heights Middle School in a working-class neighborhood of Miami:

In addition to teaching the academics, I am teaching children how to be parents. I do, every opportunity I get, especially if I see somebody from one of my classes standing around a corner kissing. I will say something to them privately because I do not like to embarrass students. I tell them there there is a time and a place for everything, but that they are too young now. I ask, "Do your parents know?" Most of the time they will say, "No."

I tell the girls that a lot of the times boys will tell them, "Honey, I love you," just to get what they want. But once boys get it, they're gone. And the girls may end up with some type of venereal disease, or pregnant. You have to protect yourself.

I tell the boys, "Be patient, join a club, play sports, run around and do something because a child needs two parents."

I had three girls in one of my classes once, all friends, all pregnant, all with the same father. The boy was an only child and he had money. I asked him why.

He said, "These girls, you take them out for a hamburger and a soda and they will give you everything you want. You don't even have to take them to the movies."

That was a lesson for my girls the next day. And I still use it in my classroom.

Ruth Prale, a teacher for twenty-six years, is now a reading specialist at Haugan Elementary School in Chicago:

A teacher today is a social worker, surrogate parent, a bit of a disciplinarian, a counselor, and someone who has to see to it that they eat. Many teachers are mandated to teach sex education, drug awareness, gang awareness. And we're supposed to be benevolent. And we haven't come to teaching yet.

We have an overcrowded curriculum. It isn't just reading and writing, arithmetic, and a little social studies and science. We also have to give them family life. They have to have counseling, and you want journal writing because you want to know if any child has any real problems. Then you have to write up the papers if you think there is something wrong with the child. You have to watch out for physical abuse and sexual abuse. It's like you are the guru in charge of everything. And then you also have to teach.

We have a tremendous gang influence that's very subtle. We've told the children here that they cannot wear earrings because that's a gang symbol. They cannot wear colors. We watch their shoes. They get around it. Now they're shaving their heads. The way they cut their hair has become a gang symbol. What are you going to do? You can't slap hair on them.

I teach out of a closet. I have a book room. I don't have a regular classroom. I notice the students as they walk down the hall. They know just how to stand so they can look into a classroom and the teacher won't see them. They are giving gang signals to a child sitting at a desk. I see them and I'll step out of the door and say, "Get to where you're supposed to be."

Some revel in the challenges. Third-grade teacher Jeff Jackson, who left a lucrative job as a senior manager with Merrill Lynch, found different satisfactions at Maury Elementary School in Alexandria, Virginia:

These kids depend on me. I guess I get motivated by that. Before, it was just going into an office, working nine to five. The paycheck did not do it. I thought I should get out before I got trapped. There is no question that this is where I belong.

Because I have twenty-three kids in this room every year, depending on me, I am constantly thinking about them. Over the weekend, I am constantly thinking, "How am I going to help this kid who is having trouble with subtraction? What can I introduce to this kid to help?" You never leave it, even in the summer. I could mentally leave other jobs. Here I can't. There is so much more at risk. I can't.

First-year teachers, as I was last year, they all go through this. They come in thinking that they are going to do miracles, save the world in your first year of teaching. I had a rude awakening. I learned that I have no control over where these kids go every day when they leave here. The only thing I can control is my classroom. That was a hard thing for me to accept, that I am limited in what I can do.

Robin Lichtenfeld is young, attractive, and not much taller than some of her sixth-grade students at Crossroads Arts Academy, an exclusive private school in Los Angeles. A refugee from the advertising world in New York City, she finds pluses and minuses in the increased responsibilities she faces as a teacher:

In a way, I really like the expanded role of today's teachers, but I think it is very sad that I need to replace absent parents. These children, for the most part, aren't getting the information because there is no one around to give it to them because parents are out working. It is not generally because there is no father at a school like this or that the mother is overwhelmed. They just aren't around.

I like it because I feel it is really important and I am making even more of a difference in their lives if I guide them in the right direction. But still, I feel that values need to be instilled at home. A lot of the most lost children, I have found, are the ones who have what appears on the outside to be the most. It is scary.

I have a little girl whose father is a very, very powerful man in Hollywood, very wealthy, and always in the newspaper. But we never see the parents here. This poor little girl was in a panic because she needed an extension on a research paper. I asked her to have her mother call me, but instead the nanny called me for the extension. The nanny came to the open house — little pink uniform and all. This family has more money than God, and twenty million horses, and houses everywhere. It is just pathetic.

Others question whether teachers are prepared to deal with the disparate problems that children bring with them to school these days. Kathy Johnson, who teaches elementary grades at a Jewish school in Miami, Florida, says:

Teachers are not prepared to handle more responsibility. They're not psychologists. A lot of them are just there to teach their subject. That's what they've learned. It's not their fault.

When I took elementary education, the last two years were devoted to kiddie lit, kiddie reading, how to teach every course — physical education, art, everything. I was not taught how to deal with the child at all.

So if you get into a classroom and have a human being in front of you, and he comes in crying because his mother yelled at him in the morning and he's having a really bad day, the teacher still expects him to do his work. The teacher doesn't understand. You can't look at that child and understand that he can't work today because he is still feeling frustrated from his morning at home. He needs a little comforting first, but does a teacher understand that? They don't even understand their own psychological makeup.

Parents should shop for a kid's teachers the way they shop for his jeans. You're putting this child in the hands of another adult for seven hours a day and you don't care who the adult is? If you have five fifth-grade teachers, go check out those teachers. Sit in the classrooms for a day and see who is going to be the best one.

Kathleen O'Neill, who teaches at Sinai Akiba Academy in Los Angeles, resents the parenting required of teachers today:

I chose not to be a parent. I love children, obviously, but I feel there is a place for parenting. I think that it confuses children when the teacher becomes the parent. And I resent the time constraints, especially when we get into moral development. I have a little problem with all of us having a say in moral judgments and being required to make them. I think it takes away a little bit of the individuality. I know it's tough on parents. I don't think putting responsibility for this stuff on the teachers is the answer. I don't know what the answer is.

When I first started fourteen years ago, I taught kindergarten in Maine and we had to allocate time for students to brush their teeth every day. I had to put egg cartons with holes in the sections where we had to put their toothbrushes, which I thought was disgusting. Every day they would brush their teeth and once a week we would give them fluoride. The town had well water, no fluoride in it.

At another school where I taught, they have a unit of sex education for first grade and I refused to teach it. I was supposed to teach the uterus. We didn't get into any male organs. I have no idea why we concentrated on the female organs. It was a program developed by parents. I guess they get to the male organs later. All I know is that I was supposed to draw it on the board and talk about it. It's not that I'm uncomfortable discussing reproductive organs or anything else with children. I don't think it's my place.

Lisa Cooper became a teacher after spending time as a volunteer in the classrooms of her young children. She is quiet and modest, worried about fitting in with the veteran teachers in her first year at South Putnam Elementary School south of Greencastle, Indiana. She also has encountered some problems she did not expect from her students, even in the first grade:

The other day I had a boy who brought in a pornographic magazine. He was taking his friends over to his locker during reading time. You know, I didn't really think too much about it. When they were out for lunch, I thought, "I'm just going to check." So I felt his backpack and it was pretty light. I thought, "Now wait a minute." It felt like there was a book or something in there, so I looked and then I panicked. I thought, "Maybe I don't have the right to look in his backpack."

So I ran to the principal's office and I said, "What rights do I have to look in things?"

"You can search whatever is in your room," he said.

"Good, because that is what I did."

It was upsetting because the pornographic magazine was really bad. It wasn't a nice one. It was a really bad one. The principal said to leave it in his backpack and bring him to the office with the backpack after lunch.

Later, when I started to go with the student to the office, I noticed that he had taken out the magazine and shoved it aside.

"No," I said, "you better bring that with you."

"It was just in my backpack when I got on the bus this morning," he said. "I don't know where it came from. It was just there."

How stupid do you think we are? I thought, and I almost laughed.

He had a letter sent home and his mother had to sign it and send it back so we knew she had read it. And he had a full day of in-school suspension, which meant he had to just sit in a room by himself and do a lot of work and eat lunch by himself. When Carol Emery, the school counselor, went in to talk to him, he cried, and that made me feel better. There was remorse there.

He told Carol that each of his brothers and sisters had piggy banks up in the top of their closets and their stepfather had gotten them and taken all their money. That is the kind of home life he has. His mother never called about the magazine, and when Carol asked what his parents did about it, he said, "Well, they beat me." And they probably did. They probably beat the tar out of him. Somebody should have beaten the tar out of them for having it in the home.

The condom lady works down the road from Cooper's school, at the junior high and high school in tiny Cloverdale, Indiana. Along with English,

Mary Ann Meyer teaches AIDS and drug awareness to grades seven through twelve. She talked frankly about these problems while smoking a cigarette in the school boiler room between classes:

In my tenth-grade class, I'm saying that abstinence is the best way to protect yourself from AIDS.

"Come on, Mrs. Meyer," says one of the young men. "I gotta have it at least once a week."

"No," I tell him. "That is animalistic. That is using sex for pleasure and that is not what it's meant for."

"You're crazy, Mrs. M," he tells me.

You find yourself thinking, "Have I missed the boat all these years?" No. Society has changed its attitudes, its morals. So I have to teach them to protect themselves, to buy the right condom, to put it on properly and take it off properly. I'm very open with them, but somebody has got to stand up and say, "Hey, this is bad."

The week after I had that exchange with the young man who said he had to have it every week, well, he came to see me. "Mrs. Meyer, you would have been proud of me," he said. "I got a condom."

We started this program right before it came out that Magic Johnson had AIDS and, if there were any qualms about it, they were silenced. We have a very conservative, very religious town. I teach abstinence. But I also teach that if you get in a position where you are going to do it, this is the way you have to protect yourself. I only want to keep the kids alive.

We should probably give out condoms here like they do in the big cities, but it will never happen. I was teaching the other day and I forgot to buy condoms to show them the proper kind. So there was a construction crew outside working on the school and I sent the supervisor of the crew out to get me a package of condoms. He was just hilarious. He couldn't find the right kind of condoms in Cloverdale, the ones that have Nonoxinol 9 on them. He went up to the truck stop and he found French ticklers and all different neon colors, but none treated with Nonoxinol 9.

So I had to go up to the Peoples Drug Store in Greencastle and here I am, a mother of five, married for thirty years, and I'm standing in front of the condom display picking up each box to make sure I buy the right kind of condom. Lots of people in town happened to be coming in and they say, "Sure, you need them for class."

You really have to like kids and love 'em and be able to forgive them. You have to remember that you've screwed up in your life. Kids are going to screw up. You just want the screwups not to be damaging to the rest of their life or, in the case of AIDS, to be terminal.

Caring about more than educating children exacts many prices from teachers, as discovered by Rita Logan, who teaches in a detention center school for young offenders in Miami:

What made these kids the way they are? They are charming and funny. That's why I love this job. You're battling wits. I mean, it's a constant battle. And they're funny. It's a hilarious job. Intellectually it's delightful.

I bring up this badness thing every nine weeks. We watch the movie *The Bad Seed* and we talk about the source of badness. They are incredibly beaten at an early age. The Hispanics, they are made to kneel on cheese graters, naked, with their father hitting them when he walks by. Every time you shift, it shreds your kneecaps. Kneeling on pebbles or rice, beating them with fan belts. The real popular punishment is getting them in the shower, get them wet, make them take off their clothes, then beat them with an extension cord or water hose or a metal hanger. This is acceptable behavior on the part of parents to five-year-olds if the kid is bad, and bad can be anything.

There's a lot of anger in these kids. They're full of rage. A kid said he hit the principal. Maybe he did and maybe he didn't. They hate the school system. The school system has done terrible damage to these kids, beyond what their relatives have done to them. Some kids just don't fit into the school system.

Now, I'm not saying we should write off these kids. A miracle might happen. Maybe because I said to one of them, "You can't hit your girlfriend," he will hesitate before he hits his girlfriend.

I don't know why I identify so well with these kids. Perhaps I have a criminal mind. I find their thinking absolutely fascinating. There was a kid who came in here three and a half years ago, when I was new here.

"Come over here," he said to me when he walked in the door. "Look at my navel. There's something wrong with it."

I go over and he's got his penis sticking out.

"That's nice," I said. "Doesn't seem to be a problem to me."

That ruined his little act. Slowly we worked on this relationship every time he was in here.

"David," I said to him one day, "if you don't straighten out, I'm going to end up at your funeral."

And I did. Shot to death. They were trying to steal his jewelry. He was the victim. He gave up his jewelry, but he wouldn't give up his car.

And sometimes the price of being willing to do more than educate the mind is actually a reward. After fifteen years of teaching in Miami's inner-city schools, Alice Golub remains passionate — caustic, caring, and devoted to the children of a tough section of the city known as "the Grove." Now a teacher at F. S. Tucker Elementary School there, she recalls most vividly the salvation of Erica:

It doesn't have to be a parent, but somebody has to care whether that kid lives or dies. Somebody has to be on their back. If nobody cares, the kid doesn't care.

I had Erica in the fifth grade. She was a little chubby and had no self-esteem at all. She was living with her mother and the grandfather. Her mother had had scarlet fever as a child and was brain-damaged. She could cook and take care of things, but she couldn't deal with money or read very well. I met her at a back-to-school night and didn't even know there was anything wrong with her. She introduced herself, looked at the stuff, and left.

A while later, Erica told me she was having trouble with her homework and didn't have anyone to help her. I asked about her mother and she said her mother was retarded. At that moment I decided she needed a Big Sister. I got the application for her to fill out and the grandfather wouldn't sign it. He'd tell her to sit down and shut up when she asked him to. How could you have any self-esteem when you are treated like that?

I just kept boosting her up all the time, and everyone's attitude toward her changed. When we had May Day, she was nominated for the court. She didn't win, but that didn't matter. The following year, I persuaded her to run for Student Council and she won. In sixth grade, she would go down and help at the office, and the secretary loved her. One thing led to another and I just never lost touch with her.

She needed help on her science project when she got to the seventh grade, and I helped. She joined the band in seventh grade and there was a band teacher over there who was absolutely wonderful and loved Erica, too. She took over where I left off. She adored her, which was just what Erica needed. At the end of the year, she was getting an award for the deprived child who had done the best in band, a two-hundred-dollar scholarship. The band teacher knew about our relationship and called to ask me to come to the ceremony.

Whenever she needed something that her mother couldn't provide, she called me. In ninth grade, the grandfather died and the mother got pregnant. These cousins made them move to Homestead, which is way south of here, because they shouldn't live alone. Erica would call. She would tell me that she got into the band in high school. She was on the basketball team. My husband and I would go to all the games and watch her. I'm her other mother. She spent two summers living with me. The child is now in college. She got there on a scholarship.

Kids aren't different today. Parents are different. I don't know what the answers are. I've been here long enough to know it's not an easy thing. But the kids have to believe that they can get out of here, that there is a better way. Erica believed that. I kept telling her she could do it, and she believed me. But if there's nobody telling and showing you, if you have no hope, what's the point? Why go to school?

CHAPTER 5

HURDLES

LISTENING TO TEACHERS talk about their own daily hurdles is a little like being a doctor as the patient describes symptoms of an undiagnosed illness: In the seemingly small, individual complaints lie the clues to the disease and to its cure.

Teachers face many barriers to success. In surveys and conversations, certain problems routinely rank at the top of the list of complaints: crowded classrooms, lack of parental involvement, ill-prepared and apathetic students, low pay, and poor support services. Others feel burdened by too much paperwork or too many extracurricular demands squeezed into the school day. Additional obstacles are matters of individual experience and personal philosophy.

With after-school jobs, some teachers say, students are cheating themselves out of the opportunity to learn because they work too much outside school. This insight illuminates a national trend: Millions of American teenagers work. While summer jobs and limited part-time employment may breed responsibility and discipline, the experts worry that teenagers are squandering their futures by shortchanging their educations. According to surveys, teenagers are twice as likely to work now as they were in 1950. Some scholars say the tendency of American students to work longer and longer hours at part-time jobs is one reason they are behind their counterparts in Japan, who are far less likely to work outside of school.

Other teachers want more time with students in class, a comment that also mirrors concerns at other levels of education about whether American children are falling behind because they don't spend as much time in the classroom as their counterparts in other industrialized countries. U.S. students attend school an average of 180 days a year, compared to 228 days in Japan. Only a handful of American schools are in session more than 210 days a year. Some schools have responded by extending the year, offering optional Saturday classes, or going to an eleven-month year.

And, of course, teachers complain about low pay. A survey by the Carnegie Foundation for the Advancement of Teaching in 1990 found that 55 percent of all teachers ranked higher salaries as the most important change needed to improve their profession. Part of this is driven by self-interest, but a great many teachers said in interviews that they feared for the future of the profession because of the inability to pay enough to attract the brightest young people.

Pay takes on a wider significance in the face of the rising problems confronting teachers today: Many people contemplating teaching careers think twice before entering a profession where the job seems to be getting harder and the pay lower. At most universities, studies find that students who express an interest in teaching in primary and secondary schools have lower SAT scores than for almost any other discipline.

These teachers' complaints reflect the profession's widespread discontent with the cumbersome and unresponsive bureaucracy of education.

Most issues described here by teachers are discussed more fully in later chapters. Addressing their concerns represents part of the solution to the larger problems confronting education.

Carolyn Langston is a third-grade teacher at Dunbar Erwin Elementary School in a working-class neighborhood of Newport News, Virginia, where she grew up and went to school:

I need more time. The school day doesn't really start till 9:30 A.M. and they go home at 2:30 P.M. They have to come to school and eat breakfast. We have to feed them because nobody is doing that at home anymore, but by the same token I don't think they can learn if they are hungry. That is a judgment call. Do you start and have a little more academic time, or do you feed them? The social constraints, like scheduling buses, are all tied up in education. Bus schedules and whether a child is fed take away from academic time.

We are talking about year-round schooling. I am sure a lot of people wouldn't like it, especially in a place like Virginia, where we depend on tourism. I wonder why high schools get out so early. They get out at two in the afternoon. Why does a teenager need to be on the street at 2:00 P.M.?

I went to a workshop not long ago and there was a doctor speaking and I think she talked about an informal study she had done about teenage pregnancies. She said that most girls got pregnant between two and six in the afternoon.

I think they should be in school. I just do. But because of buses, they aren't. You become such a caretaker for children's needs. Their health, the way they are dressed. I feel like their mother sometimes. I feel the same responsibilities for them as I do for my own children.

John Schiff, the former priest who teaches at Santa Fe Preparatory School, a private school in Santa Fe, New Mexico, says:

There are private and professional hurdles to doing this job. The professional one is not letting your ego get in the way of your objective. There are times when you would like to register personal opinions or personal feelings, when you would like to react with affection, resentment, anger to the student, pity, sarcasm to the dumb question, to the petulant student, to the grade grubber, to the undisciplined, but you know that will only get in the way of what you're doing.

You have to be disciplined enough to repress a lot of personal reaction. You just have to say, "No, this is only going to distract from what I'm trying to do." I find that, on a professional level, hard. Maybe nobody else feels it, but I do.

You sometimes want to tell a child, "That is the dumbest thing I've ever heard, and if you can't ask a more decent question you ought to go back to middle school." Or sometimes you want to say, "Look, it's Friday afternoon and it's spring. We're all having a hard time with the weather. I just don't care about one point on your test. I really don't." But you can't say that. You have to say, "Let's take a look at it and see if we can figure out why your grade is this way." You have to read the whole thing over again. All the silly remarks, all the off-base observations, all the fluff, and you have to accept it as if it were an article in *The New York Times,* because that's how the child regards it.

The personal hurdle is boredom. Terrible boredom. Tedium. For me, I think it comes from being an adult who constantly deals with adolescents, from whom you can get either an avalanche of positive feedback, or the most vitriolic of odium, depending on their mood. Teenagers are rarely in the gray area. They either adore you or just think you are the cause for the woes of the world.

I guess my real source of boredom is the complete lack of intellectual stimulation, because the kids just don't give it to me. Neither does the subject matter. I think the only thing that ever challenged me was becoming a really good teacher. That was intellectually stimulating. I really think I'm there after all these years.

I don't mind the hormonal aspect of teenagers. It's the intellectual side of it. I work with bright kids, sweet kids, wonderful kids, tremendous administrators, fabulous teachers, largely reasonable parents, but I just can't do it. I'm almost at the end of my tether. It's too boring. It's like I just want to do something more on the inside that is of a substantive nature than repetitive scrub work. Sounds crazy, but it's true.

You know how some people are very extroverted, and they live for sights and bright colors and fast cars and loud sounds and beautiful clothes and being seen. Other people live for reading and quiet and learning and appreciation. I'm in the second group. Period. I think that that does have an impact, good and bad, on my ability to be effective in a high school classroom.

I think it's good they're exposed to someone like me. But it's a relatively rare student who will appreciate what I offer them. Many students find me just mincing, detailed, overly organized, sort of like Felix in *The Odd Couple* or Mr. Rogers. They just think that the exactitude and precision and detail work that I require of them to do the scrub work properly, they just find completely unreasonable. Most of them.

Bill Walters is a mentor-teacher at Camden High School in Camden, New Jersey. With his years of experience, he shares what he has learned with other, less experienced teachers:

Having students in the classroom — absenteeism — is a big hurdle. It is students not being in the classroom every single day. That is the biggest problem that teachers have here.

You have to understand the reasons for it. It's lack of breakfast in the morning. Maybe it's getting to bed at 4:00 A.M. because you have a job. I know there are rules that say kids can only work certain hours, but they are bent time and time again. They catch buses outside the area to get back into the city. Then they have to walk to their homes. It is often 3:00 or 4:00 A.M. before they get to bed. They are supposed to be at school at eight twenty-five the next day. There may be no one home to get them up.

It is also a problem of "I am not prepared, I am going to class, but I don't have the work done." All of this sort of draws students away from academic success. There are other problems, too — home problems. Parents keep students home to watch younger children. At least 35 percent of our parents in

Camden are eighteen or younger. You have children who are parents of children. I don't really feel that children stay home because they don't want to come to school.

I think society and a city like Camden have bred a situation in which children and families have to worry about survival first. It is just that. I think our children should be rewarded because they go so far beyond that. They never give up on the fact that they have to deal day to day with getting food, getting rent, getting clothes, and yet they still want an education.

That is the challenge for me. If the kids are going to stick in there, I am going to stick in there with them. As long as I can and as long as they want me. It is more of an obligation and commitment.

Ray Devenney has always been motivated by a desire to help people. Before becoming a teacher, he worked for the American Cancer Society, the Multiple Sclerosis Society, and in several drug rehabilitation programs. After moving to Colombia and learning Spanish, he became a teacher in the English as a Second Language program at Bell Multicultural School in Washington, D.C. The name of the school reflects the diversity of its student body, which includes the children of new immigrants, mostly from Spanish-speaking countries of the Caribbean and South America. But Devenney finds that he faces problems similar to those confronting Walters in Camden:

The economic pressure on students to support themselves and their families is the single biggest difficulty that I have. A student who is working thirty hours a week, how much time can he put in at school?

I think that also there are times when the value is not placed on getting an education. Let's take a student who's entered school from El Salvador. He is seventeen, his education has been disrupted, he may be marginally literate in his first language, let alone whatever problems he has with English, and he comes from a family whose members have never attended school and are not literate.

These people lived, they survived. How did they survive? They worked. If you're from an environment where you get by by working, what do you think the value is? The value is work. Being a very hardworking man, that's good. What can your father, who is illiterate, really tell you about? What can your mother, who has never been to school, really say to you? They don't understand school. What they say is, "Work hard and be good."

Basically, I think that in many cases the value on working is also something that is highly prized in certain cultures, and that comes into a direct conflict between what your culture and your family are saying to you and what your teacher and your school are saying to you, and your counselor is saying to you: "Don't work. Stay in school." When you add on top of that that you have to pay the rent, you have to contribute to the family, you have to send money back home, how many times do you think they'd choose school?

Sandra Fernandez is a remedial reading teacher at Santa Clara Elementary School in Miami:

The bureaucracy is the biggest hurdle to doing the job. If we were allowed to come into the classroom and teach, and that was it, things would be fine. But you start getting all these memos from downtown that say you have to teach AIDS, you have to teach gun safety and fire safety. In October it's Hispanic heritage, so you have to teach about Hispanics. In February it's black history month, so you have to teach about blacks in February.

Instead of putting that all together, you get so many things you have to do that you don't have time to teach them how to read, to teach them their math or writing skills.

If I had it my way, I wouldn't have any state-adopted textbooks. I would get real literature, real books, and they could have the whole language approach. If you're a good teacher, you're going to use that anyway. But when you get all these things you have to do, all these guidelines you have to follow, you get stuck between really teaching and doing what was asked of you from downtown.

The really amazing thing is that we're told to do this by people who have never even been in the classroom. Even if you've been in a classroom, if you're out for more than three years you're out of touch. Everything changes. With AIDS, there's an office downtown where they are constructing a curriculum to teach AIDS in kindergarten through twelfth grade. They come up with a nice, neat notebook, but they haven't consulted with the Health Department or the Social Studies Department, which also cover the subject. Now this is added and separate and nothing gels together.

In a primary school, everything has to be intertwined, it has to relate to something else so that the children can retain it and remember. If it's all chopped up during the day, it's not going to work.

Gail Davis teaches fourth grade at Hilton Elementary School in Newport News, Virginia:

The biggest hurdle is unnecessary paperwork. When I first started teaching, my evenings were spent writing new lessons, checking papers, calling parents. What is happening today is that I am so far behind on filling out this form and that form, filling out something for someone above me to turn into someone out in the central office.

There is a game here by somebody above in the ivory tower, that's what I call the administration building. They are making us do all this other stuff that does not improve teaching in order to justify their existence. It is not helping the act of teaching. It is interfering with it.

Ruth Prale is a reading teacher at Haugan Elementary School in Chicago:

I think the bureaucracy is the biggest hurdle to doing my job. I get support from my principal, sometimes. He's got to be the CEO of the building, which is a big job, and our school is extremely large: seventeen hundred kids and seventy-six faculty members. And yet it's still being thought of by the bureaucracy downtown like any three-hundred-student school. We have seven hundred to eight hundred kids eating lunch and they're all eating it on their laps in the auditorium. We've been asking for twenty-eight years for a lunchroom. They're still talking about maybe building it this year. Even getting supplies is like pulling teeth.

It's such a top-heavy bureaucracy. They have never come to the realization that they have jobs because we're out here. They're in another world. Whatever we've gotten in the way of advancements, and not only financial but educational, have been because the teachers have banded together and become organized and become unionized.

Nobody down at the central office said, "Forty-six students in a classroom is a lot." Or "Thirty-five kids in a kindergarten is a lot." Or "Thirty-two children is a lot of kids if you want to read." Nobody ever said that. The teachers have asked for smaller class sizes as a working condition, and it improves education. Many of the programs are here because we said, "This is what we need." They never thought of us as being anything but at the bottom of the totem pole.

If only they knew that we are the important ones.

Marion Clermont teaches English at Tilden High School in Brooklyn:

It's the constant interference and abusive students. I feel that if they would give education back to the educators and take it away from the politicians, then there might be some radical and necessary changes made.

Politicians want everybody to have this opportunity to get an education. And by everybody we are talking about the criminally insane and the emotionally disturbed, people who belong in a separate situation, not mainstreamed with average teenagers.

I've got thirty-five students in a class and one kid in each period might be emotionally disturbed for whatever reason. I am not saying that he can't work it through with therapy and be helped out, but one person can destroy a whole classroom. The school system, the way it is set up today, can't do anything about that student.

In the old days, these kids were expelled or sent to an alternative school or a reformatory, whatever. Now they just bounce them around from one school to another. We get somebody else's headache. They get ours. It just never ends.

———————————————

Dale Kenney is an attractive blonde and one of the few white teachers at Francis Junior High School in Washington, D.C., the school that President Bill Clinton's daughter, Chelsea, would have attended had she gone to her local public school. Kenney is counting the days until her retirement and last geography class. She is overwhelmed by the problems confronting teachers at inner-city schools today:

There's just too much to do, too many kids who really need help. What's truly frustrating is that I have some ideas, and I think my colleagues have some ideas, about what we could do to make things better. If we all sat down and talked about the problems, I think we could solve them, but because of this breakdown in communication between the administration and the teachers, we're not going to be able to do anything.

A friend of mine was student-teaching here last year. She would sit in the cafeteria and say, "Why don't you talk about this? Why don't you try that?" We'd look at each other and say, "You'll find out." All the things she was suggesting I knew we couldn't do because the principal wouldn't let us do them. We sit around and have meetings, come up with a plan, submit it, and it goes right in the trash.

I've talked to administrators. From what I've heard, administrators meet downtown and they all talk about how everything is fine, that they've got everything under control. Nobody wants to admit that they're having problems. I guess there are a lot of teachers who are the same way. They aren't going to say they're having problems because it will be a reflection on them. Therefore nothing is done. The problems are not being addressed.

Ava Fullenweider is a special-education teacher at Hansberry Academy (Intermediate School 200) in the Bronx, New York City:

Teachers are a problem, too. You have teachers who don't want to work, who sit up there with the newspaper, teachers who don't value education. I don't know why some teachers got into it. Some can't wait to get out.

Some teachers are lazy, some are burned out, and some are frustrated. You can go into any school and find a lot of problems are caused by teachers themselves.

John Cook is the in-house suspension teacher at West Windsor-Plainsboro High School in Princeton Junction, New Jersey:

Defining the way to handle the problem is one of my biggest frustrations. How do you meet that particular student's needs and keep in check the superintendent's demands, the state's demands, the school's demands, the legislative demands?

All these people have demands on education, particularly from politicians who complain that they want to get the taxpayers' money's worth. We don't know what the hell they're talking about in many cases. They don't know what they're talking about either, but it's a good way to get elected.

How do we get all those things in check so that the superintendent says we're doing a good job, and the legislators say they're doing a good job, and the public feels it's getting something for its money? Everyone has answers until he becomes involved in it.

I'm out in the afternoon jogging and I hear on the local radio station, "You know, if your teachers didn't have June, July, and August off, you could do this and that." Well, once you get in there, you come to understand that the answer is not that easy.

Cathy Rieder, a language arts and social studies teacher at Miraleste Intermediate School in Palos Verdes, California, said worn-out, burned-out teachers can be some of the biggest hurdles in her profession:

Burnout. Teachers who don't contribute. Those are our biggest hurdles. These teachers want out of education but they aren't fifty-five, so they can't retire. So they stay and do a lousy job. After a while they're just pleasant at the mailboxes, if you're lucky. But they don't do a very good job in the classroom. These are people who haven't changed their lectures in thirty years and who pride themselves on giving the same exams. They tell you: "Kids aren't learning as much today because I've given the same exam for thirty years. . . ."

I don't see a lot of teachers growing and changing. Teachers, as a group, don't like it. They balk at change. Yet there is very little incentive for teacher growth. I think they need encouragement and funding to go back to school and update themselves in their subject matter and teaching methods. I fault the administration a lot for this.

Jeff Jackson, who left a business career to become a teacher, taught third grade at Maury Elementary School in Alexandria, Virginia, at the time of the interview. A bright, energetic man in his late twenties, he has since moved to Georgia, where he continues to teach:

Things that are unrelated to my classroom are the biggest hurdles. I don't know how to explain that because everything is related to my kids. It's paperwork. An enormous amount. With any job there is paperwork, I know that. And I know that all the paperwork teachers have to do is related to the kids, but sometimes people lose sight of the real reason we are here. People who may sit in administration may be kind of out of touch with what is going on in the classroom, people who are producing documents and forms to fill out to verify and justify why things are being done. You can really get bogged down in that. You have to step back and say, "What is going on? Why am I here? I am here for these kids, not to fill out these forms for twenty different people." To me that is a hurdle to getting to my real job. The kids.

I am responsible for twenty-five kids who are all learning at different levels. I am responsible for teaching them this curriculum. I also have all these other responsibilities I have to do now. "Mr. X needs this form filled out by such-and-such a day. Ms. X needs this other form filled out by such-and-such a day. These stacks of papers have to be graded. These forms by the first of the year." Where do I find this balance as a teacher sitting up till ten o'clock at night?

So I think many teachers may be taking away from teaching time in order to do this paperwork, which is unfair to the kids. But it is being imposed on us. I am here myself every day till 5:00 P.M., and I leave most nights with work to do at home.

Dwight Brown teaches fifth grade at Moton Elementary School in New Orleans:

Finances and how money is distributed within the district are my biggest frustrations. We have the magnet schools in this city. I taught at one of those silk-stocking schools. The parents, they give the teachers $120 a month to buy materials or whatever they need. Spend it any kind of way you want. Here at Moton, our parents don't have money to send and say, "Okay, Mr. Brown, here's my five dollars for this, here's my eight dollars for this." We don't get extra supplies, teaching aides, or other tools. Other schools have strong PTAs where the parents have fundraisers and they buy books for the children and other materials. At the other school I taught at, parents would write a check for two hundred dollars to donate to the school. They have resources that we don't have, in the school and in the community.

Please, I'm not trying to sound racist, but the at-risk black child is going to be locked out. He doesn't have a computer to use as much as he needs it. We have computers at our school, but they are limited and they cannot be taken home, of course. The middle-class child has a computer at home and he can work on a computer day and night. When this child from Desire reaches the twelfth grade, if he does, he will have a bit of knowledge about a computer. But the middle-class kid is ready to go on to something else, computer programming or something. We don't have that. We need more time available for kids to work on the computer. We have one computer for each class, but there is not enough time to become familiar with computers. So it becomes hard for students to get the skills necessary to break the cycle and get out of here.

When I came here from a magnet school the difference was the frustration level. The kids at the magnet school were highly motivated. They were ready to learn. They had material. They were prepared. They had a foundation. And the kids here have no foundation. They don't have the materials. They don't have the supplies. They are not motivated. It was the difference between night and day.

We have children having babies in the at-risk communities. We have mothers sixteen or seventeen years old and they are not ready to take on the responsibilities of a parent. They are not working with the children. Some of the parents are on drugs. They sit around and look at TV. They are frustrated. There are no books in the home for the child to read. They are very deprived and depressed and repressed. The minute they walk in the door they are behind. We have an uphill battle. You have to teach these kids everything — left from right, colors, their name.

"What's your name?" I ask.

"Mookie," the kid says.

"No, your name is not Mookie. Your name is Charles Brown."

CHAPTER 6

DIVERSITY

AT DOBBS ELEMENTARY SCHOOL in Atlanta, a class of third graders picked up their pencils and began an arithmetic test. It is a normal occurrence in classrooms throughout America, but this time the answers were to be written in Swahili. In the classrooms at Urban Day School in Milwaukee, a red, black, and green African-American flag hangs alongside the flag of the United States. And each day at Chad School in Newark, New Jersey, begins with the poem "A Pledge to African People."

At public and private schools across the country, there is a small but growing movement to strengthen the education of black and minority students by emphasizing their history through Afrocentric and multicultural curricula. It has not yet gained the momentum that bilingual education enjoyed in the 1970s, but it is generating a rising level of controversy and resurrecting many of the same arguments.

Supporters argue that these programs are essential to reverse decades of discrimination, improve self-esteem, and keep minority youngsters in school long enough to learn the skills necessary to break the cycle of poverty and illiteracy engulfing the nation's underclass. Poor children in inner-city schools often start their education with faith and thrive in the early years, only to lose their optimism by the fourth or fifth grade. Programs that appeal directly to them offer a way to revive their belief in education, say the backers of Afrocentric and multicultural instruction.

White children also stand to benefit from teaching programs that provide a broader, more realistic view of the achievements and contributions of racial and ethnic minorities.

Multicultural programs usually supplement a traditional curriculum with heavy doses of literature and other material from other cultures, including African-American, Hispanic, and Native American cultures. For example, when Cary Tyler teaches myths and legends to his middle-school students in Albuquerque, New Mexico, he does not rely only on Greek and Roman mythology. He also tells them the ancient stories of creation handed down by Native Americans and the myths brought to the region by Spanish and Mexican settlers. The material is not designed to replace the traditional curriculum but to enrich it.

Afrocentric schools tend to replace much of the traditional, European-based instruction with courses linked to African and African-American history. As a result, these curricula have drawn the sharpest criticism. Opponents contend that such programs threaten to increase segregation, distort American history, and leave blacks without the academic skills vital to success in the broader world. They fear a "back to segregation" movement that will erase the hard-won progress in opening doors over the past thirty years and substitute black pride for academic achievement. Even multicultural programs, which only modify the basic curriculum, worry some teachers, who already are trying to teach such an unwieldy array of topics that classes are often a mile wide and an inch deep.

The idea of centering studies on Africa has provoked one of the hottest debates in education today, spilling over to encompass questions about the long-term impact of bilingual education and multicultural instruction. Does bilingual education enhance a young Mexican immigrant's self-image and make him more likely to succeed in school by allowing him to study core subjects in his first language? Or does it mean he may never catch up with his English-speaking classmates? Will a child develop the abilities that lead to being absorbed into the mainstream without pursuing the same courses as the majority of students? Is history being skewed? Can a school system that has failed African Americans and discriminated against them for generations be redeemed by instilling in them a pride of heritage?

Traditionally, American schools have been a place where rich and poor mixed. The common school was a powerful symbol of the melting pot. But sociological forces have broken that pattern in recent years. The rich have moved out of city centers or switched to private education. Middle-class families have moved to their own distinct suburbs or escaped public schools altogether by turning to private schools. The result is that inner-city schools often have become the province of the poor, meaning primarily blacks and other disadvantaged minorities.

Pressure to create more diverse instruction programs is likely to increase, at least if population is a factor. Census projections show that the United States, always a nation of ethnics, will become far more ethnically diverse in the twenty-first century. White population growth will slow, Hispanic and Asian immigration will remain high, and the younger minority population will have more children than whites.

These changes will create new demands for educational diversity, and the challenge of fulfilling those demands will fall primarily on teachers at schools where the burden is already heavy from dealing with so many disadvantaged students. The multicultural and Afrocentric approaches are unsettling for many teachers. Despite the growing racial diversity of the schools, the teaching profession is still dominated by whites and women.

A 1992 survey by the National Education Association found that 86.8 percent of public school teachers are white, roughly the same as twenty years ago. Nearly three fourths of public school teachers are women, and the percentage of male teachers is at its lowest point since the organization began measuring the ratio in 1961. The survey found that only 8 percent of teachers are black and 3 percent are Hispanic, with other minorities accounting for the remaining 2.2 percent.

The racial makeup of teaching may make it difficult to adopt the curriculum changes necessary to make education relevant to an increasingly diverse student population. It may also account for some of the resistance to bilingual education. However, reservations about Afrocentric instruction and bilingual education are not the sole province of white teachers.

Most teachers, regardless of race, seem to favor a modified approach to the multicultural curriculum, supplementing standard classes to provide a richer education for all students. Teachers are not alone in preferring this type of program. A 1992 poll of New York State residents by the United Teachers — American Federation of Teachers found that 88 percent wanted children to be taught both the traditional events of American history and the contributions of the nation's different racial and ethnic groups. Whether it is an advanced literature class on black authors or having a high school biology class dissect sheep on an Indian reservation in place of cutting up a frog, there is a growing recognition that special approaches can make education work for more students.

In her book *The Measure of Our Success,* Marian Wright Edelman, the founder and president of the Children's Defense Fund, highlighted the value of multicultural education: "Young people who do not know where they come from and the struggle it took to get them where they are now will not know where they are going or what to do for anyone besides themselves if and when they finally get somewhere," she wrote. "All black children need to feel the rightful pride of a great people that produced Harriet Tubman and Sojourner Truth and Frederick Douglass from slavery, and Benjamin Mays and Martin Luther King and Mrs. Fannie Lou Hamer from segregation."

For most teachers, the ideal remains the common school, where students are fully integrated and are taught the same enriched curriculum. However, there are lessons to be learned from the successes of Afrocentric and multicultural schools, where early reports show that the effort to strengthen hearts and minds is raising test scores.

Zakiya Courtney is a teacher and executive director at Urban Day School in Milwaukee, a private school that emphasizes a multicultural curriculum:

Our approach to education is more multicultural than Afrocentric. I don't criticize it, but to date I don't find the type of materials that will support an Afrocentric curriculum. There are not enough textbook materials and so it requires a lot of research on the part of teachers.

We do have a traditional curriculum that follows state guidelines, but it is enhanced through our cultural experiences, and interwoven through our curriculum is self-esteem. We don't have a self-esteem class, but there are many things we do with the culture of kids with self-esteem in mind.

The children are predominantly African American. In the younger grades you see more of a mix between Native American, Hispanic, Hmong, because of the changing demographics.

We are a private school with public contracts. We have 213 kids under the choice program. The state pays us twenty-six hundred dollars to educate each of the kids enrolled in the program. There is another contract for kindergarten and day-care service.

We feel that children need to have a well-grounded view of the world as well as a good understanding of themselves and their history. Even though textbooks are getting better, they are still not good enough for all kids to feel positive about who they are. If a kid can feel good, that is just one thing you've got out of the way.

Because we put such emphasis on culture and history, the kids go home and teach the parents. Many parents come in and say what they like best is that they have learned so much about their history and culture.

Multicultural education should not take away from the academics of the school. If you have a strong reading and writing program and the assignment is literature, there are many multicultural pieces of good literature to reach the academic objective. If you are going to look at structure, you will find the same items in any piece of literature. In a letter, the components stay the same: heading, greeting, conclusion. What difference does it make whether that child writes a letter to Jesse Jackson or George Bush?

These kids don't miss out on anything. For whites to be afraid that blacks cannot function without them is asinine because we have always known how to interact. It is whites who are more uncomfortable in our environment and don't know how to function. Because of the imperialistic attitude, we don't feel obligated to know anything about other cultures.

The fifth graders asked me into their class because they wanted to know why the school wanted them to learn U.S. history. I asked one young man, "What do you want to be when you grow up?"

"An attorney," he said.

I told him: "In order to be a good attorney, like Thurgood Marshall, you have to learn the law of the land. Once you know it, you can use the law, or change that law, to get what you need for your people."

Leonard Mednick is a guidance counselor at John Dewey High School in New York's Coney Island and Bensonhurst neighborhoods. A former history teacher who is now a guidance counselor and has spent his career in racially mixed schools, he is brash, outspoken, and offers a concise review of the virtues of multicultural environments:

Multiculturalism is being able to see what every culture brings to the table, to understand and respect others. History is exposing what happened and not placing one particular group over another group. History is exclusive, and if you have only eighteen weeks, five days a week, forty minutes per period, then you have to decide what will be included in the curriculum. It is impossible to be all-inclusive. So without feeding pabulum, without watering it all down, so it comes down to this is the contribution of the Irish, and this is the contribution of the black man, and this is the contribution of women. How do you make a meaningful panorama of history so we understand where we are and how we got here? I don't know if there is an easy answer to that.

I do know that there are kids who have to know what they are about and, if you exclude that, then you leave real holes in a child that don't get better. They cause tremendous amounts of inferiority or resentment.

I have a lot of problems with some of the schools that are going to the all-black, all-male approach. I have problems with that because I think there should be an all-black men's high school and I think it is a terrible thing. I feel terrible conflict about that. I think there is a need for it, but at the same time I am angry that there is a need for it.

I never taught in an all-white environment, so I don't know what that is about.

All of my experience has been forgetting that I have a white, Jewish background and just getting down with the kids who are there. There is a tremendous need for kids to feel a part of something, not apart from something.

Look at why you have a society that is so hostile. It is because everyone is disenfranchised. Look at those housing projects. You can't go through there. There is so much anger. It is not just a white anger or a black anger. It is black-black anger, black-Hispanic anger, Hispanic-white anger. It's anger.

Carolyn Epps Jackson teaches a gifted second-and-third-grade class at Mary C. Terrell Elementary School in Chicago, where all of the students and most of the staff are African American:

I don't think there is any such thing as black English. That is a way to discriminate. Everybody should speak some form of standard English. I've worked in low-income areas where the population was not black, but all-white. The language was not perfect. They used strange idioms. You should not teach a language incorrectly. I think it is wrong to teach children the incorrect way. There shouldn't be any "He should have came" instead of "He came."

As far as multicultural curricula go, children need to know other cultures exist so that they are not strange. Also, they need to know that every culture contributes to society. I want them to know there is more to Mexican food than burritos and tacos. And all black people don't eat chitlins and collard greens. I think every culture can take something from another.

I wanted to come to an all-black school. There is a closeness you don't get in a multicultural environment. Most of the staff here is black also. You really feel good about the children. They know you care about them. It is not that you're here because you were sent here. I want to see these kids succeed, to get out of this neighborhood, to be responsible adults. I feel there is more need here, I can have more impact.

In a middle-class school, where most of the parents are professionals, those kids know they are going to college and that they will succeed, even though they may act up in school. They know that "Okay, my life is fine. Whatever I do, Mom and Dad will fix it. So what?"

No matter what I teach, these kids may not have that. I want to be sure that of the twenty-six children in here, somebody feels inspired enough to go on. At least I will know I helped somebody overcome some odds and get where they want to go.

These kids don't know how far they will get. They haven't thought past high school. Some might not make it to eighth grade. I want them to know the possibilities and that it is okay to be a black American, that it is something to be proud of, and that it is not something that has to keep you from succeeding. They need to know that, that we are okay, that we don't all shoot and kill and cut. I think I can do more here.

Dren Geer is the development director and teaches advanced placement English at Providence-St. Mel in Chicago:

Multicultural curriculum is interesting in this school because the curriculum and program in this school is very, very clear in that it is a curriculum to empower these children to compete on an absolutely even level with anybody at any time in any place. It is not watered down at all. We are not doing these kids a favor if they cannot go out and compete as equals with anybody.

Nine or ten years ago, the advanced placement literature changed the syllabus and included all the major works of African-American literature. I kept talking to the principal, saying you should really find a way of teaching an advanced placement literature course focused on African-American literature because they have expanded the program and it is really a possibility.

He agreed and what we have done is to double the English requirement. The students all take the regular English course and read all the standard works that every other student does. Then we double it. In four years, they will read every major work of every major African American — drama, plays, novels, poetry, short stories, essays.

We start with *Raisin in the Sun*. It is written about Chicago. It is written about their neighborhoods. The voice, everything is theirs. In many cases, for the first time, they are reading literature that really addresses their situation and circumstances. And it is a very serious piece of literature.

I find it very interesting that here I am white, interpreting the black, inner-city experience for ninth-grade kids. They don't object, though they sometimes correct me. You start probing if they feel comfortable about it. They haven't put those pieces together yet. They have lots of experience, lots of insight, but they are not yet at the point of maturity or age or confidence where they see the relationships between their daily experience and *Raisin in the Sun*.

That is a very important experience for these kids to begin to understand, to take somebody who has taken their experience very seriously and written a very major work of literature and be able to connect that with where they are and what they are thinking about.

I don't think we should teach just one culture or the other, particularly in a school like this. If it were an all-black curriculum, black history, black literature, and everything else, the kids might have a marvelous experience, they might write very well, but they are going to be in big trouble when they go to any college or university and try to compete. But to give them both, that is great.

I know a wonderful teacher by the name of Nguyen "Joe" Hieu, who is Vietnamese, and he teaches at Clemente Community Academy here in Chicago. He once said to me, "The children I teach are boat people, most of them. Even with all the problems they have, they have a tremendous advantage. The advantage is that they have had to learn two cultures and two languages. What happens is if you have had to learn two, you have twice the stimulus and every experience you have is doubly enriched."

Art Murnan is a guidance counselor and religion teacher at Providence-St. Mel:

It is important to know your community. In the United States today we are a multicultural community. You have to know that because so much can be misinterpreted.

For example, two kids who are arguing. The teacher will try to get them to stop, but the kids will say that they aren't fighting. You see, fighting in this community, which is all African American, is throwing a fist. If you are just verbally going at it, that isn't a fight. So there is that miscommunication of words.

You have to know the culture, the language, ideas. I can go into class and talk very formally or I can rap in the language these kids use. That is important to them because when you do that it sends off an I-understand-what-you're-saying, where-you're-coming-from message.

My principal will tell you he doesn't believe in a black, Afrocentric curriculum at all. He feels that our kids have to survive in a basically white world, so they have to read and write and do the things that are expected. Harvard is not accepting you because of your views on the African-American situation but because you're skilled in traditional education.

We are dealing with kids who are way behind when we get them. Our primary concern is to get them where they are supposed to be. It is a strong traditional education. Then we can build on it from there.

St. Augustine High School is in a working-class neighborhood a few blocks from the raucous French Quarter in New Orleans. For generations, St. Aug's has educated the city's elite black men, and Father Wilbur Atwood has taught many of them:

When a black student goes to another Catholic school that is integrated, generally the black population in that school is never more than 10 percent, if it's that. Therefore, they feel left out in many instances. There is not an active social life for them. They feel that they are always on target. Whereas with St. Aug's, they are more relaxed because they are not facing white kids and white challenges all the time. We do have kids transferring here because they just cannot put up with the pressures that they feel in these integrated Catholic schools.

Now, let me say right here and now, we would take any white student who wants to apply to St. Aug's. We are not segregated in that sense. We are segregated because of the customs of the South. White students, for the most part, would never apply to St. Aug's because it is simply not the thing done in the South. Blacks can integrate white institutions, but whites never integrate black institutions.

It is okay for whites to have blacks in their schools, providing they never get above 10 percent. You get above 10 percent, they speak about the "tipping scale." That is the point at which whites begin to withdraw. In other words, it is becoming a black institution.

St. Aug's is known as a black school, and it has played a major role in the black community. For example, Mayor Sidney Barthelemy came here and said something to the effect that he was sort of shocked and I guess pleased that when he came here they referred to him as "Mr. Barthelemy." We call kids "Mister." Most of these kids have never heard that before in their lives — to be referred to rather than as "kid" or by their first name. Because of the segregation in the South, their grandfathers, men in their sixties and seventies, would be referred to by their first name and never by "Mister." When we came here, there was a conscious effort by the staff to show the dignity of the person by giving them that little bit of recognition that they were a person with dignity. I know Sidney brought this out. While I intellectually was aware of it, it brought it home to me very realistically when he spoke about how much this had meant to him as a kid.

I think that was one of the things that St. Aug's did for these fellas. It not only challenged them intellectually to be the best they could, but also it showed them that there were people who recognized them, who respected them, and expected a great deal out of them. They went on to produce. Kids are going to react and try to live up to it.

Ruth Prale teaches reading at Haugan Elementary School in Chicago:

You walk into this building and the children are speaking Spanish to one another. We have Syrian, and we have Korean, and Vietnamese, Cambodian, Arabic, and Spanish. We have a bilingual Romanian teacher and we have a teacher who takes care of the Polish children.

You see, the rules are that if you have twenty students of a culture, you should have a bilingual teacher. We have maybe one family of Polish, we have to give them training in English. We can't give them everything in Polish. We're now looking for an East Indian teacher, and Filipino.

You see, you no longer walk into a room and have to learn English. Is that good or bad? Personally, I don't like it. My parents were immigrants. I'm a first-born American. My children are half second generation because their father came from Europe also. He came here at the age of ten. He had to learn English.

If you had given him bilingual education, maybe he'd be a butcher today, because that's what his father was. Instead he's an optometrist. He had to learn to get into the mainstream. His children are well educated and have master's degrees.

We have a very high dropout rate of Hispanic students in our schools. They're not stupid. They're very bright. But they're not steeped in English and they must learn English. You cannot go out and get a job just because you've got an Hispanic name. The adults that have Hispanic names and have jobs are verbal in English. They have the advantage of a second language. I think it's wonderful to have a second language, but that's not how the schools are operating.

I'm not telling you to give up your Spanish. I'm not telling you to give up your culture. I'd be the last one to do that. I keep my culture. I know that if I want to be part of the mainstream, I have to speak the language of the country. That's the important thing.

Affirmative action is wonderful, but you have to be qualified. I think that Hispanics are making a very big mistake by allowing their children to be taught in Spanish and not English and that they've held their children back.

When schools first started talking about bilingualism, I thought in terms of those many students, English-speaking students, who had gone to college and gotten degrees in Spanish. They would be perfect to come into our schools. They are truly bilingual, but our Board of Education will go to Puerto Rico or Mexico for teachers.

Twenty-two years ago I was in a school where they started a bilingual program. When I heard that they did this, I said, "You're holding these children back. I want these children to be teachers, social workers, lawyers, and doctors. You are going to keep them busboys and chambermaids?" That's unfair.

You have to learn English. I've done it with Korean children before we had these bilingual programs. They learned it in two or three months in first grade. Kids don't make the transition by themselves from another language to English. Teachers cannot move a child into an English program. Parents have to do it. That's difficult, because parents are visited by the bilingual teachers and are encouraged to keep them in the bilingual program.

We started out with one Spanish class and we now have nine, and our principal is looking for more bilingual teachers. We don't have self-contained Syrian or Romanian classes. Those children are in the regular classroom and they go for extra help to the English as a Second Language teacher, and she helps them make that transition. It's a way of keeping jobs for the bilingual teachers. What happens is that nine Anglos don't have a job.

Bill Walters is a mentor-teacher at Camden High School in Camden, New Jersey:

What do these world rankings mean — the United States finishing thirteenth in the world academically? What does that tell us, that we are the worst?

We are educating the most diverse population in the world. We are successful. Is that the only measure of us as a nation? We're doing okay. Aren't we still winning Nobel prizes and other awards throughout the world?

Being a democratic, diverse society, who else is going through this and doing as well? What measure can you use? If you have one culture, one group, and you focus on that and you don't have all the distractions, I suppose you might score a little higher. But that doesn't make you a better-educated person or society.

Ray Devenney teaches English as a Second Language to foreign students at Bell Multicultural School, which is part of the public schools in Washington, D.C.:

To me multicultural does not mean feasts, fiestas, and famous men. It doesn't mean the ten great books list or *The Color Purple.* I think that a starting point for me of multicultural means beginning with the notion that students are resources and students from so many different cultures are experts about that culture and they bring with them knowledge that no individual person can ever possess.

The starting point is seeing a kind of transformation of the curriculum based on the point of view of students as resources. It's a process of relating what the student brings to the learning situation with the kind of opportunities that you provide.

John Cook is the in-house suspension teacher at West Windsor-Plainsboro High School in Princeton Junction, New Jersey:

We have this group that sees education as a white thing. I often find African-American students saying, "To be educated is a white thing and I don't want to do that." That's frightening. You have to bring their attention to just what that means. If you think that being white is being educated, then obviously being black is being what? In many cases, the group that is lacking that value is also in the process of trying to gain an identity, just as many adolescents are. That identity is usually supported by what they see in the media, what they see in the streets, and what something like what the movie *New Jack City* may be about. You see this is the inner city. If you've got your gun, you're good.

We say, "My God, what have we done? What have we created as an understanding for a young African-American individual to believe in?" We don't know. That's why we have the Afrocentric way of thinking, which is questionable in and of itself, but it's a reasonable result of looking at a generation of African-American students who are lost.

The fact that that kid over there is black is just as important because that is an individual, and that culture is still very real to him. He may be fitting very well into the upper-middle-class environment, wanting to get an education, wanting to go different places? That's why he went to school. He wanted to gain some of the returns of a good education. But it doesn't mean that the African-American culture, its uniqueness, is no longer a part of that individual.

Charlie Bullock and Denise Masse taught together at the Dowa Yalanne Elementary School on the Zuni reservation until Bullock moved to another school on the reservation. For those who live and work in the remote Indian country of New Mexico, diversity has a special meaning. Masse:

The typical picture of the average Native American student in a regular school is that they are withdrawn, they refuse to make eye contact. We don't have that here because over 90 percent of our children are Native American and they see themselves as the world. That's great. They don't have a lot of the same reservations of a lot of children who are thrown into maybe larger community settings, where they lose their identity, or don't know how to hang on to identity. Here, you're Zuni. That's a real advantage.

Bullock:

On the other hand, a lot of our multicultural education is not for me to try to teach Zuni kids who they are or what they are. It is to teach them about other cultures. This year our pen pals are from Russia. Last year they were from Japan. My job is to expand this world, to build on what we have here. I don't know if everyone feels this way, but we do a lot of international education and the kids just thrive on it.

We do a lot of comparative things. As we were studying Russia this year, more and more we began to understand the contemporary role of the babushka, the grandmother, in Russian society today, and how she's becoming kind of the strength and the backbone of holding families together in a lot of different ways.

As a result, the kids wrote their pen pals about their own grandparents. So every kid interviewed their grandparents. We went to the homes and took the kids' pictures with their grandparents and every child wrote a story about their grandparents, and we made this book for our pen pals. We did the same thing on ourselves, and then on the community.

The kids ended up cooking a Russian dinner. We set up two long tables with white tablecloths and flower centerpieces, and we invited all the grandparents in. We had almost thirty grandparents here. Then they read the grandparents their stories, and talked about Russia with them. To me, that's not multicultural education in terms of my teaching Zuni kids who they are or their history, but it's helping them locate their place in the world.

Ron Cooper teaches at Van Buren Middle School in Albuquerque, New Mexico, where many of his students grew up speaking Spanish:

Bilingual education is an absolute necessity. There are different theories on this. One theory is that a kid learns Spanish first, and he is still developing his basic interaction communication, and that goes up until he is thirteen years old and then it levels out. The theory is that if he is taken out of this environment, where he is learning Spanish, and you try to teach him in another language, English, you are doing the kid a disservice because he hasn't yet developed the brain skill to work with the first language he learned. So it can become very confusing and frustrating for the kid. It is kind of like trying to learn how to pedal the bike before you learn to balance the bike. Your basic cart-before-the-horse routine.

You want a kid to be able to think and make decisions before you want him to take on another language. I say, yes, if a kid needs total immersion, give it to him. If he needs to learn a skill, if he needs to learn English through Spanish instruction, then give it to him. Make him use it, but let the natural environment work with him. When this kid goes home, he's going to a place where they speak Spanish.

Bilingual education does segregate children. It is not the right thing to do, but it is their little network, their support group, and why shouldn't they have that? Is it better for them to go and struggle? A kid has to buy into whatever he is doing. You can't force him to do anything. You can't make a system do anything either. Nothing comes from the top down that works, especially in education.

Serafin and Delores Padilla, who are married, both teach in the Albuquerque public schools. They sat side by side on a couch in their adobe-style house and talked about the best way to teach students who speak no English. Serafin:

For the first time this year, I have learning centers in my class, so I placed a child who could not speak one word of English in a center with other kids who spoke Spanish, too. This went on until December, and at that time I removed the kids around him and left him with some other kids who speak English.

I turned around and asked him a question in English, and he didn't understand one word that I had said. He couldn't even understand me and he had been there for three months. His results were coming back positive because the other kids were tutoring him, putting it in his own language.

Now another three months have passed and today he came in and asked me a question in English. He was forced to learn English when I put him in with the English-speaking kids. I'm not sure why I did what I did. I wanted to try a different approach. It reinforced my earlier feelings, that the child should be placed with kids who were speaking English. Otherwise he would still be segregated.

Delores:

We do the same thing in our groups. We always place the non-English-speaker with an English-speaker, and the kids are very helpful. Right away they want to help. They want to make sure they understand. Since they speak both languages, they are able to work with the child who doesn't. By the end of the school year, the non-English-speaking child is speaking English and he understands.

They need the reinforcement of their own language for a while until they are comfortable. Once they are comfortable, they will let you know. They take off.

Kathleen O'Neill, a Los Angeles teacher at Sinai Akiba Academy, has strong feelings the other way:

Don't get me going on bilingual education. We're just setting the children up for defeat with that. I taught at a public school here for one year in Santa Ana. Nobody spoke English.

I had a classroom of first and second graders, all Spanish-speakers. I had students in that classroom begging me to teach them to speak English, and I was told I had to teach them to speak Spanish. I'm not a Spanish-speaker. I took two years of Spanish in high school. I haven't spoken Spanish in years. It was the most frustrating situation I've ever been in. I spent two months there and said, "I'm out of here. I can't deal with this. This is not teaching for me."

I need to know that I'm reaching the students. I was just keeping the administration happy. I was baby-sitting. These students were not learning to read, they were not learning to write, they were not learning anything at a rate that I considered even close to acceptable.

And the children were asking to be taught to speak English. Even the children who could speak a little bit of English I was not allowed to teach in English. I'm totally opposed to that. I think that is one of the reasons we have gang problems, why Hispanics and Spanish-speaking people are kept down. I think that continuing Spanish through fourth grade and into junior high school is government oppression. I don't think there's any other word for it.

I know there are people who don't agree with me, who yell at me, who get on me. And it's not racist. I'd like to ask these people how they would feel if they were in another culture where they didn't speak the language and they were kept from learning it.

What am I doing for a child by not teaching him to speak English? I'm setting him up for defeat. I'm saying, "Here you go, I'm keeping you down."

Beverly Hills High School does not have a bilingual program, despite an incredibly diverse student body: Instead, principal Ben Bushman says, they substitute a program of English as a Second Language, or ESL:

We are antibilingual. We are what is known as an Option 1 school, meaning we have to prove to the state each year that our kids coming out of our ESL program do as well as a counterpart who comes from a bilingual program. It is a terrible task, and they keep making us prove it.

There is a bias in this state for bilingual education. Our concept is not bilingual education because we believe they assimilate faster that way. We double their English. I just think they are going to move through it faster. They will learn faster.

John Borsum, his tall, slender frame tucked into a metal chair next to Bushman in a small conference room at one of the nation's most famous high schools, offered a case study to illustrate the principal's point:

I always think of twins I had a couple of years ago from Korea. It was advanced algebra-trig. They showed up first day of school, fresh off the boat. These kids did not know how to say *hello, please, thank you,* or anything. They walked in with their schedules, handed them to me, and bowed. They had no idea what was going on.

They worked hard. I told them they could use their English-Korean dictionary on the tests, but that I was expecting them to be as good as any other kid in this class. I'd watch them in the tests, flipping through the pages, and they'd turn their tests in before the other kids. They got A's. They obviously came to us knowing a lot of math. The first day of school in the middle of September, they knew no English at all, and I would say by the end of October or so, I was conversing with them.

Granted, you have some intellect there to begin with, but when you are just plunged into it, you have no choice but to learn English.

We also have a girl in school who came here from Russia. She didn't speak a word of English. She has been here less than two years. The first thing she did, she was here a week or two, she got a job in the student store. Now she has been selected in a program we have called Presidential Classroom, where the kids go to Washington, D.C., for a week. To do that, she had to write a paper and go in front of a board. She is in advanced placement English. She has gone through so fast. This is a very bright kid.

Cary Tyler, the former newspaper reporter, is an English and writing teacher at Van Buren Middle School in Albuquerque:

There is something about multiculturalism that bugs me. Education should be multicultural to begin with, without any labels. We should be able to learn about each other without putting a label on it.

To me, this seems simple. Instead, we try to cram a culture into one packet. These little kids might not snap about it, but high school kids, especially those in the inner city, might just be a little resentful about it. "Well, look what they are teaching us now. Yes, I am black, what are you going to do about it? Teach me that? That isn't going to change my situation any."

Real multicultural education should begin in kindergarten and go straight through high school, although it is harder, obviously, if the schools are not integrated.

I bet there are some people who, if they heard me say this, might be upset because they'd say, "Mr. Tyler, you're black, you should be interested in this."

I agree that we should talk about our different cultures, but one of the biggest problems in this nation right now is that we don't know how to deal with people being together and working as one. We are so worried about the Japanese and the impact of their imports and we haven't even learned to work as one.

Depending upon how it is taught, multicultural education can be divisive. All along we should be dealing with our multiculturalism. There is so much left out of our history books, on any race. Someone said once, the winners made history.

Whoever won has his stuff recorded in the history books; the loser doesn't. So we need to be sure the kids know that. Our textbooks are okay, but let's expand. You do not have to make sure the civil rights unit coincides with black history month and Martin Luther King's birthday so we can get it all done at once, so we don't have to worry about it again.

Multiculturalism should be easy to teach in a school like this because you don't have to restrict it to one thing.

Linda Belarde is a special education teacher and principal of Twin Buttes High School on the Zuni reservation in New Mexico:

I think the trick is being able to use the environment and the culture in an academic way so that kids learn things that to them are real skills instead of having like a little unit on Indians. We don't celebrate Indian Day here. The school across the way does, they have dances and everything. I think every day is Indian Day.

A big part of our biology class is the outdoor world curriculum, and it was piloted in this school and the Zuni High School through a National Science Foundation grant. They are working on a lot of things here in Zuni.

One of the lessons early in the year was butchering a sheep, and looking at the organs, and the preparation lessons for it were looking at body organs. Instead of doing a frog, as they do in most high schools, they do a sheep. People here do sheep, it's a cultural thing. Feast times, that's what they do.

Richard Brough teaches in the same school as Belarde on the Zuni reservation in New Mexico:

While I believe in integrating Zuni history and culture into our curriculum, it has to be done with some perspective. You are doing a disservice to the kids if you make things to be of greater moment than they really are. I look to Zuni history and culture as being important because it is theirs, but it has to be integrated in such a way that it is in relationship to the development of the society in which they find themselves, in which they will have to learn to cope.

Sometimes I'm not sure all our teachers see that. It's as if they would like to hermetically seal the Zunis and then we wouldn't have to worry about standards. I think they'd like to return to this traditional way of life in which the kids aren't taught the kinds of skills that we need to function off the reservation, but I think this would serve to trap the children. You should use Zuni as a way to develop concepts and ideas and use it as an entrée to other parts of American and world history. It's humanity we're talking about here and accomplishments and achievements of humanity, whether it's China or the European Renaissance or Greece or Egypt.

I remember one time that I was criticized by an observer in our room. She was a white woman. We had mentioned somehow the taking of scalps and she felt that was denigrating to the Zuni people. In fact, there is an old scalp shrine right over there through that window. I think the last time it was used was eight or nine years ago for a special initiation ceremony. Of course, they don't use human scalps anymore, but it is some sort of hairpiece, probably dog. Anyway, this observer was offended. I doubt a Zuni would be offended at all.

I remember thinking at the time that you don't want to sanitize history. I guess it was Steve Martin who said that comedy isn't pretty, or something to that effect. Neither is history. There's plenty of blame to share. More blame, some might say, than noteworthy accomplishments.

Pat Maier is a teacher of French at Palos Verdes Peninsula High School in Palos Verdes, California:

I have a bit of a problem with this idea of black studies and Asian studies and Latino studies. I do not believe in this multicultural thing. The responsibility of the school is to make Americans. Not to make Asian Americans, not to make black Americans, not to make Chinese Americans, but to make Americans. If their families want to make them Chinese or Latino Americans, that's their responsibility. It is not the responsibility of the school.

There is nothing wrong with the traditional melting pot philosophy where we come up with one culture that is representative of the United States. That doesn't mean subjugating original ethnicity, but it is not the responsibility of the school or the community. We have to be Americans first.

I do think, however, that history books need some revision. Some areas have been completely left out. I think we need to rewrite America's role in terms of the Japanese internment. We cannot present ourselves as always being the best when we haven't been the best. And while we need a much more authentic look at history than we have had previously, I don't think that we should reinvent it either, just to create a history for a group of people.

Only in the United States would we teach a one-semester course on the history of the Western world. Only in the United States would we be so stupidly presumptuous that we could do the history of the world in one year, but we do American history for ten years.

For the past decade, Alan Marks has worked to open doors at the best colleges and universities for his minority students at Rio Grande High School in Albuquerque, New Mexico. An English and economics teacher, he has written and published a handbook showing his students how to choose the best school and then get in. To him, multicultural programs are a strong element of education:

I can think of nothing but praise for multicultural education. I'm feeling awkward because it's already been said so well that anything I might say would come out sounding cliché-ish. When you live in a place that is so multicultural, how can you pretend that you're educating somebody if you're ignoring 60 percent of the people who live there? That's bogus.

Also, if you're hoping that what education is about is learning how to deal with the world, it might not be a bad idea to take a look at the world around you. Given all of that, I think the more multicultural stuff we can do, the better we're going to be able to prepare people to face the world and succeed there.

The lens that you look through is going to determine the picture that you see. This is not trying to rewrite history, this is just a much different perspective. This is saying: What is the effect of history on women, minorities? This isn't saying what did women and minorities contribute and that they contributed more than anyone else. It's just, what is it like to look at what these white males did, looking through the eyes of a woman or Native American.

Robin Lichtenfeld teaches at Crossroads Arts Academy, a private school in Los Angeles:

I think a multicultural curriculum is really important and I try to do it, but in some ways, I still don't know what they mean. What exactly is multicultural education?

We had a very big argument in my class today. The theme of our literature and social studies is immigration. They are writing their family histories. They are all going to be telling their own stories.

The novels I picked out I hoped would be a good selection of books about kids from different countries. We are reading a book now called *My Name Is Asher Lev,* about an Orthodox Jew. I showed them the movie *Fiddler on the Roof,* so the children who weren't Orthodox, which was all of them, would visualize what this novel was talking about.

One of the black children came up to me this morning very angry and asked why I was showing a movie about being Jewish when I didn't show a movie about being black. We had just finished reading a book about being black in America, so why did we not show a movie about being black in America?

We have a Korean boy and a Mexican girl, too. I had the whole class participate in an open-ended discussion. I said that I showed them a movie because I wanted them to understand what was going on, but if we picked all twenty-seven of these children's stories, we would have to read twenty-seven novels because everyone has a different story to tell.

Then I asked for their feelings, if they thought I was being biased in any way. It was a really good discussion and it turned into a discussion about racism. They told this girl that she needed to see this movie, even though it wasn't about her, because you have to learn to live in a world with people different from you, that it might help her understand Jews better. I encouraged her to bring in a movie, too.

You see, multicultural means something different to everyone. You have to be so careful to avoid stepping on anyone's toes. To this young girl, multicultural education meant reading books about blacks, seeing movies about blacks. I actually told the class that I picked no books about white Anglo-Saxon Protestants and asked if they were upset since that is a group, too. You do leave people out.

CHAPTER 7

VIOLENCE

FOR PHYSICAL EDUCATION TEACHER Gary Smith, the nightmare began on the playground outside his school while he was umpiring a softball game. A seventeen-year-old boy approached from behind and swung a baseball bat at Smith's head. Nobody was sure how many times he was struck. Maybe ten. Maybe fifteen. His life was saved only because another teacher kept him breathing with CPR until he reached the hospital. Seven operations later, Smith had a metal plate in his head, a glass eye, a significant hearing loss, and a change of heart about teaching.

For Ava Fullenweider, it began in the sanctity of her classroom. A student who had been thrown out of class earlier in the day returned with the padlock from his locker. He beat her on the head with the lock as he dragged her screaming into the hallway. Although her physical injuries were not permanent, two years later she still found herself walking against the walls in the hallways and often waiting until they were cleared of children to venture out of her room. Rarely does she turn her back on the door to her classroom without a subconscious chill.

For Barbara Mendez, it began on the stairs as she walked toward her basement classroom. Mendez was twenty-three years old and excited about her first teaching job at the Brooklyn high school from which she had graduated five years earlier. Walking back to her classroom from a lunch break, she was shot in the shoulder. She had been on the job less than two months.

The circumstances differ, but each incident is linked by a common thread: All three of these teachers were attacked on school grounds. Just as changes in society have burdened teachers with more demands, so has the increase in violence and crime across the country translated into more dangerous schools. Our increasingly violent society has translated into increasingly violent schools.

Assaults, drugs and drug transactions, robberies, and threats with knives and guns have moved from the streets into the schools. A 1991 U.S. Department of Justice report characterized the situation with frightening clarity: "Gunfights are replacing fistfights, and 'bullet drills' are replacing fire drills on many campuses."

About three million incidents of street crime — rape, assault, robbery, theft — occur inside schools or on school property every year. Most often, the victims are students. Nearly three hundred thousand high school students are physically attacked each month at school. Nearly one in ten students at urban junior and senior high schools miss at least one day of school a month because they say they are afraid to go. More than a third of those students report that someone has threatened them at school.

For students, danger and disorder at school mean they have no sanctuary. If minimal physical protection cannot be provided at school, the message to children is that they are not safe anywhere. If school is a place of terror, students have little chance for the learning and training necessary for future success.

But this atmosphere of terror — that is not too strong a word for some schools — also victimizes teachers. More than five thousand high school teachers are physically attacked at school every month, and one teacher in twenty is assaulted every year.

The violence and fear, the verbal assaults and disrespect take a toll on teachers, too. Twelve percent of teachers in one survey acknowledged that they hesitate to challenge students who are misbehaving because they fear reprisal. Countless others have left the classroom or the profession after being attacked or out of fear that they will be attacked. A teacher with eighteen years' experience says she is contemplating her mother's offer to buy out the remainder of her contract so she can quit the profession.

"As violence, drugs, and exotic weapons proliferate on the streets and seep into our schools, safety has never been more important to this union," says Sandra Feldman, president of New York City's United Federation of Teachers. "It is an uphill fight, and we aren't anywhere near satisfied with the commitment of money and resources."

So a nation that already spends more municipal tax dollars on incarceration than education must use some of those scarce education funds to make schools safer. At schools large and small, administrators and teachers have been forced to trade the freedom associated with childhood and a learning environment for something that more closely resembles a medium-security prison. Doors are locked once students and teachers are inside in the morning. Employees wear photo security badges. Visitors are screened at the front office before they are allowed into the school for conferences with teachers. Drug-sniffing dogs are led up and down the hallways, and security guards patrol the perimeters.

In New York City, a roving team of security police carrying metal detectors visits three high schools a day on a random basis in a search for weapons. There are no hard figures for how many guns and knives wind up inside schools, but a 1992 study by the National School Safety Center found that 25 percent of the nation's fifty largest school districts deemed the problem so severe that they use metal detectors to try to keep weapons out of schools.

"Figures such as these send a message that there is enough concern about weapons and violence that strong actions are being taken to defend schoolchildren and teachers," says Ronald D. Stephens, executive director of the nonprofit center, which is affiliated with Pepperdine University in Malibu, California.

Problems are not relegated to the biggest schools. A study by education professors at Texas A&M University found that many rural schools, particularly those near big cities, have even worse violence problems than the national average. In a survey of one thousand students in the eighth and tenth grades at twenty-three small Texas schools, the researchers found that more than half the boys and a fifth of the girls reported having been in at least one physical fight involving weapons during the previous year. One in four students said they had carried a weapon to school during the past year, and 40 percent said they could get a handgun if they wanted one.

Guns are epidemic in some schools, with security guards reporting confiscations of everything from Dad's antique pistol to state-of-the-art Uzi submachine guns. According to the U.S. Justice Department, an estimated one hundred thousand students bring guns to school each day, and forty children are killed or injured by gunshot wounds on an average day.

"Regardless of race, family income, or region of the country, no child in America is immune to the fear or insulated from the possibility of random, indiscriminate, and senseless violence," Keith Geiger, the president of the National Education Association, said in 1993 when he issued a call for tougher enforcement of federal laws that make it a crime to carry a gun onto school property.

In Wichita, Kansas, an undercover team from ABC-TV's *Prime Time Live* discovered that they could buy a .22-caliber pistol from a thirteen-year-old. Their middleman was a fifteen-year-old, too young to drive them to the location of the deal.

Only about 12 percent of the violent crimes in school buildings involve a weapon. However, the same erosion of discipline and respect and increased aggression of students that spawn the influx of guns and knives create an atmosphere where baseball bats, locker padlocks, and fists become weapons.

Schools also are forced to protect themselves from the violence around them. Evening athletic events are shifted to daylight for protection. Children in South-Central Los Angeles, where drive-by gang shootings have become commonplace in recent years, go through "drop drills" in which they are taught to dive under their desks at the sound of gunfire. In Long Beach, California, a $160,000, ten-foot-high, eight-inch-thick, nine-hundred-foot-long concrete barrier was constructed around the playground at Charles A. Lindbergh Middle School. Bullets fired during gun battles in the surrounding streets had been flying into the playground, wounding a student one day and narrowly missing teachers and students on other occasions.

Concern over violence to students and teachers alike prompted Baltimore to set up alternative schools for problem students in high school and junior high school. The classrooms are small, with no more than fifteen students per teacher, and each school is served by counselors, social workers, and psychologists.

"It is not there to be a place to warehouse disruptive kids," says Irene Dandridge, president of the Baltimore Teachers' Union. "We're hoping that, with smaller classes and all the support services, the children will eventually be able to return to their home school."

Just as these deadly lessons create new worries for parents and students, so they add a frightening dimension to the job of being a teacher. Just as students cannot learn when they do not feel protected, so teachers cannot function effectively when they are not sure they are safe. Privacy laws in most states mean that teachers never even find out that a new student has a history of violent behavior — until it is too late. As a result, even teachers who have never been the victims of violence or even witnessed violence find their lives on the job altered by its presence in the lives of their students.

In New York City, former teacher June Feder is the head of a program established by the school system to provide assistance to teachers who are victims of school violence. It is an attempt to avoid what Feder calls "a second injury," which comes when teachers are portrayed as instigators rather than victims. There is a stigma that attaches to a wounded teacher, not unlike that of a rape victim. Too often, school administrators and boards of education are paralyzed as they try to determine whether the young offender is a victimizer or a victim. The result is a world in which serious crimes escape punishment. Everyone in that dangerous territory — teachers, students, and society — pays a price.

Gary Smith was teaching physical education at Roberto Clemente School (Intermediate School 166), a junior high school in New York City's tough South Bronx, when the violence of that neighborhood spilled over into his life and changed it forever:

Nineteen eighty-eight was not the first time I had witnessed violence at school. I was a dean for nine of the eighteen years I taught there. I dealt with all kinds of violence — the fighting, the kids with weapons, the robberies. A kid was even shot in the school. But I never felt vulnerable at all. I could walk the neighborhood anytime. That's why, when my incident took place, there was so much reaction from so many people — because it had happened to me.

Another teacher said to me, "Gary, you're probably as street-smart a person as there is in this school. For you to get taken from behind with a bat like that, well, it's hard to believe."

What happened was very troublesome to me, mainly because of the effect it had on my family, friends, and colleagues, and because it made me leave the job. I never ever saw myself leaving that school. I saw myself getting to retirement age there.

I turned down an assistant principal's job in that school. I turned down a special ed supervisor's job. One semester I was acting assistant principal because the assistant principal was on sabbatical and I had the license to do the job. I hated it. It was the spring of 1983. I hated everything about it. I hated the fact that I was in less contact with the kids. And I hated the fact that I wasn't teaching. I saw that this wasn't where I could have a real effect on kids. But if I'd taken those jobs, assistant principal or special ed supervisor, I wouldn't have been injured. I wouldn't have lost my eye. That's the trade-off.

The program was called after-school intramural sports. It was May 26, 1988. I was outside and it was the last day of the program. We were playing a championship softball game between two boys' teams. It was a nice day and we had all been looking forward to the championship game. I got out early and swept the field and got the water jug. People came from three blocks away to see the game. Now, in the South Bronx, when you go three blocks down you're in another neighborhood, and that had a lot to do with the situation.

So, I'm down there and the kids show up and we get ready to go. We'd prob-ably played twenty minutes and this guy comes onto the field, somebody I didn't know, a seventeen-year-old. I had had the kids throw their book bags in one spot on the bench over there, just so they could stack them up for security reasons. It's right there where everybody sits.

This kid came onto the field, walked right over, and started going through the kids' book bags, opening them up, lifting them up. He did it quickly and he was bigger and older than the kids. You have to remember to get back to street law now. The guy could turn around and pull a gun and before you could say a word you'd be over. Objections don't come quickly.

So I walked over and said, "Could I help you?" He didn't say a word, but he stopped. He stayed around the field, walked around the outfield. We continued playing. Then he went over and picked up a bat. This was five to seven minutes later. We continued playing. I was keeping my eye on him now, though.

I was umpiring from behind the pitcher's mound. He walked behind me, close behind me. I said, "Look, are you looking for something? Maybe we can help you." I said that because I had to say something.

"Somebody has my ring," he said.

"Nobody here has your ring because I got here first and the kids came after-ward and there was no ring around here."

It turned out that he was there earlier in the day and he probably did lose the ring, but he lost it earlier. We continued playing, and he ended up leaving, taking the bat with him. I was kind of relieved. It belonged to one of the kids, but I told him not to worry. I would give him one of our bats. Nobody disagreed.

What I didn't know until later was that he had circled around in back of the school. He came charging from the back, where I couldn't see, and he came down full speed. A pitch was thrown at the moment he was coming toward me, so a kid, Tracy Rivera, yells to me, "Mr. Smith! Mr. Smith! Look out! Look out!"

I turned around and I got it right across my face, but I was able to block it partly. My face closed up with blood real fast. I started backing off, trying to regain my balance, and he hit me and knocked me out. Then he supposedly hit me ten or fifteen times.

The kids were about thirteen years old. Some of them just got scared and ran. A number of them were frozen in their tracks. Then he took off, running toward where the other children were. They just ran, and he left the area. The kids raced back to the school and caught one of the teachers who was there late. He hap-pened to be a person who knew CPR and emergency lifesaving techniques. He was a volunteer medical worker where he lives in New Jersey.

It's amazing he was there. He just got in his car and drove onto the field. He opened up the air passage in my nose and then he and another physical education teacher started giving me CPR. The kids flagged down a fire truck. They got in front of it and told them that a teacher was hurt, and the firemen listened. They helped.

At the hospital, they put me on life support. I was in a coma for twenty-four hours. After I came out of the coma, it looked like I was brain-dead. Some doctors said it was amazing that I survived. I was moved to a neurological unit, and I was there for five weeks. I had surgery for the skull fracture and another surgery to remove an eye. It was shattered.

My wife is a teacher, and she did not want me to return. She was scared for me. She said, "If you stay, you're going to do the same things you did before. You're going to go out to that field. I know you. You'll be cool. They'll ask you to do the after-school program, and you won't say no, because of the kids."

The day I returned to work, February 1 of 1989, the first thing I did was I went to the field. My wife had taken six months off work to help me, and she drove me to school that day. I got there real early, seven-thirty in the morning, before I had to come in, and I walked onto the field. The same drug hangout guys were already out. It was cold. They were still out. My wife stayed in the car. I wanted to do it. So a kid walked by, I didn't even know him, but he said, "Yeah, you're the guy." I stood there. It was freezing. I walked to the spot by the pitcher's mound. I walked around a little bit. My wife kept watching from the car. It was like chills going through your spine. The reason I did it was to say that I'm going to walk through here because I'm going back now, and I want to go back with a clear knowledge that it was over.

When I left work after that I could have gone home another way, but I always went down that street. I really don't know why. All the good things that I had done kind of got destroyed on that spot. But I was going to make it back. It kind of kept motivating me.

But when the time came, I had to quit. My wife was afraid that she was going to lose me. I had to respect her wishes.

In many cases, teachers are blamed when they are attacked. The implicit question is, "What did you do wrong with this child?" In my case, that did not happen. People tried to make me a hero. The union, United Federation of Teachers, has given me awards. I was only doing my job. I wasn't going to knuckle under and say nothing if a kid was going through somebody's books.

In New York City in a lot of schools, teaching has become a hazardous job. I want you to know that there are so many schools, and so many days, when everything functions tremendously, when it's what you'd expect a school to be. But the acts of violence against teachers are increasing. There are supervisors who will say to a new teacher that being a teacher is like being a policeman. It's just awful, horrible.

Kids today are more prone to violent acts, more prone to not having any remorse about what they do. It's the environment they live in, it's the breakdown of families, it's the way they grow up, it's a combination of things. I hate to think that the end result will be a generation without a conscience.

Ava Fullenweider was beaten over the head by a boy at the middle school where she teaches. The student had recently been transferred into her class because of his violent behavior:

On November 8, 1989, I was teaching in a classroom with students who are labeled as emotionally handicapped, but the class was very still, very okay. A new student came in and said he didn't want to be there. He had already assaulted another teacher in our school, but the administration can't just move them to another school because there is only a certain amount of jumping or movement it can allow in a certain district. It's politics. So the kid was to remain with me until an evaluation. That is his right. He is to remain in school, no matter how much he assaults, no matter how much verbal abuse he gives.

He had terrorized his previous teacher until she just couldn't take it anymore. She almost had a nervous breakdown. She begged the principal, literally, not to admit the boy back into her classroom. Well, he had to put the boy someplace, and I am known as a strong, positive teacher, and he thought I could handle this young man.

He started by throwing a bucket in the room. It was the bucket I have there to wash the boards. I was mortified, devastated. The crisis intervention teacher was in the hallway and she removed him. He threatened to come back and get me.

Now remember that I had been teaching for nine years. I was used to being threatened and cursed at. That's the norm. It shouldn't be, but it is. Verbal abuse we take every day. So his threats didn't mean much to me, but this time he did come back to get me. Just four periods later.

The floor was empty because it was lunch period and I was standing in my doorway talking to another teacher. He had a padlock from somewhere. He approached us. The other teacher stepped out and asked him to put the lock down. He called her all sorts of names. Then I told him to put it down. He just came around and beat me across the forehead, behind the ear. He dragged me out the classroom door down to another teacher's room, continuing to beat me. The other teacher was screaming. She tried to stop him, couldn't, and ran to get the crisis intervention teacher. It seemed to take so long. Then there were eight people over us, pulling him away. It took all eight teachers to get him away from me. Other teachers got hurt.

I had a concussion, a blood clot, a black eye, but I was still conscious.

They arrested him. So what? I went to court and he was there with his mother, calling me names. I had to leave. Two years later, I don't really know what happened to him, although I heard that he was locked up for two days because his mother wouldn't come down to get him. Then I heard that he ended up in Bronx State Psychiatric Ward because he beat his mother up a month later and she ended up in the hospital.

When a teacher is attacked she becomes a victim ten times over. I was blamed for the incident. I got a note from a student advocate in our Board of Education office, saying that I had committed corporal punishment. I was devastated. Apparently while he was beating me, I scratched his face. The fact is that while he was beating me, if I could have hurt him, I wouldn't have cared.

My physical recovery took five months, but I stayed at home for two years because I am recovering emotionally still. I came back because I can't sit at home anymore. I still have something to say to the kids. I still have to give whatever was given to me when I went to school, but I find I am afraid of the kids today. I find myself walking down the hallway with my back up against the wall. There are times when there are kids in the halls that I can't bring myself to leave the room.

Even teachers who are not assaulted themselves confront the effects of rising violence on a daily basis, as Bill Walters observes from his spot as a public school teacher in Camden, New Jersey:

There is growing violence in our schools, but society is changing and it is a reflection of the very thing going on in our cities. We have babies having babies and they are coming into our school system today. As we build a society where we leave people to fend for themselves, it is going to happen. I am not sure how I would react if I felt trapped and I didn't have rent money, no home, no food, and I couldn't go to college even though I had the ability, if people looked askance at me as if I was lazy and that was my reason for being where I was. It's like social Darwinism. You're there because you're the most unfit.

Therefore it is going to happen, and it is going to come into the schools. Have I ever been attacked at school? No. You learn as a teacher how to address these things. You don't force a student into hitting you. You try to defuse situations. You don't box a kid in. You learn skills to survive yourself.

Donna Madath is a third-grade teacher at Wadsworth Avenue Elementary School in South-Central Los Angeles:

The gang problem is horrible. They run the city. I'm afraid. I won't look at a sixth grader wrong or reprimand a sixth grader. It's not worth the risk. I don't think it makes me a bad teacher. I think it makes me a cautious, smart person. You just don't pick a fight when it's not necessary.

We have drop drills at this school. I think of them as the new generation of bomb-shelter drills. There is one really long bell. I think it rings for ten seconds. The kids have been taught that when they hear that bell, they drop then, flat on their stomachs, and slither like snakes away from the windows. Then the announcements come over the intercom that we're in a lockdown situation, and that means that no matter what, don't let a child go to the bathroom, do not answer your door. Yeah, sometimes the gangs come tearing through the schools.

A friend was telling me, if you're in the army and you're trying to dodge bullets, you're supposed to walk three steps to the left, and three steps to the right, then three steps to the left, and zigzag. That's too hard to teach children when there are a million things going on. So if you teach them to drop and slither like a snake to their destinations, that's fine. My kids mainly just have to drop on their stomachs until they are told to get up.

Simply the prospect of violence on one particular day drove Tom Starnicky to transfer from a school on the South Side of Chicago to a safer school on the North Side:

The Blackstone Rangers, a street gang, were recruiting three miles away from the school. We had some incidents on our school grounds, roughing up children and children being forced to pay.

One day, rumors were flying around that the gang was coming to take over the school. There was a police officer who was working part-time in the school, being paid by the Board of Education. He carried a gun. I went with him to check through the school because someone from the gang had supposedly been inside the building. We went downstairs and into this catacomb beneath the building where steam went through. We were walking and he just pointed to his back, under his jacket, and he lifted the jacket and he had his gun there.

"If they get me, drop them," he said to me.

I never got into teaching to be a policeman, and I had no intention of dropping anyone — unless, of course, they were shooting at me. It never happened. There was nobody there, but that incident really turned me as far as what I was doing in education at that time. I wanted no part of it. I didn't want to be fighting the street fight.

Jessie Thrasher teaches remedial math and reading at the Miami Lakes Technical Education Center in Miami Lakes, Florida:

Last year, I was covering for another teacher and I had about ten kids in the room. We do a lot of individual work because a lot of the material is on the computer. This particular student had been having a lot of problems with his family and he had been on drugs. He came into the class and started screaming at me. He called me every name in the book, everything you could think of, and then he said, "My mother is going to come in and punch you in the face because you are not helping me." Over and over again. He used the M.F. word a lot.

I said, "It is time for you to leave now. This is not the kind of language we use here. There is the door. Go." Then he started ranting and raving again. He was fifteen. It went on a long time, but finally he left, swinging the door so hard he almost broke it. I got on the phone immediately and called administration. The kids were really upset. A couple of them had tried to stop him. I was scared because, as a nurse before teaching, I had worked with drug abuse patients and I knew how volatile he could be.

Often teachers find themselves on unfamiliar ground in dealing with violence in the lives of their students, as Ron Cooper discovered at Van Buren Middle School in Albuquerque, where he teaches special education and critical thinking:

We were talking about how a person could join a gang. I didn't understand it. I was thinking that I wanted these kids to know there were options. We were talking about why you join a gang, and the assignment was to go out and ask kids they knew who were in gangs.

When the papers came back, I read stuff like:

"Because my mom and dad don't really care for me."

"Because I'm lonely."

"Because I need friends."

"Because they will back me up if somebody does something to me."

Don't you see something inherently wrong when a kid says things like that? So, I'm sitting up there in front of all these kids thinking, "Okay, I can explain this." I fell flat on my face. I could not give them a reason not to join a gang. I resented that. All the tricks I have and I could not give those kids the options. I was saying stuff like, "If your family doesn't like you, what else can you do after school?" I was trying to get them to take responsibility for themselves and to find the real friends they need.

They were good kids. They didn't shoot me down. They had a good discussion, but when they walk off campus everything changes because I cannot guarantee them that they do not need the safety of a gang.

I learned something really, really important. I can't change their reality, but I can make them realize the odds they face, that if they join a gang they are likely to be dead before they are twenty-five. When I said that, one of the students, Tony, had his head down on his desk.

"Tony, you're in a gang," I said to him. "That is going to happen to you."

I am asking him to think about it. I am not trying to change his mind any longer. It is my job to teach kids to take responsibility, so I try to deal with issues that are real to them. I confront them. I am not trying to tell these kids that it is going to be okay, that if you don't join a gang your family or God is going to take care of you. Mom and Dad aren't. Who is God?

Some teachers learn that any confrontation with certain types of students can turn into violence. Although he is not a big man, history teacher Bruce Williams at Jefferson Senior High School in Los Angeles dealt with a potentially explosive situation in a manner that was calm but forceful:

Just outside the door to my classroom is a line of lockers. It was after school. I was putting stuff on the board for the next day, and I heard a lot of metal banging and loud voices. After a day in a middle school, you don't want to hear a lot of noise, so I went outside and asked them to lower their voices. They immediately started giving me shit. It was one of those moments when I wanted to return the favor, so I walked up and said, "Whose locker is that?" No one would fess up. So I swung the door to see the number on it and wrote it down.

I got the idea that they were trying to break into it. There was something in the locker they didn't want me to see, so this kid, I guess he'd had enough of my interference. So he said that I'd better get out of their way or he was going to knock me out. Now, that sounds harmless, but it means that physically he is going to lay me out. I said, "If you do, I'll see you and your parents in court." They left, shouting obscenities the whole way. I wrote the whole incident off. I didn't give it another thought because that happens on a daily basis, but what I didn't know is that it was just the preface for what was going to happen the next day.

The next day I'm coming back from lunch and I hear a voice shouting, "Hey, you!" I didn't think I was the you, but I clearly was. By the time I got to my room, he came up behind me, grabbed my neck and yanked me, and said, "I told you yesterday that I was going to lay you out and I am going to tell you just once more, get out of my life."

I froze. The hall went quiet. He was a very big eighth grader. I am not an average-size adult. I put my hand up to create some distance and went right about my business. I don't know where my calm came from. I turned my back on him and got out my keys while he stood there shouting, "I'm going to beat the shit out of you after school. I know what kind of car you drive." I immediately got on the phone and called security. They came, and that was it.

From what I understand, the law is clear, it doesn't matter what the kid said if your perception of fear is real. It wasn't like it was just an adolescent blowing off steam. He had sought me out in front of a whole bunch of witnesses. Enough is enough. Then I had to decide if I was going to stick to my words. So I did. I took him to court, and sure enough, he was already on probation.

See, we as teachers are supposed to know that. The law says that if there is a child in your classroom who has already been convicted of a crime that if he had been an adult would have been a felony, the teacher has to be notified, but teachers are never notified.

I don't know what the information would do for me as an instructor. Certainly I would have been more cautious. However, by withholding the information, the administration is saying, "We don't want you to make prejudgments because we don't trust your judgments."

Craig Lancto retains the humor that marked him as a cutup when he was a student. His English classes at T. C. Williams High School in Alexandria, Virginia, are often scenes of good fun. But when it came to school violence when he was teaching at the junior high a few years ago, Lancto found that he could be as unyielding as the cop on the beat:

Trespassers came here to beat up one of our students because he had pushed the younger brother of some high school students in the library. There were no administrators around. Me, Mr. Macho, went down the hall and told them to leave.

They all suddenly jumped this kid. I grabbed the kid and moved him to the side and they just nailed me on the beak. I heard this awful noise, my nose breaking.

The next morning the principal came to my room and said the boy and his mother were here to apologize. The principal said to me, "I just want you to know, whatever you decide to do, we're behind you."

The boy said, "I'm sorry I hit you."

I said, "Great, but I'm still going to press charges."

His mother said, "You can't. He apologized."

There was no way that I would back down on pressing charges. He was expelled and given two years' probation by the court.

Donna Dial, a language arts teacher at Miami Beach Senior High School, blames administrators for failing to provide teachers with all the support they need to deal with potentially violent students:

I am not suggesting that every little problem needs to be known, but if the administration knows that a child presents a potential danger, I really think that morally they are obligated to tell us.

At another school, I had a kid who all the other kids in the class said was a drug burnout. He came in late in the year and he was obviously not from this planet. One day, he put his jacket over his head and put his head down. I came along and pulled his jacket back and asked, "Is anybody in there?"

He jumped up and said, "If you touch my jacket one more time I will cut your throat."

When security came, every assistant principal in the school came too. There were about eight adults in the room. What they knew but had failed to tell me is that he had been institutionalized at a state institution for two years and had been diagnosed as being violent. He had a whole history. They had said that they would try him one more time in the public education system before institutionalizing him permanently. This was a guinea pig class and they didn't even bother to tell me.

It wasn't just me they were endangering, but the whole class. I don't think this is an isolated case.

The contrasts are sharp between big-city schools and places such as Warsaw, Indiana, the small town where Jane Starner is head of the high school's English Department:

I am always shocked when I hear of violence occurring at schools. I don't understand it. I have never been frightened in school. All the doors at our school are unlocked. We have people wandering around and you just say, "Hello. May I help you?"

There are teachers who have had vandalism done to their homes. We had a kid who set a fire in a rest room, and the implications of that were kind of scary, but those are the only things that you worry about in a place like this.

I can't imagine teaching if you went to school scared. I can't comprehend that.

Marion Clermont, who teaches in New York City's public schools, works in a starkly different environment:

Teachers are terrified. I've been lucky for the last few years. I had my baptism by fire sixteen years ago when I first came into this school system. I was working as a sub in a little neighborhood here in Brooklyn, and within the first couple months I was pushed down a flight of stairs, but I grabbed onto the railing and actually flipped over to the next landing, like a commando. I wasn't even hurt. I was young then, very spry. I turned around and everyone was running in different directions. I couldn't see who did it. I didn't even report it. I just said, "They are not going to get me down and intimidate me."

The next week was Halloween. I was at the front of my room, writing on the board, when the back door was kicked in and I was bombarded with eggs. If you saw the movie *Carrie,* you know how she looked with pig blood. Well, I looked like that with the yellow egg yolk all over me, and everyone was hooting and hollering, laughing and clapping, jumping up and down. I was frozen stiff, waiting for the bell to ring, not knowing which way to go. Because I was a sub, the principal didn't give a damn.

Then I had an incident at Eli Whitney School where I worked. A girl was banging on the door, trying to get in, and I wouldn't let her. She wouldn't stop, so finally I went to the door to tell her she couldn't disturb the class. She spit right in my face. So I went to the dean and reported her. The next day she was stopped in the hall because one teacher overheard her say to another student, "Look in my bag, this is for Clermont." The teacher looked in the bag and there was a meat cleaver. They managed to nip that right in the bud. They got her right out of school, she was arrested, and I never saw her again.

So I have had some close calls teaching, but this last time was the first time they actually drew blood. Again, it was some student trying to kick in the door during class. As I walked to the door, he threw something, and it — a piece of chalk, a pencil, something like that — hit me right between the eyes. It hit with such force that I bled. One girl got me some paper towels and then went to get the security guard. The rest of the kids were all laughing and clapping. There may have been some kids who were scared, but with all the blood and my own disorientation, all I could hear was the laughing. It was a circus. I am pretty tough, but seeing their reaction was too much for me, their callousness and delighting in my pain.

I found that I wasn't ready when I went back to school. Every time someone peeked in the door, I got a lump in my throat, butterflies in my stomach. Some of the kids yelled, "Ugh, she's back!" One kid had to be dragged out of the room because the substitute who had my class had come in to identify some kids who had thrown a book and a bottle of soda at her. When the sub pointed out one girl, she jumped up and got angry at me. The assistant principal had to hold her back and she screamed, "I wish you would have died when you got hit!"

I have always had an open forum or rap session in my classes, but lately they just get out of control. It just gives them an excuse to yell, talk, fight, and ridicule. In one class, someone started pounding on the door from outside the room. The guy banged on the door and cursed and screamed. I wouldn't go near the door. The kids all laughed, saying, "She's afraid, afraid to go near the door." I was.

They are getting shot at eleven, twelve, thirteen, and losing friends, cousins, and brothers to street violence. This is an everyday thing with them, especially in this class structure, in the projects. For the first time in my life, I'm struggling with this issue, this black-and-white thing. I don't want to be unreasonable. I don't want to be a bigot, a racist. I've lived too long to turn into somebody like that. But what is going on here?

We, as teachers, do not want to lose sight of our humanity. There is no room for prejudice in anyone's heart. These are things I feel deeply, and I have to struggle to keep from slipping into an area where I am going to be closed-minded.

———————————————

CHAPTER 8

DISCIPLINE

FATHER WILBUR ATWOOD's history class at St. Augustine High School in New Orleans is hushed and orderly, with nearly thirty teenage boys sitting silently at their desks listening to the teacher describing the lesson plan for the following day. When the bell rings ending the class, the boys get up quietly and move into the hallway. Even in the rush from one class to another, the slamming of lockers, and the jostling of bodies, there are no shouts, and there is no running.

"We don't really emphasize the paddle," says Father Atwood by way of explaining a central feature of disciplinary procedure at the school. "It's there. It's an ultimate."

Discipline is not an apparent problem at St. Aug's, one of the leading high schools in New Orleans, but the availability of corporal punishment is a small part of the reason. There is a sense of order and mutual respect in the way the school operates and the manner in which students and teachers deal with each other.

The instructors at St. Aug's have some advantages over most other teachers in the country. Because it is a private school, the teachers can administer punishments pretty much as they see fit. Because the school has traditionally provided a means of improving the lives of its graduates in dramatic ways, the teachers have the uniform backing of the parents of their students. Because it is a religious school that draws primarily from the city's black Creole population, the teachers can count on a foundation of shared philosophy and community.

Still, few students graduate from St. Aug's without having felt the sting of the disciplinarian's paddle at least once.

For better or for worse, corporal punishment is not in the arsenal of most teachers; a majority of states prohibit its use, and in most places where corporal punishment remains legal, it is seen as an anachronism that must be employed sparingly. At the same time, however, other remedies for punishing inappropriate behavior have been eliminated, too. Many school districts prohibit simple disciplinary actions such as keeping children in from recess, and more serious measures, such as expelling them from class.

There are teachers who lament the decline of corporal punishment, but there also are teachers who believe that violence begets violence and would not spank or strike a child regardless of the rules. So how do teachers instill order on unruly students and create an atmosphere where young minds can be stimulated? The answers vary from teacher to teacher and from school to school, and so do the success rates.

Discipline problems confronted by most teachers today reflect the changes that have occurred in society at large. A study conducted by the California Department of Education in 1992 compared school discipline problems of the 1940s with those of the 1980s. The leading discipline problems in the 1940s included getting out of place in line and not putting paper in baskets. The leading discipline problems in the 1980s included drug abuse, pregnancy, suicide, rape, robbery, assault, arson, and bombings.

As a result, some teachers measure their success simply by escaping unharmed at the end of the school day. Imposing silence on students prone to cuss at teachers is beyond imagination; striking a child could land the teacher in court, or in the hospital if the student retaliates. However, the majority of America's teachers find some way to impose enough discipline on their classrooms to make learning possible — and the best of them regulate conduct without robbing students of their self-esteem.

Common threads are apparent from discussions with teachers who have developed effective means of instilling discipline in their classrooms. Indeed, these elements are the real reason for the success of schools such as St. Augustine. First, teachers must respect students even when they discipline them; the most effective punishments are those that do not demean the student. Second, teachers need the support of administrators and parents to be effective disciplinarians; the chances of success in the classroom are reduced each time a teacher is reversed outside the classroom by an administrator or dismissed by a parent.

This does not mean giving teachers a blank check in meting out punishment, but it does imply that they have the trust and consent of administrators and parents alike when they are making honest, fair efforts to cope with disruptive behavior. In the end, everyone benefits from a well-run classroom.

*   *   *

In a collection of trailers behind Miami Beach Senior High School is a unique enrichment program for public school teachers in Dade County, which encompasses the Greater Miami area. It is called the Dade Academy for Teaching Arts (DATA). Teachers are selected to spend nine weeks on minisabbaticals, studying issues of interest to them and sharing ideas with colleagues. During a long interview on a day on which rain deluged the school campus and played on the roof like a metal drum, teachers sat around a long table to debate many issues, among them discipline.

Donna Dial is an aspiring writer and a language arts teacher at Miami Beach Senior High School:

When I first started teaching and we had corporal punishment, I was under the impression that it was more symbolic than punitive. Then one day I sent a little girl down to the office for being a jerk, and the assistant principal took out a paddle and hit her three times so hard that she went across the room each time he hit her. I couldn't believe it. She was a ninth-grade kid, about four feet tall. If I had been a parent and known what was going on, I would have taken my child out of that school immediately.

We had an incident a couple years ago, just before corporal punishment was abolished, where a principal beat a child so severely he was hospitalized.

What do you tell a kid when you beat him? You are telling him, this is power, when you get bigger than me you can do this, too. It sends such a terrible, terrible message. I never sent another kid down to the assistant principal. It amazes me today that people are still beating children. It seems like the Dark Ages.

Evelyn Campbell, a capable, mothering, and gentle woman, is the director of the program and a veteran teacher with thirty years in the classroom:

Not in this day and time, I don't think corporal punishment will work. We've seen violence among students escalate in this district — kids carrying knives and weapons, kids with Uzis in their cars. A teacher dare not take that risk to hit a kid. For that reason alone, we need to stay away from corporal punishment. It could endanger a teacher's life. When they gave kids rights and parents rights, it meant hands off. We still have detention, expulsion. That's all we can do.

Ruby Wanland, social studies teacher, Miami Beach Senior High School:

I think generally that teachers who have discipline problems have asked for them. They have pushed kids into a corner. Teachers ask for trouble when they do that.

The best teacher I ever had in my life was a philosophy of education teacher. In Illinois, you could be a teacher and a principal at the same time, and it wasn't uncommon. He was on the South Side of Chicago, a rather small school. Corporal punishment was acceptable. Some kids had acted up in his class and he was going to take them down to the office and, as principal, put the "Board of Education" on their "seat of knowledge."

Now there were gangs on the South Side and he had one of the gang leaders and a member of his gang there. The guy looked at him and said, "Dr. Lawson, I'll be goddamned if you are going to lay that board on me." Lawson looked at him, ignored the language and everything else, and said, "If you're too chicken to take it, I bet your buddy isn't." And then he went ahead and proceeded to paddle the other one.

The next day in the classroom, he had his back to class, writing on the board, and it became way too quiet. When he turned around, the one he hadn't paddled, the gang leader, the one he had made to look like a jerk, had a gun on him. He would never tell me how he got out of it, but he did say, "If he had pulled the trigger, I would have deserved it because I had left that student no way to save face. There was no place for him to go."

That has had a big influence on how I deal with kids. I am very careful. I know that I am an adult. I am careful never to push a kid in the corner. I have watched teachers, I've watched administrators, I've watched policemen. The ones who get in trouble push kids in the corner. Just like you and me, kids are going to come out swinging under those circumstances.

Jerrilee Harris is a special education teacher at Miami Beach Senior High School:

When you get to the point that there is a problem, you start a dialogue with that student on how you are going to deal with it. At that point, you sort of take responsibility and you know that how I deal with this child is going to affect how this child deals with me. But I cannot agree that the discipline problems that arise in the classroom are tied to the teacher putting the kid in a corner. Many do, but sometimes things just happen.

Children bring a lot of baggage to school with them. You don't always know what they are bringing. You can try to learn as much as possible about your children. Quite frankly I don't think you are a good teacher if you don't. We are beyond the time when you could stand up in front of the classroom and teach strictly the curriculum and have nothing to do with the child as a person.

But even with all that, there are days when a child will come into the classroom and you won't know what has happened before, and you are going to say something as simple as "Open your book to page 46," and that kid is going to fly off at you. You have no control over that.

Paul Hirko was a math teacher at Miami Beach Senior High School but is now assistant principal of Westview Middle School, in Miami:

You have to be creative. Sometimes discipline can be something very simple. If a kid is misbehaving, you simply tell him to get up and place him in another teacher's room for the rest of the period. That's all. You don't penalize him with grades, you don't bad-mouth him. I've found kids hate that. I've done this in inner city schools, suburbia. It doesn't work with every kid, but often enough to make it worth it. You have to try different things.

You also have to recognize what doesn't work. Try something else. I used to find that I'd give F's in conduct, and the more structured I was the less happy I was, the less successful I was with correcting misbehavior. I found that when I deal with the individual child and adjust, I am pretty successful.

You got a class acting up, you take one kid, the ringleader, and move him. That's the end of your problem. The rest of the kids say, "Oh, I'm next." That's the end.

Ricki Weyhe teaches language arts at Miami Beach Senior High School:

I don't like to be the villain. I like peer pressure. If a kid is acting silly, I don't have to acknowledge them. Someone else will. So what happens is, if anyone is behaving poorly, some kid will speak up and say, "Salvadore, you're acting like a jerk." I don't even become an angry ogre. It hurts more from a kid.

At the beginning of the year I say, "Here are my standards." It is necessary to have standards of excellence early on. I rarely have a discipline problem, but when I do, everyone knows it. I am not patting myself on the back, but it doesn't happen often.

If by eleventh grade they are acting silly or foolish, I don't have the time for it. I tell them that early on. If that is your mode of behavior, you don't belong here. If I am pushed to the limits, I must admit that I try humiliation. That isn't a nice thing to do.

But Richard Garcia, science teacher at MAST Academy, the Marine and Science Technology High School in Miami, was quick to interrupt:

That's intellectual corporal punishment. I do it also.

Weyhe defended herself with another example about Salvadore:

Yesterday, Salvadore was jerky. We had been talking about Holden Caulfield and *Catcher in the Rye* and lay psychiatry. I said to the class, "Now what do you suppose Salvadore has been lacking in his life to produce this kind of behavior?" The kids all started answering. Of course, it was humiliating for Salvadore, and I apologized afterward, but I tell you something, he was terrific today. He sat quietly and he behaved.

Donna Dial:

And someday he's going to pull a gun on you.

Some teachers try to defuse potential discipline problems with humor rather than sarcasm. Darlene McCampbell teaches high school English at the Lab School at the University of Chicago:

I try to prevent problems from happening. Humor, lighthearted stuff, works here. I talk with kids privately if I think they are doing something inappropriate. The most destructive thing a school can do is to take anyone's belief in himself, whether it's a kid or a teacher. This is not a new thing. I can hear Bruno Bettelheim, who is one of my mentors, saying that the word "discipline" comes from "disciple." You must know what it means for someone to develop controls, guidelines, boundaries, in order to generate principles on which to act. I think very few people have thought through what that means.

Merri Mann, a former high school English teacher, is now assistant director for the Department of Professionalization at United Teachers of Dade. Because of her position with the teachers' union, she hears a lot about teachers' concerns:

Teachers are very unhappy about discipline problems. It's probably the number one issue for teachers. Teachers have kids in their classrooms who are unruly, who are verbally abusive, who swear in class, and then you send them to the office and the office will turn around and send them back to you. Then you have to deal with their anger, too.

If you suspend a student or put him in a center for special instruction, where you remove him from the class, then you also have to do all of the work that student needs. You have to make up the work that the student is missing when he is not in the classroom. It's a double burden for the teacher. Also, it's not a long-lasting approach to discipline. It does nothing.

We have a program in a pilot school. It comes out of California, and they work on something called developmental discipline, where they help the children to learn to be caring members of the community. They try to impose an internal kind of discipline. They don't think the checks and stars system is long-lasting or that it has an impact as kids grow up. However, if you can teach them to become a giving, caring member of a community, it may last.

Bruce Williams teaches history at Jefferson Senior High School in Los Angeles:

The discipline issue does contribute to the ills of public education. There is no doubt about it. The lack of ability to set discipline standards and enforce them and so on. I hope that I'm not coming from a dictatorial point of view here when I say that. However, getting the kid to become responsible is a key element of school. School doesn't just exist for learning when a certain war was fought or how to break down a sentence. We're trying to create good citizens.

So here's my point. Regardless of the fact that all those things are true — yes, we, as teachers, have been emasculated by society, yes, we don't get parental and administrative support — but that still does not excuse us from the debate. It still doesn't mean that we are powerless. It just creates a whole different problem.

What can we do? It forces us to examine alternative ways to keep them in line. I've met with a good degree of success by just changing my own attitude and starting to respect differences of opinion from a kid. No child cusses at me and tells me to go get fucked — except occasionally. Do I tolerate that? Absolutely not. To say that I wouldn't tolerate it doesn't mean that the day after I suspended that kid for doing it that I won't be back to that child and stroke him and honor the fact that he was angry with me and that he has a right to that anger.

That is not the issue. The issue is that there are alternatives for dealing with anger. It takes a whole lot of work at the beginning of a school year to establish a rapport with kids, as a group and as individuals. I am not trying to blind you with the halo over my head because I don't succeed as often as I would like, but I do succeed to a larger degree than most of my colleagues.

When I get angry at you, too, you're supposed to honor my anger, respect it, not debate it. Let's deal with it when we're both calm tomorrow, or after class. It goes both ways. That is one of the principles that I try to operate under: I won't break a rule that I hold the students to.

A perfect little example, and my colleagues won't like me for it, is that I allow my kids to chew gum. It's a school rule that they can't, but I learned a long time ago that there are a lot of things more important than whether or not a child chews gum. Plus, I chew it all the time. I could not possibly go through a day without it. This is trite, I know, it's silly, but it's a good example.

I just tell the kids, "Look, I'm chewing gum and in no way could I expect you not to, so you will never hear me ask you to pitch it out unless you crack it, or I find it stuck on a desk, or the wrapper on the floor." I always make sure that the first time I hear a crack that I make an example and that's when the school rule kicks in for a while.

It's learning how to talk so kids will listen, and how to listen so they'll talk back. Most teachers fear the hell out of kids talking back, but it's the number one need of students.

Tom Lachias, who once taught in the public schools of Los Angeles, is chairman of the History Department at Crossroads Arts Academy in the same city. Discipline problems are very different at the private school:

Discipline is not an issue at Crossroads for two main reasons. First, we can kick a kid out. And second, we select the kids. We have one space for every two applicants. Therefore, the kids who are going to be a problem are not going to be accepted in the first place.

Public schools, on the other hand, are a whole different situation. A friend of mine who works in a public high school had a knife thrown at her. The principal suspended the kid for two days. Another friend of mine who teaches at a junior high had a kid take out a knife. He confiscated it and gave it to his principal. The principal, however, returned the knife a couple days later because, after all, it was the child's property. Explain that.

What you need in the public schools first, is the ability to kick kids out. And you have to do that selectively. You have to decide which individuals are providing the models for the lousy behavior, which ones are slightly psychopathic. You target them and get them out. The rest you can work with.

Second, the public schools need a clear system of consequences. And they have to be gradual. You can't have a choice between expulsion and nothing. Third, if you set high academic expectations, kids respond. They get a sense of achievement from that.

And finally, a lot of administrators need to be sacked. The idea that a kid can get away with pulling a knife on a teacher without serious consequences is absurd. An administrator who does not respond to that situation deserves the contempt of everyone who works in that school and every kid who attends it.

Alice Golub teaches third grade at F. S. Tucker Elementary School in South-Central Miami:

There have to be consequences and we are doing children no favor if we don't let them know that. I don't think that corporal punishment is all that bad in a neighborhood like this. I think that with some of these kids, it's the only thing they know. That's what their parents do: They beat them.

Providence-St. Mel's caters primarily to students from the public housing projects on Chicago's West Side. Because there is so much disorder in their lives outside school, order is essential inside the building, right down to the clothes they wear, as two teachers there explained in separate conversations.

Dren Geer:

We have only 34 teachers for 540 kids. The classrooms aren't big, but everyone works all the time. The kids come to school at eight in the morning and they are in class until school lets out at three. There are no free periods. When you take kids from the chaos of the inner city, where there is no structure, no habits, no discipline, you don't have the luxury of saying, "Okay, we'll be nice. We'll be persuasive." If the school is going to work, from the moment the student comes in the school there has to be a safe, somewhat rigid, but absolutely predictable environment.

The teachers in our school are not just teachers. You have heard the term, used for first and second graders, that this child needs structuring. Teachers in this school are marvelously skilled structurers, and that structuring is in every aspect of our school, in terms of homework and simple patterns such as our dress code.

Art Murnan:

Most kids will tell you that the rules aren't strict. That's because they abide by them. It's the kids who break the rules who find it extremely tough. Skirts must be knee-length. Braids may be worn by girls only. No earrings for boys. In fact, if you come to school with an earring on, you just got your transfer out of here. I wear an earring, but I never wear it to school.

We're concerned that they are dressed appropriately so they don't attract any attention on the streets. We also tell them that we are preparing them for later on. There are certain jobs for which the way you dress is very important. If you are going to be a garbageman, you can wear an earring probably and dirty overalls, but if you're going to be a corporate vice president for IBM, they will expect a certain image.

We have really high expectations and strict behavior requirements. Here's a form that might interest you: If you get five tardy slips, you are at school for two hours on Saturday and you pay ten dollars. Tardy means not in your seat with your book open when the bell rings. The kids don't have the money, so the parents have to come up with it, but how many times are you going to give your kid ten dollars for this? Once? Exactly. One of the things we are doing here is making parents accountable.

I have never been threatened. I have never seen an act of violence in this school. I have heard a couple of threats against teachers and those students cleaned out their lockers instantly and were transferred to another school.

Schools have to give out very clear messages to kids. Schools are not democracies. To me, as a social science teacher, democracies only work with an enlightened adult population. Kids don't understand democracy. You are a parent. Are you democratic with your kids? Do you let them make any decision they want to make? No, of course not, because it is a learned process.

There are certain decisions that have to be made for kids. You must explain to kids that with freedom comes responsibility, and if you cannot be responsible, then you cannot be free. Freedom is not free, just as schools cannot be democracies.

You want to teach a democratic process to kids, but kids have to know that they are not making decisions. When a student crosses that threshold, democracy ends on the other side. This is a dictatorship and I am the dictator. I decide what will happen here. Yet I involve kids in the process, slowly bring them in. You don't have a choice about whether or not to do homework in my class. You are doing homework. You don't have a choice about whether or not you can just get up and leave the room when you want. I do allow my kids to get up and go to the washroom, but that is something that comes with time. When you get to that point, if you have to go, just get up and go. Don't abuse it. If you have to sharpen a pencil, don't raise your hand and disturb the class, just get up and do it.

You make the decision. You work with kids. As a teacher you have to instill a lot of things. It's the way you do it. If you come across too strong and not caring they will fight you at a certain level. They'll do certain things because they know the school will enforce you on the rules, but they'll never give you their heart and soul. If you really want a kid to do it, it has to be just a mental thing. It has to be holistic.

You are not just teaching a mind, but a whole person. You're working with the development of the individual. You have to care and be sympathetic at times, but at the same time you have to be strong.

While violence is not restricted to public schools or big-city schools, the biggest discipline problem facing Joan Iverson at St. Isaac Jogues School in the affluent, tree-lined suburb of Hinsdale, west of Chicago, would be the envy of teachers at many other schools:

One big thing in my classroom is having good manners, not being rude, not interrupting, to wait if two people are talking, unless, of course, it's an emergency. I think today people have gotten a little bit away from that. We're practicing good manners. Of course, in a Catholic school you can take it even further and say, "What would be the Christian way?" Or, "What would Jesus have done?" Right now we're studying about our saints, so we can ask, "What would your saint have done?" Still, it does come down to good manners.

Marla Sculley also is a teacher at St. Isaac Jogues:

I am a strict disciplinarian because I believe that children innately crave discipline; they don't learn in a free-for-all situation. They like order. They like organization. They don't want to walk into chaos. Yes, that's one of the problems kids are having today: There's more chaos in the world, in their homes. I don't believe that you are really free until you understand your own basic controls. And when you know where to draw the line.

Ron Cooper uses a behavior modification technique to bring order to his special education students at Van Buren Middle School in Albuquerque:

My management plan is "interdependent group contingency management." Basically what it means is that I have rules and, when the rules are broken so many times in a certain time frame, this is going to happen. It is a logical consequence. It is not punishment. In fact, it is completely different from punishment.

I do not say, "Goddamn it, what the hell are you doing? Why are you talking to me this way? You're bad." You want to send children a message that doesn't reinforce their behavior, especially in special ed, because they have gotten the negative enforcement already way too often. Parents who hit are teaching kids to hit. You are playing the kid's hand.

Instead I say, "Louis, you didn't pay attention in class. Pull a strip." Now, there are five strips. In my class, in one period, if you lose one strip, you lose passing period. If someone else loses a strip, he loses his passing period. If a third person loses one in the same period, it is complete loss of all privileges for everyone. Everybody loses. So we don't go out to play basketball. So there is group pressure here. That way I don't have to work as hard. It's reality. It is a range that is accepted.

In my opinion, the biggest thing I can teach them is realistic discipline, so that when they go out into the real world and they know that when you are working with a group and you show up drunk, or you show up hung over so you can't work as hard, you're not carrying your weight. They'll say, "Hey, man, what's wrong with you? You're hung over? That hurts us. Why did you drink last night?" Or maybe it'll be that you're fired. That's reality. I always try to make my class run like the reality they may know. I don't close doors on them.

To deal effectively with discipline, teachers need support from administrators and parents. John Perelli, an American history teacher, applied a creative and effective approach to handling discipline at Rush Henrietta Senior High School in Henrietta, New York. It was too effective for the administration:

I used to get a lot of hall duty. It's worse than lunchroom duty, because in a cafeteria at least the kids sit down. For hall duty, you're supposed to patrol the halls and look for trouble.

The school was having a lot of trouble at the time with kids smoking in the bathrooms. But we couldn't catch them because the bathrooms were at the end of long hallways and the kids would post a lookout. As soon as one of us walked around the corner, the lookout would stick his head in the door, yell "Teacher!," and the kids would drop their cigarettes in the toilets, rush out of the bathrooms, and disappear around the corner.

I used to like the old cop show *Starsky and Hutch*. I sort of look like Michael Glaser, and my partner for hall duty looked like the other guy. We got water pistols and stuck them in our belts and decided to work together like Starsky and Hutch. We synchronized our watches and, while my partner waited to stroll down the hallway, I positioned myself around the corner in a dark spot with my squirt gun in two hands over my head, just like Starsky.

At exactly fifty-seven minutes past the hour my partner turns down this hallway. This kid yells "Teacher!," they drop their butts, and go flying around the corner. I'm waiting for them. I yell "Freeze! Put your hands on your heads!" My partner comes up behind them and we march them into the office. Then we went out on patrol to make more busts.

We were bringing in forty or fifty kids a day by working together. The principal called us in and told us to split up and go back to the old way. The system couldn't handle that many kids.

John Cook has developed a special program for in-school suspensions to cope with discipline problems at West Windsor-Plainsboro High School in Princeton Junction, New Jersey:

The point is that our schools have drifted and it is very sad to see what is happening in some. A whole generation is losing, and there's a sense of Where do we go from here? Often it is related to a political mind-set: "Well, if we just put another twenty-eight million dollars in here . . ." That's bullshit. The answer lies in value. The answer lies in home development. The answer lies in giving value to young people to believe that they can do things. We don't have to change school systems. We have to change our value of family systems, our value of saying that you can gain something from it.

I myself came through school with my mother and father saying, "You're going to go to school and you are going to get something out of it." I decided school was important because my parents said it was. Plus, I had a sense, no matter how poorly or how great I did in school, that I was important because of my parents.

By and large, the only institution still reasonably intact is education. Our religious institutions have failed us. Our families have fallen apart. We don't have extended families anymore. Our peer group situations have all kinds of problems. So these problems come to us at school and we need to find a means of dealing with them.

The purpose of our in-school suspension is to take the student out of the school environment. We operate from the premise that most students enjoy being in school, and they do. Being sent home is boring. So when a student is involved in behavior that is inappropriate, we suspend him from the main population. Historically, you would send him home, which is obviously of no value to the student. So we suspend him in school, and he comes to a specific room out of the regular environment.

They are required to do all the academic work they would get if they were in school, but they have been suspended out of the main enjoyment, the friends, the going to the bathroom, passing notes, the cafeteria, all the fun little things they do all day. They go to the cafeteria to pick up their lunch, but they bring it back here to eat. They spend their whole day in this closed environment and they are not allowed to communicate among themselves. They are required to meet my academic standards, and if something comes in that is not as neat as I believe it should be, they do it all over again.

Then we have group discussions. We have developed a problem-solving exercise in which we go to a step-by-step process as to what occurred to get a kid in here and what they can do in the future to avoid a repeat. We also have learning packets designed specifically for foul language, fighting, and vandalism. You can really get kids to buy into the system.

When you get a kid excited and involved in the intrinsic value of education, that is what education is all about.

Kathleen O'Neill teaches in the lower grades at Sinai Akiba Academy in Los Angeles:

Discipline is not a big issue in our school, but then we get a lot of support from administration and parents. We're allowed to impose real consequences. When I first started teaching, I was more negative than I am today. I guess I was imitating what was modeled to me. Then, over time, I realized, wait a minute, this may be working, but it's a scary thing. Getting yelled at or getting my name written on the board is threatening and makes school a scary place. So I tried different things.

The room can be total chaos and I'll walk over to one student and start talking quietly. I'll say something like, "I really appreciate . . ." and everyone wants to hear what is being said. It's like magic. Everyone wants to hear you say these positive things. Then I go around the room and everyone loves to be recognized for doing something well.

Gail Davis teaches at Hilton Elementary School in Newport News, Virginia:

How do you teach good citizenship and responsibility? At the beginning of the year, we discuss the classroom rules. I also discuss the importance of doing your best, to be honest, kind, helpful. I read a series of thirty-five books on value tales. One is about Terry Fox, and it is the value of facing a challenge. He is the man who was dying of cancer and he ran almost all the way across Canada.

All the children get five blue strips every Monday. If they don't have a homework assignment, I take one, and then they have to sign the blue book explaining why they have lost the strip. At the end of the week, if they still have four blue strips, they get a sticker on the good citizenship chart.

If they don't get the sticker, we can open up the blue book and see what happened. They can't just shrug their shoulders. We can talk about what they need to do to improve. It is really concrete. With twenty-five children, I don't like to say, you can't get a sticker this week because it doesn't seem like you behaved. It is more exact. This is fair.

It is good for conferences too. If a parent asks, "Why is my child not a good citizen?" it is documented. Parents can't really challenge this because it is in the child's handwriting. If a child has a problem that comes up in the meeting, the parent can write a note explaining that something happened and ask that he make the work up. When that happens I still take their blue strip but I give it back to them when they make it up the next day.

It's funny, when we start checking work, and a child doesn't have the assignment, they don't wait until I come to the desk. They get up automatically and put the strip in the container and sign the book. I also send home "work-to-do strips" so the parents know they have not done the work. It has to come back signed the next day. If it doesn't, they lose another blue strip.

It does bother me if I have an outstanding student who does everything all the time and they forget something. I still have to be consistent and take that blue strip, and I have to send a note home. That is okay. They can lose one blue strip and still get a good citizenship sticker.

I also use compliments. "Gee, I saw you did that, helping someone. That was very kind. Thank you very much." These children understand about being kind and helpful. When someone is absent and needs to borrow a notebook to get caught up, they automatically say "You can borrow mine." Or with a child who is having trouble with subtraction, I will get someone else to help. They are glad to. I always say thank you for helping this child. Or if the child who is having trouble does well on a test, I remember to thank the helper: "Thank you, your help helped this child do better."

Peggy Proctor teaches Spanish at Crossroads Arts Academy, a private school in Los Angeles:

Discipline is a major issue here. Teachers are really powerless. For instance, this school has an attendance policy that infuriates me. I take roll. I write down who is absent and tardy and then I turn it in, and nothing happens to them. If they believe it is an important issue, and I certainly believe it is, they ought to do something.

Tardiness, to me, shows a lack of respect. It's the kid's loss. The kid comes in ten minutes late, he's not going to learn what happened in the first ten minutes of class. It's going to catch up with him eventually. In a sense, it doesn't hurt me, but in some ways it does because it is showing that the kid doesn't respect me or the other kids in the class whom he has disrupted.

Rules are necessary. There is a tendency to overimpose rules, to use them excessively, to become obsessed with them. It is sort of like a group — we are in this together, and if you're not here it hurts the group somehow. These rules teach social responsibility. Down the line, in bigger situations, where it really does matter, if you're late for an interview or picking up your kids, it can mean you don't get the job, or it can even be dangerous.

I think kids do have power in this school, maybe too much. Here we are on a first-name basis with the kids. The child is our equal — our project, almost. We feel a real responsibility for the children in this school. It's like, let the child learn what he wants to learn, experiment with what he needs to experiment, let him screw up every once in a while and learn from his mistakes. I think that is good. You do have to be allowed to fail. Here the problem is, there's this tendency for us teachers to pat them on the back afterward and tell them it will be okay. We're handing a lot of responsibility to people who sometimes don't want it or can't handle it. Should there be a stopping point?

In his thirty years there, Father Wilbur Atwood has learned that parents often see discipline as one of the selling points of St. Augustine's, in New Orleans:

Many years ago, a man came in one evening when I was still at the school. This man looked like a stevedore from the waterfront. He was a big man, rough-looking. He had a fourteen- or fifteen-year-old kid in tow.

"I understand you people around here use the two-by-four," he said. "I can't do anything with him. Would you take him?"

Parents know what we do, that we still employ corporal punishment. If they don't want their kids to be subjected to this, they don't send their kids here. The parents who send their boys here know that discipline has to be part of their lives. Whether or not they use it, they want somebody to use it. St. Aug's has remained constant in these things over the years, even the decades.

I don't really know how you would go in and teach in a class that was disruptive, with everyone doing their own thing. It seems to me that, before you can get their attention, you have to have a little order, quiet, and discipline so that you can get your message across. Not to be able to do that, I really don't know how you could teach.

One of the things that we might use a paddle for is if a kid talked back to a teacher. We just don't accept that. For example, this morning I chewed out a kid who was not on the page that we were dealing with in the book. I was walking up and down the aisles as we were discussing the subject, and he was not on the page. So I stopped and chewed him out. If the kid had talked back, then there would have been reason to use the paddle.

Artie Sinkfield has taught for twenty years, mostly science to junior high students at Brownsville Middle School in North-Central Miami, where she now chairs the Science Department, and she finds value in fear:

Discipline disrupts the whole learning environment. I told my daughter, who just finished school last year, that if she acted up I would give them permission to paddle her because I couldn't stay home every day with her if she were suspended. I would much rather have her get two or three whacks than to have them put her in jail or have her go out and commit some serious-type crime. Really and truly, two or three whacks won't kill you, but it will keep you in line because they hurt and they are meant to hurt.

When children fear no person, when they don't even fear a police officer, how can you expect them to fear you? People have different values about paddling and spanking, but I know one thing: Society is a terrible place now because children have so many rights.

I tell children, "Until you work and earn money, you have no right to tell teachers what to do. Your parents are in charge." In the same way, the teacher is in charge of the classroom, and they should have the right to say what goes on. That's the way I feel.

I'm not saying children shouldn't have rights, but their rights should be limited. I am saying that you give children choices, and within those choices they have the right to choose the ones that set with them, but there must be limits. There are things that we can't do. You must learn early. That's why people commit so many crimes. Children grow up doing what they want to do, so when they get older they continue. I think we're doing them a disservice.

In enforcing such simple elements of discipline as attendance requirements, John Borsum gives failing grades to the parents of some of his math students at Beverly Hills High School:

*   *   *

In order for a school to run efficiently, you have to have certain rules and enforce them. Unfortunately we have, because of parents' complaints and everything else, difficulty enforcing anything nowadays. So what rules you do have become sort of silly.

I had a real nice kid once say to me, "Mr. Borsum, don't you know the rules don't mean anything?"

The main reason we have problems in schools is the discipline in the home. How can you discipline them at school if it is the only discipline they get? We probably do a better job with discipline than a lot of parents.

Last year, a boy on the football team was a good player, but he was extremely arrogant. I was talking to his mom and I told her that he had missed an entire day of school the day before and we had a test.

"I know," she said. "He told me to excuse him."

"Was he sick?" I asked her.

She said, "Well, the game was yesterday and he wanted to make sure he was feeling okay for it."

I said, "If you don't think he's well enough to attend school, do you really think he should be playing in a football game? That is why I am calling you. He wasn't in my class to take a test, but when I was at the game, there he was playing."

These are kids and they don't know what's best for them all the time, and unfortunately their parents don't either.

Mickey Gilbert deals with rules from the bottom up with her sixth graders at South Pointe Elementary School in Miami:

I have always had children help generate the rules. Ninety percent of the teachers I've observed start the rules with negatives. Don't chew gum. Don't run. Don't talk. If the child realizes there are ten things they are not allowed to do, they know that they are not that welcome right from the start.

The first day, we sit in a circle and build a list of rules. This year, for instance, it was very interesting, as always. They talked and came up with eleven rules. "No running in the hallways." Or "No food in the classroom. We don't want ants." Then the drama started.

I said, "I don't know about you, but I can't cope with eleven rules. My brain won't handle it. Can we throw out some? Narrow it down."

"Yes, yes, we can combine some," they said.

They condensed eleven down to six. I still said that I couldn't cope. I said, "It barely fits on the chart, so let's narrow it down some more."

For one hour we deliberated this. Crossed some out. Combined others. Made a new chart. Finally, in my room now there is a chart with one rule. We narrowed it to just one. It is "Show respect."

If you show respect, you are not going to run or throw your books on the floor or use a really loud voice. They came up with the conclusion that one rule is easy to remember. You just have to think about all of its dimensions.

It came from them. They won't forget it. They have ownership in it. You have to trust and give them the opportunity to succeed.

————————————————

CHAPTER 9

RESPECT

PEGGY PROCTOR's fall from grace was swift and mercifully temporary. After graduating from an Ivy League school, she did not follow her sister into investment banking in New York. To the disappointment and confusion of her parents, she became a teacher.

"For the first two years I did this, my family just thought it was a phase I was going through," says Proctor, who teaches at Crossroads Arts Academy, a private school in Los Angeles. "They put out this much money for an education and it is not as if I will ever earn it back teaching."

Eventually, however, her parents came around. They saw the joy she derives from her work, the commitment she brings to teaching. "They saw how much I really loved the experience," says Proctor, "and they can say with pride in their voices, 'My daughter is a teacher.' "

Not all that long ago America revered its teachers. In his best-selling biography of Harry Truman, David McCullough recounts the president's love for his teachers. "The influence of his teachers on his life, Harry later said, was second only to that of his mother, and when crediting a Tillie Brown or a Margaret Phelps for all they had done for him, he did so with the assumption that everybody of his generation had a Tillie Brown or Margaret Phelps in their background and could therefore understand how he felt."

Since Truman attended school in Independence, Missouri, a century ago, America's attitude toward its teachers and teaching has deteriorated. Part of this can be attributed to the general decline in esteem in which the nation holds public service today. Teaching has suffered the same public alienation that affects working for the government or being a social worker.

But that does not explain it all. Some of the blame lies directly on the doorstep of America's broken education system. With justification, the public has grown alarmed about the deterioration of America's schools. Yet they have not forced politicians and policymakers to pay a price for this failure. After all, it is difficult to blame the distant government for its bungled efforts at reform and refusal to provide the funds necessary to help revitalize the schools. It is equally difficult to grasp the complex social factors that have multiplied the burdens on those schools. So as the random anger accumulates over the faltering education system, the most obvious and nearest focus is your child's teacher.

On a gray afternoon in late winter, Antonio Gil sat in the classroom where he teaches Spanish to students at West Windsor-Plainsboro High School in New Jersey. He is short, handsome, and an outspoken liberal. Over the years, he has had a lot of time to reflect on the differences between the way teachers are regarded in America and the way they are viewed in his native Spain.

"If you are a high school teacher in Spain, you are called 'Professor,' " he says. "It is a position that instills a lot more respect within society."

Yet when Gil goes to a social gathering in this country and the subject of jobs arises, his is a conversation stopper. "I say that I'm a teacher and then the conversation ends there."

Teachers have never been well paid, although their salaries used to be firmly middle-class. However, they have traditionally been regarded as vital members of the community. The pay these days has slipped to below the level that many teachers regard as middle-class, and the sense that teachers are essential citizens has slipped, too. These twin changes are making it harder to attract top students to the profession.

In a survey of teachers nationwide in 1990, the Carnegie Foundation for the Advancement of Teaching found that more than four of every ten teachers feel this is a poor time for a young person to begin a career as a public school teacher, although other surveys have found that those already in the profession are relatively happy. Three of ten teachers told the Carnegie survey that they had seen a decline in community respect for teachers in the past three years.

The survey also explored the reasons behind those sentiments. For instance, rather than the cushy work hours imagined by the public, a majority of teachers said that they "subordinate all aspects" of their lives to their jobs and spend more than forty-seven hours a week doing their job. A majority also ranked higher salaries as the most pressing change to improve their profession, and a staggering 96 percent of the teachers spend their own money on classroom supplies, averaging $250 a year. What other profession requires its members to provide their own working tools?

The consequences of declining esteem for teachers are enormous for the country, not simply because it means that teachers are paid less, but because education will not improve dramatically unless the best people are attracted to the field and the best of those already on the job remain. If respect for teachers is destroyed, if students no longer regard them as worthy instructors, the unraveling of the system is doomed to continue.

Jim Hosney is a teacher and head of the Film and Video Department at Crossroads Arts Academy, in Los Angeles:

Teachers don't get any respect in this culture because I think we live in a culture that values money. The fact is that you are defined by how much money you make. Stephen King is considered generally to be a greater novelist than William Faulkner because he makes so much more money. When Faulkner won the Nobel Prize, most of his books were out of print.

I think success is defined by how much money you make. It leads to ridiculous things. I don't understand how anybody in good conscience can say that acting in a movie is worth seven or eight million dollars. That boggles my mind. That would make actor X two hundred times better than most teachers. It is hard to swallow.

Bonnie Blader is a language arts teacher and sponsor of the school newspaper at West Windsor-Plainsboro High School in Princeton Junction, New Jersey. During a conversation in the school's noisy lobby, she made an important point about how teachers feel:

It surprises me that there can be so much disrespect for the people who are probably the second most important people in their children's lives.

Leonard Mednick is a former teacher who now works as a guidance counselor at John Dewey High School, in New York City's Coney Island and Bensonhurst neighborhoods. With a mixture of humor and resentment, he remembered the time he was invited to a meeting of education's elite to discuss strategy for winning a three-million-dollar grant from Washington, D.C., to design a dream high school:

There are two former heads of high schools, including the dean of Columbia's School of Education, several retired superintendents from the Board of Education, seven principals, and two assistant principals. There was one teacher there, the wife of one of the principals, who was not invited. And, of course, I was there, a guidance counselor.

Developing a school with all of the suits present and no teachers? Most of these people have been in the system for years and were positive that they had an answer, but they haven't been in a classroom in I don't know how many years. Imagine, no teachers.

There was no sense of what is really going on.

Donna Madath teaches third grade at Wadsworth Avenue Elementary School in Los Angeles:

I go to dinner parties with my husband and people will say, "What grade do you teach? Third grade? Oh, then next year will you be promoted to fourth grade?"

My good friend Terry teaches kindergarten, and they say, "Does she make as much money as you?" They think that you start out at kindergarten and that you get paid more and promoted from grade to grade, year to year, until finally, after you reach twelfth grade, you can go teach college.

Or they say, "You teach third grade? Oh, how sweet. How cute. You must love children. How many children do you want to have?" And I think, "What if I am working on a cure for cancer? Would that make me more intelligent?"

I think that's what is wrong with society. There are people in business who could go into the schools and help. Or people who have as much money as the Kennedys — I've been to weddings where they said it cost a hundred thousand dollars and I think, "Why don't you spend twenty thousand dollars and give the rest to charity?"

Some people, like Abraham Lincoln, who was self-taught, can do it alone. Most people need a teacher. I want a bumper sticker saying, "If you can read this, thank a teacher."

Kaye Furlong teaches third grade at Vista Grande Elementary School in Palos Verdes, California:

I had a Korean parent come in, maybe two weeks ago, and she said, "Joe wants to bring lunch, but he's embarrassed." And I said, "Oh, no, he really doesn't need to bring lunch.'' And she said that in Korea they do a lot for their teachers, they bring lunch for them, they do their laundry. She said they have a laundry and they would do my laundry. I told her, ''No, but thank you very much.''

Anyway, one day little Joe did show up with lunch. He's a nice boy, but he didn't want anyone to know he was doing it. I thought he didn't want anyone to know because he would be embarrassed, but he told me later that he wanted me not to tell because he wanted to be the only one who does it.

I like to get nice notes. I do a lot of extra things for my students, a lot of extra creative writing, art, stitchery. A lot of times you do the extra things and you wonder if the people care.

The district gives you awards and plaques, and you still wonder. When you have a superintendent going around saying he makes $115,000, and then when you add up all of his benefits, plus his car allowance, you realize he gets about $150,000. That makes him the fourth-highest-paid superintendent in Southern California. Teachers, however, we're forty-second out of forty-three. Teachers are second from the bottom as far as pay goes, and he's fourth from the top.

We can't get new young teachers, and a lot of people are going to leave. When we go, what is going to happen to these schools?

Why do we need a superintendent for $115,000 for one high school, six elementary schools, and two intermediate schools? You could hire a lot of teachers for that. We wouldn't have to have such large classes. We lost our curriculum director. They decided they would show a good example at the administrative level and fire two people. They fired the one person in charge of testing, which doesn't bother any teachers, but also the curriculum director. She brought in all the innovative things. She had time to keep up with it. She made sure we were up on the new things and that we had money. She's gone. And that superintendent? He's got two assistants, at $95,000 plus each, plus benefits.

It makes teachers angry, very angry.

Sherrill Neale teaches reading at Patrick Henry Elementary School in Alexandria, Virginia:

I really believe that if our profession weren't so female-dominated that we would not be looked down upon the way we are by the rest of society. Because you are a woman, you are a caretaker, not an educator.

I get respect as a teacher from friends, girlfriends, but from men only when their wives are teachers. People just don't know what is happening in the schools. All they hear is the bad stuff. They hear what the Harvard professor and the politicians are saying, but that is not reality.

Parents just pick up on the idea that we are glorified baby-sitters. After all, they think, we get summers off, holidays off, and we get off by 3:00 P.M., but I haven't been home before 6:00 P.M. this week.

We have after-school programs. We teach after school. Never mind the time we spend trying to get parents on the phone. Weekends, I spend at least five hours doing schoolwork. Holidays, at least a couple of hours a day. My husband's attitude is, "You aren't getting paid for this? Why are you doing it?" I wonder, too.

Frank Tobin teaches inmates at the Cook County Temporary Juvenile Detention Center in Chicago:

When people move someplace, what is the first thing they want to know about their new home? It's how good are the schools. Yet when you say "Do you want your kids to be teachers?" they say, "Hell, no." I just don't understand. It boggles my mind why people don't understand and appreciate the importance of the teaching profession.

If parenting is recognized as the primary important thing in raising children, then teaching is next. After parents, there is no one more important in the development of the human person than the teacher.

Kathleen O'Neill teaches first and seventh grades at Sinai Akiba Academy in Los Angeles:

Money is terrible. I work a lot of jobs to make ends meet so that I live adequately. I work at the Britannica Learning Center, tutoring two days a week, and I do private tutoring several other days. Every now and then I even baby-sit, but I'm trying to get out of that. A thirty-six-year-old baby-sitter! I find it a little bit embarrassing, but you have to do what you have to do.

John Cook is a teacher at West Windsor-Plainsboro High School in Princeton Junction, New Jersey:

Oftentimes when you hear the teacher-bashing it's coming from someone totally unaware of the complexity of the profession. They like to criticize things like tenure and say that tenure incorporates mediocrity. In most cases, most people have no idea what tenure is about. They see the surface — it means that you can have a job the rest of your life, no matter how bad you are, but that's not what tenure is about. Tenure was a law developed in order to permit the freedom of expression inside a classroom so that the administration couldn't come in and dictate what went on. It had nothing to do with whether you had a job for the rest of your life.

That doesn't mean that there aren't bad teachers. Of course there are. There are bad politicians. Bad presidents. You hear the argument "Let's get a national exam." But as one of the presidents of the New York teachers' union pointed out, when it comes down to who's going to be a teacher, the line gets smaller and smaller. Who's going to take the emotional drain that comes from 7:30 A.M. till 2:30 P.M.? Who's going to stand up and run the risk of being shot walking to your car? Who's going to stand up and run the risk of having a pencil come through your jaw?

Who takes the abuse from parents? From the students? Who gets insulted on a daily basis? Who stays up at night and prepares lessons? Who is emotionally upset when the student doesn't achieve because you've used every known trick to help that kid get that concept?

Teacher-bashing usually comes from people who have never been in a classroom.

Jeffrey Blowe teaches second grade at Dunbar Erwin Elementary School in Newport News, Virginia:

People just don't respect teachers as they used to. When I was growing up, if I saw my teacher in the store, outside of the classroom, it was like instant fame. My heart began to beat and my stomach got all quivery. That doesn't happen now. Teachers are just ordinary people. Maybe not even that good.

Robin Lichtenfeld teaches sixth grade at Crossroads Arts Academy in Los Angeles:

By teaching, I feel that I am giving something important back to the world, yet I hate it that I don't make a lot of money.

My father works on Wall Street. That was an option for me, too. I had to think about it a long time: Did I want to make a lot of money, or follow my heart? It was a hard choice. It is still a frustrating choice because teaching is as important as being a doctor, and certainly more important than being a lawyer.

Ron Cooper left a job in business to become a teacher at Van Buren Middle School in Albuquerque, New Mexico:

I used to date a woman from Taiwan. Her father told me that in Taiwan, teachers, professors, are highly revered, highly respected. They drop on the ground and worship them in Taiwan. He told me that in his country my profession is highly honorable and that I should always feel good about what I do because what I do is changing society more than any other profession can.

Ruby Wanland teaches social studies at Miami Beach Senior High School in Miami Beach:

Teachers have always been looked down upon. I had a friend who was dating a congressman occasionally. Then for some social event, she brought a teacher to a party as a date. She was told, "My, my, you're really scraping the bottom of the barrel."

Mark Mattson is an art teacher at Francis Parker School, where his students come from Chicago's most influential families:

Until society changes its priorities, we are going to have trouble with education in this country.

A little story about my tenth year of teaching. I was still young. We had moved to an apartment building, my wife, my kids, and I, that was owned by a Greek immigrant. Now for some reason, this fellow thought of me as a sort of a plum for his building. He called me "the professor."

I was just a high school teacher, but he had this respect for educators that was European, not American, and he brought me down to this little store, a little restaurant, a Greek deli, on some pretense that we had some business to attend to one day. Really the point was to show me off to his friends who sat around drinking coffee in the deli.

I was amused by the whole thing. It was very curious. It was a compliment. But I thought, It's too bad that American educators don't get this kind of treatment very often.

We can put up with the low pay. We don't go into education for money. We can put up with the long hours, the large classes, and so forth, if we had some sense that anybody appreciated what we were doing. It is very rare, especially in public schools. It is what keep us from burning out.

Linda Wood is a social studies teacher at Van Buren Middle School in Albuquerque, New Mexico:

I remember very clearly the first time I got a paycheck. I had forgotten that I got paid for this job. That was a message to me that I really enjoyed what I was doing, if I would consider doing it without getting paid.

Now, I don't like that statement, because I think that is what society expects. That somehow people go into teaching with some kind of dedication and a willingness to sacrifice to help shape young minds and therefore money isn't important. I think money is important. Otherwise it is a matter of being "just the teacher."

Mary Bicouvaris, a former national teacher of the year, teaches at Hampton Roads Academy in Newport News, Virginia:

I wonder why it was that it was so much easier for my generation to allow our teachers to teach us things about the world without challenging with disrespect who they were. Today these students are challenging knowledge.

They like to challenge even the very basic principle that a teacher is a learned person who has spent an entire lifetime learning something.

They probably do the same thing at home with their mothers and fathers. I assume that the children who are rude and challenging to the teacher usually will do that with their own parents. There is an undermining of teachers today.

Bruce Williams teaches history at Jefferson Senior High School in Los Angeles:

Teachers fear the "professionalization" of their profession because they have never known anything other than being treated by administrations as tall children.

One of the most defining moments in my professional life, the catalyst for me to become a political union activist — not in the traditional sense of working conditions and salaries, but changing this whole damn system — was the time I asked a question in a faculty meeting about the use of our classroom wall phone. I admit that I used some degree of sarcasm because she [the principal] had said that she'd pick up the phone on her desk and call so-and-so. I was trying to make the point that when we picked up our phones we can't even dial. They are preprogrammed — because teachers can't be trusted not to abuse the privilege — to ring the switchboard automatically. Then we have to beg that person's permission, usually a student or a clerical person, to be transferred to some office. We get asked, "Aren't you teaching?"

Anyway, I was so furious at the setup that I asked, "Why can't these phones be reprogrammed?" I had already talked to the phone company and I knew that the technology was capable of it.

The principal's response was that I was rude, impertinent, and out of line during a faculty meeting. She called me into her office the next morning and called me unprofessional and actually put it in writing in my personnel file. I've been called many things in my life, most of them true, but never unprofessional. That's audacity. Thus, my quest.

Here's another example of being treated like a child. I had a key to the main building of my campus, the so-called administration building, but the administration took it away. In my several attempts to get an answer about why, the answer was always the same. It comes back to the issue of security: There are too many keys floating around here, you know. Your colleagues lose the key so we've had to change the locks. It's like the president always blanketing everything with the national security issue.

I said, "How long have I been teaching here?" Nine years. I was the mentor teacher and department chairman. "In that time have I ever lost a key?" I asked. I've earned my key. Not that I should have to earn it. In any other profession, you'd have a key to the front door, a telephone, and a computer on your desk.

CHAPTER 10

FRANK SINATRA AND OTHER PUNISHMENTS

D URING the average seven-hour school day, teachers rarely escape their young charges except to slip into the boiler room for a cigarette or relax for a few minutes in the teachers' lounge. Every school has a teachers' lounge, and students have been intrigued for generations about what goes on beyond those forbidden doors. In fact, life in the lounge can be pretty mundane. The best moments in teaching are always in the classroom.

No job that requires an adult to spend so much time with children, even big children, is without its moments of joy and humor. Even if it is stimulated by some inane version of potty humor, few sounds are more melodious than the laughter of children. This can be true even when they are laughing at you, as many teachers have discovered. Only the sourest of teachers can spend much time in a classroom without accumulating memories of the incidents that help soothe the complaints and frustrations.

Teenagers are the toughest audience for a teacher. Teenagers are bored by everything. As humor writer Dave Barry has noticed, show a teenager an actual volcanic eruption in progress, with lava flowing and ash spewing, and they will respond by mumbling, "Gee, this is *swell*." So teachers who have evoked laughter from teenagers are especially proud of themselves. A sense of humor is essential.

Roger Bowen first taught during a stint in the Peace Corps. Today he is the thoughtful director of the upper school at St. Stephen's and St. Agnes School in Alexandria, Virginia. But his funniest story comes from his days as a teacher at St. Albans School, across the Potomac River in Washington, D.C.:

I was teaching a fourth-grade religion class a few years back. We got to the covenant between Abraham and God, and the symbol for that is circumcision. This is an all-boys' school. So I said, "You guys understand what this circumcision business is all about?"

They all looked at each other. There were a few giggles and elbows going back and forth. And finally little Oliver in the back of the classroom pipes up: "Oh, oh, oh. Mr. Bowen. I know. I know."

I said, "Oliver, please explain."

And he said, "Circumcision is when they cut off your old testaments."

Bruce Janu was twenty-four years old and in his second year of teaching in 1992 when his sense of humor landed him a one-paragraph notice in *Esquire* magazine. He teaches American history and Western civilization at Riverside-Brookfield Senior High School, west of Chicago:

A friend of mine in college and I were both Frank Sinatra fans and we both talked about teaching. I guess that is where the roots for this idea lie.

At this school, we have a system of detentions that keep kids after class. I just wanted to have something a little bit memorable about my detentions and something that would make detentions a little easier on me. You see, when I give a kid a detention, it's like giving myself one, too. After all, I have to sit there with the students.

So I had a specially made tape with a wide variety of Sinatra songs, from his early years on. I found that it makes detention more enjoyable for me and less enjoyable for the kids. Sometimes they bring their own music and ask to listen to it. No way.

I seem to have fewer detentions now than during first semester. I have no way of knowing, however, if it's because of Frank or because they are getting used to me and know what I expect.

I've always told the students that if they come into detention and can sing a Sinatra song all the way through, they can go early. No one has taken me up on it yet. I had one student who had eight detentions and after a while he was beginning to know the songs. He got so he couldn't even stand to hear the name. That is not exactly the effect that I wanted. I would have liked to generate a little appreciation.

As with every job, teaching develops its own form of black humor. Jim DeCamp has been an English teacher for twenty-five years. He now teaches advanced placement classes at Rush Henrietta Senior High School in Henrietta, New York, where he spent a lunch hour prospecting for funny stories with three colleagues who preferred anonymity, for what became obvious reasons:

What struck me as amusing was how unfunny their stories were. The first guy said, "I once had a student who wrote a note about me in class that was very unflattering, but he spelled my name wrong. So I sent it home to his father that night for his dad to sign. Instead, his father backhanded him over dinner and broke his jaw."

I said to him, "You think this is funny?"

I turned to my other friend and said, "What about you?"

He said, "I remember sitting in the principal's office one afternoon with a kid who was kind of out of control. When the principal turned around for a second, the kid jumped out a window. Fortunately the office was on the first floor."

Finally, I turned to the woman who was eating with us, and she said, "Remember the blind English substitute? Remember the time that all the kids were tormenting her and the whole class left because she couldn't see them? Well, she decided to report them all, so she sat down at the typewriter she kept handy to take notes and typed out all the names. The problem was that they also had taken the ribbon out of the typewriter."

A lot of my stories involve a legendary principal, who must remain anonymous.

This guy was actually a former social studies teacher. He really liked to make announcements on the public address system. One time he was dealing with a problem of kids loitering in the hallways, talking, and being late to class. So he used the PA system to talk to all the students about this and he finished by saying, "I don't want you kids conjugating in the halls anymore."

The same guy began a faculty meeting one day with an announcement about a woman who had been injured at the school. I guess he was making the announcement so anyone who wanted could send flowers or sympathy notes. He said she had fallen and broken her scrotum.

We had the same principal during the 1970s when there was a lot of political unrest. We had several students who were political activists, who were what some people might call hippies. They had a lot of protests. One day a group staged a sit-in in the cafeteria. When they got dragged down to the principal's office he asked them why they were doing what they were doing. They told him that they were following the nonviolent policies of Thoreau and Gandhi. The principal said, "Who the hell are these people? I bet they don't even live in our school district."

A woman friend of mine was teaching a class of moderately slow kids. Her lesson was a complicated one, all about natural resources and how countries have to take advantage of what they have to trade and barter for what they don't have. At the end of the lesson, she cited the Arab countries as an example.

"They have plenty of oil, but not a lot of other resources. What can they do under these circumstances? How can they survive?" she asked the class.

One girl raised her hand and said, "If it's Crisco, they can use it to fry chicken."

During the 1970s we were hiring teachers like crazy, right off the street, as long as they had some kind of degree. The school district was building schools, we were expanding. A friend of mine was teaching social studies and one day the teacher from the next classroom tapped on his door to ask a question. He said, "I have to get this straight before the next class: Did we drop the bomb on Germany or Japan?"

Continuing with DeCamp's general themes of legendary principals and PA systems is his friend and colleague at Rush Henrietta, history teacher John Perelli:

We were giving an achievement test at school one day, the Lorge-Thorndike test, which is given annually by certain school districts. Our principal used the PA system to say, "Today we will take the Large Thorndike test, which must be administered anally."

Student misspellings are great, too. Right now we are doing a unit in history on imperialism. I had a kid tell me in class that the United States is expanding into the Pacific Ocean and wants to acquire the Fallopian Islands. I think he came to history straight from health class.

I once had a kid write a wonderful essay on snuggling. It was supposed to be on smuggling, of course. He wrote that one of the most serious problems during the late Colonial period was unrestricted snuggling. Snuggling was so common in the Massachusetts Colony that instead of going into the Boston Harbor, where they would have to pay taxes, ships would go secretly to distant coves to snuggle under the cover of darkness. The report said that the British were aware of the rampant snuggling and sent special tax collectors who captured the snugglers to prosecute and punish them.

Once I was correcting the New York State Regents exams in American history. I don't recall the exact question, but generally the student had to identify three technological developments and assess their impact on how war was fought. A good question.

I'm reading this one paper, and first the kid comes up with the airplane and explains its use for reconnaissance, dogfights, and the bombings and mass destruction of World War II. Wonderful. His second choice was the nuclear bomb. He goes into nuclear energy, Hiroshima, and the ensuing Cold War. Terrific. The kid is working on a full-credit essay now and I'm getting psyched. On to number three. He chooses the invention of the shoe. Then he proceeds to write how with shoes on soldiers can march faster over rocks, that they aren't as crabby when their feet don't hurt, and that with shoes they have more energy to fight battles. When they are not busy picking sticks and stones out from between their toes, he wrote, they could watch out more easily for moving arrows. The well ran dry.

Linda Smith is on sabbatical from teaching high school science and is working as a mission commander at the Challenger Learning Center of Greater Rochester, New York. Perelli and DeCamp are her friends, and she has her own PA system story to tell:

One day I walked into the high school and I heard the vice principal blast on the PA system, "Okay, all of those students going to jail, please report to the bus now." It was a field trip.

Years ago, when I was young and fresh to teaching, I had a junior high school biology class. We were dissecting frogs. I decided to play a small trick on one of my students, although I didn't know which one. So I placed a small incision in the body cavity of one of the frogs and put a small note in there. I passed out the frogs and the dissecting trays on which they were supposed to pin the frogs down. The kids were busy saying, "Oh, gross." I was so happy, wondering who was going to get the special frog. They were all going along with me, carefully cutting. I was waiting and watching. Suddenly I looked and one of the kids found the paper. I watched him unroll it. It said, "Kiss me. I'm a prince."

Craig Lancto was an English teacher at George Washington Middle School in Alexandria, Virginia. He has since moved to T. C. Williams High School there:

I had a kid once who kept unscrewing the desk legs during my English class, booby-trapping it for the next student. Finally, I sent the kid to the principal with a note. It said, "He fills my mind with scorpions." You know, *Macbeth?* I thought, "There, that's a nice English teacher touch." So the principal shows up panting at the door. "Where are all the scorpions?" he yelled.

To learn vocabulary, I used to have the kids choose a word from a current story and do a demonstration that would embed the word permanently in other kids' minds.

During one presentation, a boy pulled a chair into the center of the room and asked for a volunteer. Me. I asked what the word was, but he said to wait.

He pulled out a rope. I asked what the word was. He said I'd have to wait. He tied my hands to the chair. I was beginning to perspire. Then he pulled out a scroll and announced that his word was "scourge," to whip or scorn. He proceeded to pull out another rope and hit me with it. I was brutalized in class.

Another girl doing a demonstration wanted to tie me to a chair. I declined, saying that I had had a bad experience with ropes and chairs earlier. She said, "Don't worry."

She and two of her friends tied me to the chair, pulled me out into the middle of the hall, and left me. The associate principal walked up, nodded hello, and walked on. I thought, "What kind of reputation do I have?" The girl finally opened the door and said, "Are you blushing? My word was 'embarrassed.'"

I've been held hostage by terrorists with squirt guns. They sent a ransom note to the principal, and the hall monitor came back with a note saying, "Blow him up."

For "harangue," a boy whose father was in the Episcopal seminary came in with full ecclesiastical robes and stood on a desk, giving a long oration.

Then there was the day some kids wanted me to close my eyes. They sprayed my hair green. The word was "bizarre."

Avis Harris is the administrative assistant to the principal at Van Buren Middle School in Albuquerque, New Mexico, but she remembers best an incident at Polk Middle School:

We had children in the sixth through ninth grades. I was an educational assistant in a math class. The ninth graders used the F-word a lot — all the time, actually. The teacher would be up in the front of the room, I'd be in the back, helping different kids with their work. And I could hear them talking to each other, "F-this" and "F-that." I used to say quietly, "Please don't use that word. I really don't like it."

One day one boy said to another: "I need a F-ing pencil. Give me yours."

The other boy said: "Shut your F-ing mouth. Ms. Harris doesn't like you to talk that way."

Like all jobs, teaching has its share of gallows humor. Pam Lubitz teaches first grade at Maurice Hawk Elementary School in Princeton Junction, New Jersey:

I had a really difficult year once, with a group of children that had a lot of problems. One of the kids had been raped by her stepfather. When her father found out, he moved her here. Not surprisingly, the little girl had a lot of emotional problems and needed a lot of counseling. She told a lot of stories.

Another child in the class had a lot of neurological problems and was blind in one eye. The glass eye used to fall out all the time. I'd send her down to the nurse and she'd put it back in.

Well, one day, the mother of the child who had been molested and told a lot of stories came in. "I've had it with all the stories," she said. "Yesterday she came home and told me that an eyeball rolled across your room."

Barbara Ruggles teaches third grade with Gordon Kridner at Black Hawk Elementary School in Park Forest, Illinois:

We had guinea pigs for years and years, and Gordon had talked to the children about how one was a male and one was a female. One day, the "male" gave birth, and one little first grader walked in and said, "Isn't that nice? The dad had the babies this time."

It's lonely and windswept on the Zuni reservation in New Mexico where A. J. Gillard teaches at Twin Buttes High School, but humor survives:

We have a drug-sniffing dog. I don't think the dog has detected anything in a number of years. His smell may be shot. He sniffs lockers and students for dope. I don't know if it's constitutional, but the dog comes in monthly.

One day, the dog went nuts. He was pawing like crazy at a locker, and the administration thought the dog must have found a cache of drugs. They were somewhat disillusioned when they found a hamburger in a coat pocket.

Sanford Bearman is a math teacher at North Miami Beach Senior High School:

I had a student once who was a relatively bright kid, but a real troublemaker. He was in his junior year and he was in my trigonometry class. The school had a bake sale for the junior class, so he made some brownies and he said he'd made a special batch for his favorite math teacher, Mr. Bear.

Me, like a dummy who is a chocoholic, ate them, every one of them. I ate the brownies during homeroom and right in the middle of my third-period geometry class they tell me I was singing and dancing and having a great old time.

They were hashish brownies.

When I first got to Beach High, I was totally unprepared for that school. My job interview had been after school, and the kids had all left. So I arrived my first day wearing a tie. At my previous school everyone wore a tie. When I got here, the only other person with a tie on was the principal, so I realized very quickly I was out of place. You couldn't walk up the stairs looking up, because if you did you'd embarrass yourself with all the short skirts, microskirts.

My first course was taught outside the building, in a portable classroom on the physical education field. It was a real rough class, and their first teacher had been a young woman with a master's degree in math. Because she had never taught before, instead of giving her some decent courses, they gave her these basic-level classes. She lasted two weeks. Then there had been a series of substitutes. Then I came along. So I walked in at the beginning of week number five. I was barely in the door and they were challenging me about how long I was going to last.

The first two or three days I was afraid to turn my back on the students. When I wrote on the board I wouldn't turn my back because they would throw something — pencil, eraser, book, anything that was loose, would come flying. So I had to write at the board without looking at it. These kids weren't really bad. They had just been allowed to run free for a month.

As I began the third day, I was walking backward toward the chalkboard, I tripped and fell ass-first into the wastebasket. These kids went crazy. They were laughing hysterically. I thought we'd have to call the rescue squad for some. I had to laugh, too.

The whole rest of the period they had just one big howl. I never got them back that day. But the fact that I showed up the next day made me a hero. They couldn't believe that I came back. They expected me to quit and disappear.

So when I walked in the fourth day, we all had a good laugh for the first five minutes and then they let me teach. I was a hero. The story spread all over the school about this new teacher, but I lived it down.

I normally would walk in the door and walk up the left side of the room. Three months after that incident, for some reason I went around and walked up the right side. About three quarters of the way up the room, I went right through the floor up to my hips. It had been eaten away by termites. Luckily it was a cold day and I was wearing corduroy pants. I got some scrapes, but I was okay. A couple of kids got up and helped me out. Again, they were hysterical.

After living those incidents down, I figured I could get through almost anything. That became one of my secrets of success as a teacher — the ability to use humor in the classroom. Not as a major instrument, but to tell a joke now and then.

Kathleen O'Neill teaches first and seventh grades at Sinai Akiba Academy, in Los Angeles:

Two years ago, I had a student give me a grenade, a real grenade. It wasn't loaded, but I didn't know it at the time. It scared the daylights out of me.

About two or three days before that we had been at recess and, believe it or not, we had seen empty bullet shells. I picked them up, and then the kids got going about it. These were fourth graders. So I thought we should have a little discussion about responsible behavior with guns.

Two days later, all morning long, the kids kept saying, "Miss O'Neill, Bradley has a grenade." I was thinking, "Yeah, G.I. Joe plastic." So I said, "Okay, I don't want to hear it. I don't like that kind of stuff in class." And the kids kept saying, "Miss O'Neill, Bradley has a grenade."

It kept on and on, and in silent reading period, this nice little kid, Bradley, who did a lot of off-the-wall things for attention, just walked up to my desk and kind of dropped the grenade on my desk. I froze and said, "Oh, my God, it's a grenade!"

I didn't know the guts were out of it. I think there was a pin in it, but the underneath part was kind of hollow. I didn't know that. I'd never seen one. There was an aide in my classroom working with one of the students, and I just said, "Excuse me, I'll be right back." I picked up the grenade and walked down to the office.

English teachers rushed in and out of the teachers' lounge at T. C. Williams High School in Alexandria, Virginia. Occasionally one would stop to share a funny story, and eventually it became a game, with each teacher trying to top the others.

Rebecca Buckbee, whose smile lines indicate a love for those funny stories, is the head of the English Department. As with many teachers, she finds the PA system is a constant source of laughs:

When I worked at Hammond High School, we had a football team that was not scored against one entire season. It was legendary. I remember our principal introducing all the people who had some kind of input into making it happen. So she was getting ready to introduce the athletic director over the PA system and she said in a loud, clear voice, "Here now is the biggest athletic supporter in the school."

Once at our middle school, one of the secretaries who was very southern and very elderly came on the PA system with her fine, southern voice and said, "Would anybody who can't hear this announcement please send a runner to the office?"

Breezing into the lounge from duty monitoring the cafeteria, English teacher and author Patrick Welch offered a breezy anecdote:

One of my hoodlum students — he's probably doing drugs and all sorts of things — walked into my class and picked a book off my desk the other day, a book that the advanced placement class was reading. He got really excited and I couldn't understand why. He's in the lowest English level and it wasn't like him to get excited by a book. It turned out that he read the title not as *Light in August,* but *Fight in August.*

Julie Haivemenos taught family life at T. C. Williams for nine years. When she needed a change, she switched to English:

I was teaching a family life course about anatomy or maybe it was birth control. Anyway, it was something that involved talking about male and female body parts. This one student who has since been in serious trouble with the law, but was a big teddy bear with his teachers, was listening very intently. It was clearly the first time that he had ever really been given permission to have an okay conversation about the sexual parts of the body in a serious way. He kept asking question after question. And other people would ask questions. And he watched me, staring at me so intently. Finally I asked him, "Is there something you want to ask me?"

He said, "Well, yeah. Are you married?"

I said, "Yes, I am."

Another pause and he said, "Does your husband know you do this?"

Rebecca Buckbee:

Remember Harold Brown? He wanted to be called Hash. You know? Hash Brown. This was twenty years ago. His science teacher told him to use "metabolism" in a sentence. He said, "I bought some metabolism at the store." She said, "No, no, no. Harold, you can't buy metabolism. It is impossible." So Hash said, "All right, I stole some metabolism."

Jean Wiggins is a teacher's aide in a kindergarten class at George Mason Elementary School in Alexandria, Virginia:

These are just little kids. We let them play with any toy they want in the classroom. The rule, though, is that when you are done with a toy, you put it away before getting out another.

One little boy just didn't like that rule. He chose a toy, he played, but he did not want to put it away. So I chose a toy, sat on the floor nearby, and played with it. When I was done, I said, "Well, I'm done with this toy, but before I get another, I'm going to put this away."

He just looked at me and said, "I knew I wasn't going to like this place."

CHAPTER 11

TRADE SECRETS

MERRI MANN taught high school English for sixteen years. She is now assistant director of the Department of Professionalization for the United Teachers of Dade County in Miami. From this vantage point she has a good view of the components of quality teaching.

"Being out of the classroom and being exposed to lots of different ideas and approaches makes you see things in a different way," said Mann as she sat at a cluttered desk in the union's nondescript offices. "You can't just love your subject matter. You have to like the kids to make a connection between what you know and all the exciting possibilities for them."

Relevance can be as simple as showing students that grammar is essential to shaping sentences so they can communicate clearly and effectively. "If you're teaching grammar for its own sake, I don't know what that relevance is," she said.

Mann acknowledged that there is no easy formula for an effective teacher, no list of ten easy steps or essential attributes. Good teaching has an element of mystery because it is so personal. A good teacher knows his students. They know him. There is a mutual respect and trust. Good teaching is an art, and as such its ingredients defy quantification and its practitioners will not be pigeonholed. Some trade secrets are individual, created to respond to the needs of a particular student or group of students.

In conversations in classrooms, lunchrooms, and living rooms with teachers across the country, teachers shared stories of their own learning and how they came to be better teachers. Some common qualities emerged. Good teachers demand a great deal of their students. Good teachers don't necessarily have to like children, but they must respect them. They demand a great deal of students without establishing goals so high that they set up students for automatic failure. They allow children to fail, however, because failure can be a learning experience. Yet they always temper that failure with optimism and encouragement. Good teachers are adaptable, recognizing that techniques that work with one child or group of children often need to be tailored to meet the different requirements of another group.

Distilling these qualities into a simple definition of a good teacher is not possible. But Molly Donohue, who teaches third grade at Francis Parker School in Chicago, offered as good a description as any when she said, "To me, a good teacher is a person who has a big set of values, can accept lots of things from people, and can recognize that the world has a place for everybody."

For instance, when Helen Mrosla found herself teaching at a school in the backwoods of Kentucky, she soon discovered that book learning had little relevance in this world. Her students had little use for anything that did not relate directly to the way of life in their isolated hollows, places where families have remained rooted to a single location for generations.

"We opened a gas station and a minimart and the students ran them both," she explained in a soft voice tinged with fondness for those long-past days in Butcher Hollow. "Students learned mechanics and they learned to talk to people outside the hollow by waiting on people. And they learned math by counting change."

In the stories of their successes and failures with various teaching techniques, teachers provide insights for their peers, for parents, and for anyone else involved in trying to discover ways to improve the schools.

Helen Mrosla taught for thirty-seven years in elementary and secondary schools and in the education departments of two universities. Early in her career, she discovered a teaching technique that she never stopped using, but it wasn't until years later that she learned its true impact. She is a member of St. Francis Convent in Little Falls, Minnesota, and even now she cannot tell the story without crying:

I was teaching at St. Mary's School in Morris, Minnesota. I had a darling group of third graders, and Mark Ecklund was one of these students you never forget. He would always smile and say, "Thank you, Sister, for correcting me," or "Thank you, Sister, for helping me." But he talked a lot in class.

One day I had to tell Mark that if he said one more thing I was going to put tape over his mouth so he would be quiet. Before I got back to the front of the room, Chuck raised his hand and said, "Mark is talking." Because I had said it in front of the whole class, I had to follow through with the discipline.

I got the masking tape out of the drawer and went back and put it like an X over his mouth. Students were snickering and, when I got back to the front of the room, I turned around and Mark winked at me. I went back and took off the tape and said that we were friends.

I know now that one never corrects a student in front of an entire group because then you have to live up to what you say.

Later I was moved from the third grade to teaching seventh-, eighth-, and ninth-grade math. Eventually I had Mark in math class again. He hadn't changed. He was not malicious. It was always an enjoyable sort of remark that he would make. In those days, we had to be strict in class. Today we would say don't squelch him.

One day in his class things were not going well. It was on a Friday and we had had a difficult week. I didn't want the students leaving for the weekend feeling bad. So I just stopped teaching math that day and I asked them to get out a piece of notebook paper. I told them just to look around the room and write down the name of each student in the class and write down one good thing about each.

They did that. Then I spent the entire weekend listing all the things that were said about each student. I had a yellow legal-size piece of paper with each student's name on it and below the name I put the anonymous comments of their classmates. It took me hours and hours because I had thirty-four students.

By Monday morning, they each had their paper on their desks with these phrases: "Always smiles," "Is a good listener," "Always tells the truth," "Tries hard all the time." The reaction that morning was just terrific.

They read their papers and there was a general murmur throughout the class. One after another, they were surprised about the nice things that were said about them. It made quite a difference for them.

I continued to do that in the next years. I even did that on the university level one time.

Years later, I was working at an inner-city school in St. Paul. The mother of one of my former students had given me a trip to the Bahamas. When I came back, my folks met me at the airport and my mother said, "The Ecklunds called last night."

"Oh, isn't that wonderful," I said.

My dad kind of cleared his throat and he said, "Mark was killed in Vietnam and the funeral is tomorrow and they'd like to have you come for it."

I can still see the spot on the highway where my dad told me. Every time I go to the airport I pass that spot and feel a sense of loss.

The next morning, we got up early and made the trip of about a hundred miles to Morris. We got to the funeral parlor before the Mass and went in. I had never seen a military funeral before, never seen a soldier laid out in his uniform. I could just picture Mark with that X taped over his mouth. To this day, I regret having done that.

After the funeral, we went out to the farmhouse where Mark's friend Chuck lived. When I got there, Mark's folks came right over to me and said, "We want you to see this." His dad pulled out that yellow sheet of paper that had all those good things about Mark on it and he said that it had been in Mark's billfold.

"You can tell this meant a lot to Mark," he said. "It was with him when he died."

His classmates were all around. One of them said he had his slip. Another pulled his out of his billfold. Another one said she had hers in her wedding album, and another said hers was in her diary. All the students who were there said they had saved their sheets of paper.

Teachers make a difference in many ways. Frank Tobin, who teaches inmates at the Cook County Temporary Juvenile Detention Center in Chicago, was nominated for a teaching award by an inmate at Statesville Prison, who wrote, "If I had known Mr. Tobin as a teacher before I had committed a major crime, I never would have ended up where I ended up, which is serving twenty years in a maximum-security prison." To reach such unusual students, Tobin employs some unusual techniques:

I had a kid here the other day, a fifteen-year-old kid who was supporting his mother by pushing drugs. He is very honest. Now, here's an example of something good about the kid. He is very concerned about his mother and he is tough. He carried a gun. When you are pushing drugs, you have to carry a gun because someone will either hold you up for the money or the drugs or try to take over your territory. Somebody came after him and he said, "I just had to take care of business." He killed somebody. If you understand the environment he came from, he is basically a good kid.

So I talk to this boy about the mathematics of pushing drugs. "How much is a kilo of cocaine?" I ask him.

"Over $25,000," he says.

"So if you split it this way and that, how much will you have?" I ask.

I tried to show him that if he didn't know decimals he couldn't divide it up accurately. We worked out a problem where he had to divvy up this cocaine and sell it and determine how much he should pay for it in buying it from me.

Well, in about a week I ripped him off by about $180,000 because he didn't know what the hell he was doing with mathematics. It was a way of getting him interested in math. He knows that I am death on drugs, but he got real interested in decimals and he is working very hard at it.

About a week ago, he came to me and said, "If I get out of here, do you think you can get me back in school?" So there it is, the desire to be good and save yourself.

Dren Geer, a former principal, teaches advanced placement English and is director of development at Chicago's Providence-St. Mel:

One of the great tragedies of American education is that we aren't paying people enough and the universities report that the best people are not going into education.

So do we try to upgrade teaching? Get better people? No. Instead, we create a connect-the-dot curriculum, and safe teaching situations that don't really demand responsibilities of teachers so that they can't make mistakes, so they are buttressed by huge fences of rules and regulations, practices and procedures.

And as soon as you do that, the relationship between the teacher and the students begins to deteriorate incrementally.

Mark Mattson is an art teacher at Francis Parker School in Chicago:

The more we know about the human mind and the complexity of how children learn, the more difficult our job becomes. We're being told every day that there are fine distinctions among learning disabilities, and there are differences between learning disabilities and behavioral disabilities, and there is a difference between an economically deprived child with learning or behavioral disabilities and an economically advantaged child who has been abandoned to the two-job family and the television set and has become inured to just about anything.

The subtleties we have to deal with are becoming more and more difficult and there is a greater need for specialists in schools to help us sort these things out. Yet there is still no substitute for good, old-fashioned common sense. You can drive yourself nuts trying to sort out all these peculiarities in children when, in fact, some good, enthusiastic cheerleading for that child will probably get him through it. Common sense still counts.

I was an art school student and I still like to think of myself as a painter. Therefore, I think of education as an art form, not as a business form, not as a psychological thing or a set of social rules. Artists know there are rules out there for what a picture should be, or what composition is, or how color works. But every great work of art in some way changes the rules, challenges the rules. That's what a good school does. That is what a good teacher does.

Jim Hosney is head of the Film and Video Department at Crossroads Arts Academy, a private school in Los Angeles:

It's really interesting when you teach something and the impact goes beyond anything you imagined. One of the experiences I had was teaching my students a form of guerrilla theater, something that was prevalent in the sixties. I assigned the students to do this project and I had assumed they would clear it with me, but that's ridiculous, because it goes against the whole idea of guerrilla theater.

So I'm sitting in a faculty meeting and somebody comes running in, asking, "Why are these students blockading the entrance to the school?" And then someone else came running in, really outraged, yelling, "And they said it's for their English class." I just slowly sank down in my seat, noticing the headmaster's veins in his neck beginning to bulge.

The kids had blockaded the mothers from leaving, sitting there in the drive with surgeons' masks on their faces, with big signs that said, "Cars Can't Pass."

I heard stories later. One of the mothers said, "I was at Berkeley. I understand what you're doing, but I have to get my kid to the orthodontist." But they wouldn't let her through. So you teach something and they actually put it into practice and suddenly it comes home to you, the power of teaching.

Carolyn Langston teaches third grade at Dunbar Erwin Elementary School in Newport News, Virginia:

I had a mother come in because her little child was not reading at all in second grade, yet I found her to be very intelligent. I couldn't figure out in my wildest dreams why she couldn't read. So the mother finally came in for a conference and we talked. The mother was very young, had other little ones, told me she was a dropout.

I said, "I'll tell you what I am going to do: This child has got to read when she leaves this room. I'll write out all the vocabulary words on cards and I will send them home."

You see, you can't send home books anymore because we don't have the money to replace all the ones that never came back. Remember how you used to take a reader home and you'd read it with your mom because you didn't want to be embarrassed the next day reading out loud without knowing the words? Well, I bought a pack of recipe cards and wrote every word in the reader on it. I sent them home and the child could read them in three days. Then she sat down and read the first reader. Then she moved on to the next one. She was so thrilled with her mother.

"Oh, my mother and I do these every night," she'd say.

If I missed giving her cards, she'd remind me: "You don't have any new words for my mother and me."

Then I bought a bingo game with words and I wrapped it up for her and she has never failed to bring it back. She and her mother were doing something together. She is reading, not yet on the second-grade level, but by George, she is reading. And her mother feels she has contributed something.

It is just that simple. Educators make it so complicated. I am not sure why, except to make themselves feel important that they came up with another new theory, I guess.

Despite being confined to a wheelchair because of multiple sclerosis, Doug Burris teaches classical guitar and rock ensemble at Miami Beach Senior High School in Miami Beach, Florida. The handsome teacher with a close-cropped beard sits in front of a hushed class, speaking gently into a microphone. Like his exact ear, his control over the forty or so students is perfect. For many kids, Burris is an educational lifeline; he offers them something they love, which in turn keeps them in school and gives them a reason to stick with other classes:

Any teacher has to love what's he's doing. If he's a math teacher, and he really loves math, those kids are going to learn. He's going to figure out a way to turn those kids on to math.

When I started teaching here twenty years ago, teaching guitar, I needed something else for my own excitement, rather than just five classes of guitar. I went to the principal and told him that I'd like to put together a rock group. He said to go ahead. He's a very progressive kind of a guy.

We have plenty of kids in that group, very bright kids, who will go on to be doctors, lawyers, and that kind of thing because that's their thing. They're not going to make music their life-style, but they're very talented and interested in the group. They're enjoying it because it's exciting.

But this program also can help those kids who aren't doing well in other aspects of their education. It helps them stay in school. We have so many kids throughout the years who have come through the program that the counselors have told me wouldn't have stayed in school without it.

One kid grew up in a drug-infested family. This kid could have joined that whole thing, but he came to my class. He became a technician and eventually got interested in really listening to recordings, saw different effects and how things were recorded, and started reading books.

This kid couldn't read. The teachers thought he was dyslexic but he wasn't. He was pushed through the educational system like a lot of kids are. I got him in a class at Criteria Studios, which is a pretty well-known studio here in Miami, and at that point he was taking some recording classes, and while he was there the Bee Gees were recording *Saturday Night Fever*. He got in on some of those recording sessions and later the Bee Gees left there and built their own studio a few blocks away. They took him with them. He became their top electrician, actually fixing equipment, highly technical equipment. He learned to read, I think, because he started reading magazines and periodicals that had to do with electronic music.

Last year, he went on tour with the Bee Gees, and also Phil Collins, the drummer, took him on tour. Today, when he's not on tour, he's building recording studios for the top guy here in Miami. That's one kid that I really feel who, without that rock class, probably would have just said forget it, maybe joined the rest of the family.

John Schiff teaches at Santa Fe Preparatory School in Santa Fe, New Mexico:

I teach in a private, nonsectarian, nonboarding school. It prides itself on stimulating the student educationally. Our school doesn't reduce education to data mastery. We insist on appreciation in the humanities, in science and mathematics, in language, in fine arts.

The community-service aspect of this school also is very strong. We believe that real education involves the whole student, and that means educating them as members of this society.

Every Thursday, all of our students, as a part of the requirements for graduation, must contribute two hours of community service to some agency in the city: services for the blind, the orchestra, the school system, the National Park Service, various things. They probably have thirty-five or forty agencies where the kids can pick what they want to do. The senior students are allowed to make up their own program. In addition to that, occasionally the entire school takes an afternoon off to go down to a section of the city and clean it up. This year it happens to be the area around the river, and we're going to take plastic bags and shovels and do it.

We feel that social consciousness, and making it a reality, is an important part of being a member of the democratic society, and an important part of understanding, for example, Locke and Hobbes. I mean, those are realities in the world. They aren't just abstract, historical figures. This is the way to make them live.

Alan Marks teaches English and economics at Rio Grande High School in Albuquerque, New Mexico:

My mission when I came to public school was that I never wanted to look at a person who was going to college. I never wanted to teach one, I never wanted to deal with one. I figured they would get good teachers in college, to hell with them. They're going to do fine. I was worried about the kids who don't go to college. I wanted to make sure that they had the skills, and the confidence, to fight their battles, to demand that society not run over them but provide them with their fair share of the benefits of this society. And that they know how to work their way through the morass, the bureaucracy, of daily life. I want them to have critical skills, to feel that they're entitled. Entitled in the sense that, if they can articulate, and argue, what their rights are, then they have to be respected. That's what I wanted. That was my mission and intention when I came into teaching.

It has changed in several directions. The first four years I stuck with that, I became less interested in content, more interested in process, and more interested in skills than I thought I would be. I didn't think I cared about skills. But dealing with these low-level kids, if they couldn't read and couldn't write, what good did it do for me to get involved in all this nifty content? All of a sudden I realized that it was very revolutionary to teach somebody to write really critical, argumentative essays, and if they could do that I felt that, my God, I've done something. So that became my mission with these regular kids who weren't going to go on.

But then I started looking over my shoulder and see all the people who were graduating at the top of their class and doing nothing with their lives, so eventually I succumbed to beginning to work with them somewhat. I worked for four years, took a year off, lived in Manhattan for half the year and in Nepal for half the year, and in France for a bit, and then I came back, worked the second four years with more advanced kids, left at the end of that time, and went to Stanford Business School so I could check up on my seven kids who were at Stanford to make sure they were actually getting something out of it and not just being humiliated and intimidated in this elitist environment.

Then I came back this time and said I would come back to my original mission. I said I'd work a little bit, but not teach these advanced kids. I want to teach the regular kids. I want them to understand what is going on in society and I want them to be able to do something. So now I've kind of come full circle. I still do a little bit with the advanced kids, but mostly on my own time. I don't get paid for it. I did create a class finally where I could do some of that within the structure of a class. And I do teach one enriched economics section, so I'm able to work with some of the kids there. I've got my tenth-grade people that are in the minority program, and I kick their butts. Everything else that I do is with the regular kids. I'm very concerned about them. I just don't worry too much about your kids. They're going to do fine. They've got parents, they're going to go to college.

Pam Lubitz is a first-grade teacher at Maurice Hawk Elementary School in Princeton Junction, New Jersey:

When I had been teaching only a year, my administrator let me go visit a very dynamic teacher. That was it. I wanted to emulate her style, even her personality. She was really involved with her children. She wasn't the sort of teacher who stands up front with the children in the back. In fact, you wouldn't know where she was when you walked into her classroom. She was involved with play with her children. I'll never forget her saying to me, "If I've said more than fifteen things during the day, then I've said too much. I should be listening and observing." I was so inspired from that moment on that I looked at education differently.

Father Wilbur Atwood teaches at St. Augustine High School in New Orleans:

What we want, what we are hoping for, is men. That's the first thing. We want to graduate men, not boys. Men who are men of faith, but men who are conversant with the world in which they are going to live and who have the skills necessary to deal with that world.

We are primarily a college-preparatory school, and 80 percent of our kids go on to college. So therefore we've got to give them skills, an ability to read and to comprehend, an ability to write reasonably well. And men who are capable of thinking reasonably and logically. If we have at least equipped them with those skills, then we feel they are ready for college and ready for the work world.

We use numbers for tracking: 401, 402, 403, 404, and 405. What you do is group together people of like ability. This first started out as the results of their testing, what the tests showed of their ability. Then, as we see their ability in practice, we begin shifting them around.

It used to be that the one real big criterion was math. If they showed a good ability in math, then they went into the A track. But now, if a kid shows real good ability in say social studies and he is not so good in math, we will move him into the A track, realizing that in math he is going to be pulling up the rear.

For example, I had a kid who was moved into 301 this year and he is a fine, fine history student. He is a lousy math student. But they moved him into the upper track because they saw his ability. His strength is that he does a great deal of reading. However, he doesn't really like to do all the work that is involved in preparation for math.

We had a lay principal here at one time who did not like the system, but it is our system, and we insist on keeping it. Frankly, I don't know how you go in and teach a class where you have people of different abilities. It seems to me that it would then become like a one-room schoolhouse where you separate your kids and teach them individually or by small groups, but you don't treat them as a whole.

This principal didn't like it, I suspect, because he was a product of the University of New Orleans, and they don't like it. This is death in the public school system because in theory we are educating people for democratic living. But, as you and I know, people are segregated even in democratic living.

So what this principal did was, in the homeroom he mixed everybody up and started putting them together alphabetically — A's, B's, C's, and D's in one room. He was thinking that he was breaking down the class structure. Well, what we noticed happen was that in those homerooms those that were in the A track tended to mingle together, those that were in the B track tended to mingle together, that they themselves segregated themselves because they had likes and they talked the same language. Consequently, they sought out one another even when he was attempting to break it down. When he left, we went back to doing homerooms the way we always had.

The first year I taught before I came here I taught in a parish school up in Natchez, Mississippi, and there was just one class. You divided by girls on one side and boys on the other. You ran the gamut in that classroom.

For example, there was a boy who was very great at mathematics, a guy by the name of John Hogan. Now, John later went on to college. There was another kid in the same class who was hardly literate. The thing is that in our parish schools we are educating men and women who are going to be parishioners. These are children of God who are going to be active in their parishes. This kid who was semiliterate had a right to an education as well as John, who was going to go on and do great things.

But I discovered in that class that I could talk to John and miss this fellow, or I could talk to this fellow and bore John to tears. I could not talk to the two of them at the same time. So here at St. Aug's, what we have done is group them together by ability. I must admit that I can hardly believe it when people in the public schools say that they do not track. I had a teacher one summer in adolescent psychology who had been a principal in a public school and who said that they did it surreptitiously. I cannot believe that it does not go on through some kind of subterfuge because I cannot see how you can possibly teach people of widely varying abilities in the same room. It seems to me very inefficient and wasteful. But I've been in enough situations where, when people hear about the system that we use, they are horrified — scandalized, really, in some instances. But I don't really understand how you can do it without tracking.

Ron Cooper teaches special education and critical thinking at Van Buren Middle School in Albuquerque, New Mexico:

My junior year I had a job working as a teaching assistant in the San Diego city schools. It made a real impact on me. The kids liked me and liked the way I handled stuff, and they didn't like me just because I was being nice, but because of the way I treated them. It was kind of a natural thing that I had learned from being coached in tennis.

There are two types of coaches. There is the kind of coach who teaches you how to do it and then pushes you really hard and he doesn't care about your personality or the issues you're dealing with. I never wanted to be a coach like that. Then there is the coach who gives you the skills and then he works on the motivation. He brings the two together by building your self-esteem, and some people just take off with that.

I returned to Albuquerque, my hometown, after graduating and worked for a truck-leasing company and I really didn't like it. Then I went back to school and took more education courses. I got into the master's program at the University of New Mexico and I came to this school as a substitute teacher one day. The kids had done a really good job in class that day, so I took them out to play basketball. I figured that was the best way to reward them. The principal saw me doing that. He hired me because he had seen me interacting with the kids.

That is what led me into teaching. There was no big decision. There was no great decision to change the world, but I guess I am an optimist. I have this ability to find the good in anybody and that is why I am teaching special education. I really think that I am here for a reason. The hardest, most screwed-up kid, I can take that kid when nobody else can and give him or her what they need to do the things that they are going to have to do in life. I try not to control a kid. Control is really easy to do. My philosophy is that of a facilitator.

Barbara Knowles teaches sixth grade at a private school, Hampton Roads Academy, in Newport News, Virginia:

I've taught in public school and private school and also at the university level. It is interesting that I didn't find much competition in public school. In fact, there was almost no competition.

But I looked at those kids and wondered what they were going to do with their lives. I was trying to teach those eighth graders what I am teaching now in a sixth-grade class. Nothing was working. I had discipline problems, I had kids drooling on their desks, kids without pencils and paper, who couldn't care less.

I backed off and thought that there was zero competition here, and asked myself, what am I preparing them for? I wasn't preparing them for reality. Because their reality isn't what mine is, or what my kids' is. And I'm saying to myself, thank goodness.

Finally, I remember going around and getting McDonald's and Wendy's applications, and in my mind I was thinking is this as high as my expectations go for these eighth graders? So I showed them how to do those applications, and that is the only thing I accomplished that year.

I realized that following the curriculum wasn't doing the eighth graders any good and it wasn't doing me any good. So we learned how to fill out different applications and write a brief biographical paragraph. It has been a real pleasure in years since then, that I have seen many of those kids, at Hardee's and McDonald's, taking orders. The parents that I dealt with at that school, that's about the kind of job that that parent had. So if you had parents who aren't modeling an education and a business, and competitiveness (which I'm not saying is entirely healthy), where are you going to get these priorities?

Craig Lancto taught English at George Washington Junior High School in Alexandria, Virginia, before moving recently to T. C. Williams High School there:

When I first starting teaching, I always thought a silent classroom was an efficient classroom. I remember one time we were doing prepositions. Talk about something that is the heart and soul of excitement. I was saying, "So it can go — " and the kids would yell "in" or "out" or "around."

Eventually the principal heard the noise and came in and stood against the wall and just watched. I said, "Maybe we can get a volunteer from the audience. Mr. O, give us a hand." I explained that we were studying prepositions and said, "The man 'something' the stool, and we will see if the volunteer can do it."

So the kids said, "The man walked over the stool. The man walked around the stool. The man walks under the stool."

Well, the man had not said a word since coming in the room. At the last command, he just snapped his fingers at two students. They stood and held up the stool. He walked under. The kids were screaming, whistling, stamping their feet. They went wild. I learned later that Mr. O went to the room next door, the nurse's office, and asked, "You hear all that noise?" The nurse nodded, and he said, "I did it, it's my fault. I caused it all."

I realized that noisy is sometimes good. I don't know what good prepositions do them, but we have to teach them, and they learned them that day. Now, when I look around and see the child who, at the beginning of the year, was a troublecauser and he's talking about sentence structure with another student, or I see the child who couldn't write a sentence helping someone else, I think this is good noise. I've come far from thinking that the silent classroom is a learning classroom.

Jane Starner is head of the English Department at Warsaw High School in Warsaw, Indiana:

Sometimes it seems like teaching is getting harder. You want to get kids excited and say, "Let's do this," and they just sit there. I teach a class called "Art and English." We are studying Christo. We started with Robert Frost and "Mending Wall" and we led into Christo. We studied the Wailing Wall. We went to a synagogue and we studied the Chagall windows at the Art Institute in Chicago and the Vietnam Wall Memorial. Then we got to Christo. Then we talked about what we could do. We talked about wrapping something in school or making a wall. Sometimes the kids said that it sounded like too much work, like, "Don't bother us with this. Are you crazy?"

We have this gorgeous new school, beautiful stairways, courtyards. It cries out to say, "Let's take this area and do this with it." It would be so great if they wanted to do this and would work in teams or as a whole class. But I am not really optimistic. I guess it is just a lot harder to try to get them to do anything that isn't writing papers and doing study sheets and taking tests.

Michelle Kaufman teaches fifth grade at Anna Howard Shaw Elementary School (Public School 61) on New York City's Lower East Side:

I remember the things teachers did and said to me twenty years ago — the kind word, the nasty thing. I remember it like it was yesterday. I think a teacher has to remember that words and gestures are powerful. And that they are in a very powerful position in relation to children. Once you say the words, it's very hard to take them back. They're like arrows. You must weigh what you say and do.

I tell my kids today that I will never embarrass them. If they make an error at the board, big deal. I'm not going to eat them alive. They are learning. I will never humiliate a child.

Sherley Keith teaches eighth-grade English at St. Stephen's and St. Agnes, a private school in Alexandria, Virginia:

Teaching is a very pleasant job. It is a very demanding job in that your ego is on the line all the time. You have to be pumped up all the time to be a good teacher. You just cannot go in bored. You can go in tired, but you better know what you are going to be teaching. And you better consider the makeup of each individual class. You can't necessarily do with third period what worked in first. You have to be sensitive to the way each group learns and present the same material in a way that will be stimulating for each bunch.

For me, this is a ministry, a sort of spiritual calling. It is what pulled me back into teaching and keeps me here. There's no way around it. A sense that I really think my colleagues and I are really touching lives and changing them. I don't think anything ever means any more than their school experience. It is the most profoundly shaping force in a child's life, after the family. We are nurturing something precious in each child, helping them find something valuable.

Kathy Johnson teaches kindergarten at the Katherine and Jacob Greenfield Elementary School, part of a Hebrew academy in Miami:

Teaching is bringing children out of the school who are socially responsible human beings. Teaching them values and morals. Setting up a classroom of trust where a child can feel free. Setting up an atmosphere of learning, getting a child to think. It doesn't matter how, presenting situations and problems, teaching them to think, to be socially responsible human beings.

A child should learn patience. We don't allow a child to wait. They want it now and we give it to them now because we don't want to hear the whining or the crying or we don't want to see them sad. It's a developmental stage that they go through at about four years old. The child who is allowed to develop that patience does well as he gets older. It's a matter of beginning when they're young. They want a drink now. Tell them it's okay, you're on the phone, trust you, in five minutes they'll get their drink. It's allowing them to have a period of time when they have to wait, and then they see that they waited and yes, it still came to them. Nothing bad happened in between. They occupied their mind with a toy or a book, and then the period can get longer. They have to wait ten minutes, thirty minutes. I was not one of those who thought, God forbid that my child should have any uncomfortable feelings. We don't allow them to be uncomfortable. And I guess that's where it starts.

Tom Starnicky teaches science in grades four through eight at Walt Disney Magnet School in Chicago:

There's a tremendous amount of really interesting, vital teaching going on, but what scares me is the lack of learning at the other end. We have a large number of children who are below level. Seventy-one percent of our black males in this school are underachievers. I know there are a lot of social problems out there, but we're teaching all the children, and they're not learning like the others. What can we do to change it so that we can get them learning and moving at a faster rate?

We don't know the answer. We're trying a different approach to reading. We're trying to get them to write, to express themselves more. We're doing much more writing. We're trying to get books, short stories, and get each one of them a copy so each one of them can have this book in their own hands, to read this and write their reactions and feelings. Get them writing, get them involved, get them doing. Hopefully the reading will come up, and the grammar can come, and the spelling will come after that.

John Scott turned to teaching after working as a road manager for jazzman Miles Davis. Now an English teacher at Hampton High School in Hampton, Virginia, Scott still finds a relationship to performing:

You get a chance to do five numbers a day for forty minutes a time. Five forty-minute sets and you go home. If I could teach this way, I would probably teach forever. If I could give my papers to someone else to correct, I'd do this forever. That part is fine. I don't mind the questions, the explaining, anything else. It is just the intrusion that this profession makes on your life. You end up with papers, and you need strategies, rationales, and administrative dance.

I used to be the most impatient teacher in this school. I'd zip through a lesson in three days. That's it, next, just like the barber shop. Now I take my time. What we cover, we cover very thoroughly. What we don't cover, that is an experience you will have to delay to another time in your educational development.

Good teachers grow with the job, as Darlene McCampbell, who teaches high school English at the University of Chicago's Lab School, discovered:

This was not exactly my best moment in teaching, but it was deeply important. I had assigned a review, asking the students to write a little paragraph to prove one point with evidence from the text of the story. I was starting to evaluate what they had written partly by the substance of what they were saying.

On the bottom of one paper I wrote, beginning with an apology, "If I am wrong about this, John, forgive me. But you have already shown in the last couple of paragraphs that you know how to use the form and shape a paragraph. Now it is time to use that form to say something."

It was a pretty ruthless statement I had made. The boy came up after I had returned the papers and he was pale and upset. He looked me in the eye and said, "I worked on this for two hours. I don't know what you want." I went home that night. I had been teaching at that point for ten years. I was puzzled and didn't understand what he meant by not knowing what I was after. I tried to pin down what I was after for myself.

The next day when I went to class, the story we were working on was James Joyce's "The Boarding House," and I read the first sentence out loud to the kids. It went something like, "She was the butcher's daughter."

I asked the kids what they knew from that first sentence. They said, "We know her socioeconomic status." End. And then I asked them, "What do you do when you read?" What emerged was that they read for the plot. I had been teaching literature for ten years and I didn't know that. They said that once they knew what happened, it was over for them. That was all. And then what I hadn't bothered to find out, or what I hadn't been bright enough to know before, came clear and then I started to have some notion of what to do. At once it connected for me what reading meant to them.

I said for them to close their books. I put the word "butcher" on the board. I said, "Forget that we have been reading the story. Forget literature. What are your associations with the word 'butcher'?" We filled the blackboard with their associations: cleaver, bloody, meat, food, chopping, parts, whatever. I said, "Don't censor. Let the source of your insight go."

At some point in the discussion, I don't know how long we went on, one girl raised her hand and said, "May I open my book?" She said she wanted to find something, it was a line in the middle of the story that went something like, "She dealt with moral problems the way a butcher cleaves meat."

For her, and for me, that was a real beginning. That was also a really painful moment for me. But when that boy came up and said, "I don't know what you want," I had to question all the years I had been teaching. If I didn't know that he didn't know that, what did I know? I couldn't begin to help him get better. He confronted me with my own ignorance.

I had been teaching a long time and I had thought I was a pretty good teacher. Anytime when there is the beginning of what turns into a profound change, an illumination that forces everything into re-sorting itself, it is very painful. In a way, I associate those with best moments, not the initial painfulness, but the later growth.

Sherrill Neale teaches reading to fourth, fifth, and sixth graders at Patrick Henry Elementary School in Alexandria, Virginia:

Effective teachers are people who can be given a goal and told to go ahead. A teacher who is not as effective does it only by the book. My test scores in Charles County were as high or higher as any other room, and I did it my way. If we were doing dinosaurs, we did dinosaurs. We did reading, we did research, and no one said, "Mrs. Neale, you have to be on page sixteen tomorrow."

There are counties in Maryland and Virginia where you are rated on what page they're on at a point in the school year. That's an administrative choice. Don't you find that hard to believe? Isn't that scary?

Ricki Weyhe is a language arts teacher at Miami Beach Senior High School in Miami Beach, Florida:

Early in my career I assumed everyone was equal and the same and they should learn everything the same. I made every student memorize a Shakespearean monologue. Several years ago, I came home, pulled into the driveway, and a voice boomed from what I thought were the heavens, saying, "All the world's a stage and all the men and women merely players."

I looked up and there was a power-line man up there. He looked down and said, "Mrs. Weyhe? I knew I'd get to use that someday." It humbled me. He had no need to know that, really. I think we have to look at kids as people and realize there are differences, and that whether Kenneth knew Shakespeare or not really didn't make a lot of difference ultimately in his job career and his life.

Paul Hirko taught math at Miami Beach Senior High School but is now assistant principal at Westview Middle School in Miami:

Teaching can be equated to the skills of salesmanship. A lot of people, when we talk about sales, get a very negative image. But if you take a lot of ideas from the salesmanship seminars and tapes, the motivational material, and apply them in the classroom, they all work very, very well.

Listen to Zig Ziegler on "Meet You at the Top" and you take some of those ideas and start talking about win-win situations and putting kids in situations where you get what you want out of them and they get something out of it in return. Kids respond. They learn as a result.

Molly Donohue is a third-grade teacher at Francis Parker School in Chicago:

I had a little boy in my class who, because of the way his brain works and the way the genes came together and his body is functioning, gets lost. He's lost a good portion of the time. So he needs to keep putting himself back into the world in the right way, finding out where he belongs and what is expected.

I walked into my room, saw him stumble into three desks and fall over two kids, and then I started to talk to the class and I watched his eyes glaze over after a minute or two because he was still processing what I said before. By the time he was done and he came back to the class, I was three steps down the way and you could just see the fright start in his face.

Some teachers can ignore that. I'm no good at observing classes because I can sit there and start feeling the people who are dying. I think it's because I died in school. I know that feeling. Inside my body I know that fear. I'm not sure if you can empathize with that if you didn't experience it somewhere in your life. It didn't have to be in school, but somewhere you were not able to do something the world thought you should be able to do. If you've ever been unacceptable, and not of your own making, then you'll never miss that feeling. You can feel it in the air.

So here's this boy. He's dying. He wants to be good. He wants the world to see him, know him, hear him. Help, he can't process it. And he's a bright kid. So what you do is start on this, and after a couple of things I'll say, ''Oh, wait a minute. What is it we're going to do first?'' So I'll act out what his confusion is. Or I'll say, ''Oh, wait a minute, guys. Did I say, 'Help me out here, I don't know where I'm going next'?''

When you teach you have to be able to judge a situation and immediately move to it, and you have to have the skill to make those readjustments constantly. It's like playing a game where there's an offense and a defense. You have your agenda: I want them to learn quotation marks, but I can't make them learn quotation marks unless they're with me. So I'll say something, and then I'll watch, and if they're not there I'll readjust what I'm saying to bring them back again. It's not hard work.

My maiden name was Molly McGuinn, but there is this Mrs. Donohue character who teaches. I have no idea how she knows what to do. I have no control over what she does. There are no words attached to what she does. I can walk up in front of a class and she just takes over my body. She responds and reacts and thinks of things to say, and it's like being an actress. There's this person I create for the kids. It's not Molly McGuinn who has three children who she screamed at every afternoon as soon as school was over. It wasn't the Molly McGuinn who got a divorce after fifteen years. That person is a human, still struggling along.

But this Mrs. Donohue character who has been in the third-grade room for sixteen years, who kids think of as understanding and being able to help them learn, is another lady. That lady has the ability to judge situations very quickly and respond in lots of different ways to the same thing.

The problem with most teachers, I think, is that they don't have a wide enough set of personal experiences to encompass all the kinds of children they have in their classroom. They can only teach to part of their class. I think that my growing-up experience helped me relate to a lot more kids. I had the learning disability troubles, so those kids who have difficulty with the codes of our society, I know their feelings. I had an alcoholic father who never worked from the time I was in third grade, so those kids who have family issues going on, I understand. I was the youngest of four children, so I know what that was. My mother's family has been in Chicago since 1850 and were fairly prominent people, so I know those pressures of how you're supposed to behave and what it means to be a so-and-so. We grew up every summer on the farm, so those kids who love the out-of-doors and are physical, I know those people. That's a part of me.

————————————————————

CHAPTER 12

WHO IS TO BLAME?

THE ROBERT TAYLOR HOMES, a two-mile-long stretch of high-rise buildings running parallel to the Dan Ryan Expressway, has the dubious title of being the largest of Chicago's nineteen public housing developments. Shootings, rapes, and robberies are part of everyday life for the fifteen thousand people living there. As far back as 1968, a presidential commission on urban problems described Chicago's public housing this way: "The . . . child caught in such a social environment is living almost in a concentration camp from which he has little chance of escape."

Not much has changed since then, and the slim chance of escape for the children of this camp is usually found at school. For many of those who live in Robert Taylor Homes, their first school is Mary C. Terrell Elementary, a low-rise brick building surrounded by a tall security fence. However, by the time children reach the relative safety and order of Terrell Elementary, many are so far behind that they never catch up.

Sitting in her office one day, principal Reva Hairston told the story of a single child whose deficiencies were emblematic of the troubles confronting not only the teachers at Terrell Elementary but also teachers everywhere dealing with large numbers of disadvantaged children:

We have kids starting school without the givens. You assume that kids know their colors, that they know their first and last names, something about their birthdays. They know Mommy's first and last name, or a telephone number and an address.

Our children, if you say "Where do you live?" they will either say "a red building" or "a white building," based on the color of the brick. It is not important to them to know their address. So we have to say, "Suppose you get sick. We need to know the number on your building and what apartment you live in."

Two years ago, the most amazing thing happened. It was a Friday. Everybody had gone. It was getting to be 4:00 P.M. and I wanted to get out, too. This kid was sitting in the office, waiting to be picked up, a little kindergartener. He didn't know his name, he said. Of course, he didn't know his address.

I said, "Well, what's your teacher's name?" He didn't know. At that time, the two kindergarten teachers were white, so asking if she were a white woman wouldn't help me figure this out. I was looking for a clue to his identity.

I thought I had a brilliant idea. I said, "Does your mommy have company? Do people come by to visit her?" He said, "Yes."

I said, "And they knock on the door. Mommy opens it, and she says 'Hi' to them. What do they say?"

"Yo bitch," he said.

The child was crying. So was I.

It is fashionable these days to discuss the "accountability" of teachers. Most often, the word is wielded as a weapon by administrators, parents, and experts. They demand that teachers be held "accountable" for the decay of public education. Proposals are advanced — and, in some cases, implemented — to link teacher pay to the test scores of their students; the scores become the measure not so much of the children but of their instructors.

As in any profession, teaching has its great teachers, its competent teachers, and its poor teachers. The problem, however, with teaching is that the stakes are so high, making the price for incompetency too steep. Parents are understandably angry and frustrated when they find their children in class with an incompetent teacher. The reaction intensifies when they discover that getting rid of a bad teacher is almost impossible.

As Linda Raines, a second-grade teacher in Greencastle, Indiana, aptly described the responsibilities confronting every teacher, "If I fail, I've wasted a whole year of a child's life."

Yet the problems in removing poor teachers have been illustrated dramatically in Rochester, New York. An attempt to rebuild the ailing public schools there linked teacher pay with incentives for reform, such as improving test scores and weeding out weak teachers. By 1992, five years into the program, the personnel chief for the schools estimated that only two of the two thousand tenured teachers had been removed, and test scores had improved only modestly.

Current teacher evaluations are arbitrary and superficial in most districts. When congressional investigators looked into the subject in Washington, D.C., they found that all but 621 of the city's 5,909 public school teachers had been rated "very good" or "outstanding" in 1991. That same year, 3,000 students dropped out of the capital's schools.

However, there is merit to some arguments for evaluating teacher performance on the basis of student performance. There is no chance of reversing the decline in American schools unless teachers do a better job and are held accountable for what occurs inside their classroom. The question is how.

This recognition that teacher performance must be improved is the force behind the movement toward creating a national board to set professional standards for teachers. While other professions have established standards for admissions, efforts to promote a national certification program for teachers have languished — or been actively blocked by powerful teachers' unions.

Even implacable foes of national standards concede that teachers must be accountable for teaching children the skills that they need to improve the future for themselves and the country. The best teachers are the angriest at colleagues who have lost their enthusiasm for education, who show up late regularly, and who rely on the rote of lesson plans. At Terrell Elementary, Reva Hairston says that she would put a third of her teachers up against the best in any school district in the country. Another third, she says, are satisfactory. A final third, however, Hairston vows she would fire today, if only she had the power to do so.

Any time a group of teachers gathers to gripe about their jobs, the issue of accountability will arise before the conversation gets too far along. Perhaps more than any of the criticisms heaped on them by parents and politicians and education officials, teachers are most angered by the notion that they must be accountable for the total performance of their students. This notion, they argue, makes teachers responsible for factors outside the school grounds over which they have absolutely no control.

"Accountability doesn't take into account where these kids are coming from, and that's not fair," fumed Alice Golub, who teaches at a public school in Miami.

As in so many areas of education today, the key to improvement lies in understanding that teachers and parents are not natural adversaries, that the system will work only when there is an alliance between educators and those outside the system. A central element of that alliance depends on the ability of parents, education officials, and others to recognize that account-ability does not rest solely with the teacher.

"For far too long, teachers have been seen as part of the problem, not the solution, but when all is said and done, excellence in education means excellence in teaching, and whatever is wrong with America's schools can-not be fixed without the help of those already in the classroom," says Ernest L. Boyer, president of the Carnegie Foundation for the Advance-ment of Teaching.

One of the teachers Hairston would put up against the best anywhere is Carolyn Epps Jackson, an articulate young woman whose silk dress brushes the floor as she sits in the classroom at Terrell, where she teaches a class of second and third graders:

I think that the accountability, the way it is now, is unfair. If you take a group of children and at the end of that school year they can read, write, and do whatever math is appropriate for that grade level, then you have succeeded. If they come in way below level and they gain a year or more in your class, then you have succeeded. They know considerably more than when they walked in your door. It has to be relative. If you can't read at all and you're twelve years old, but by June you can read a first-grade book, you have learned. Even though it is not ideal, and it is certainly not where you should be, you've succeeded.

We must all be held accountable — teachers, parents, school, the commu-nity. I have them for only seven hours. If nothing is going on at home, then that means my job is harder. Then I have to do the things that the parents should be doing. Politicians are at fault because they don't want to provide enough funds. I can only do so much with limited resources. I have twenty-six children, which isn't a bad number in a public school, but ideally I should have fifteen. I should have more computers and all sorts of books. I should have things to make it more interesting, and then easier. There should be all sorts of labs the children could go to. But the money isn't there, or at least it is not being spent on these things.

I would like a rug on the floor. We should have tables instead of desks. It would be nice if we could have an art center. You can go broke buying your own art stuff, but you find places where you can get special things — like a pound of feathers, sequins, buttons. Teacher aides would help because that way, if a child needs a little extra, it's possible.

When people say teachers, they only work eight to three, they get summers off, it's an easy job, I want to kill them. I want to say, "Hey, come in here for the day." Actually, I used to think that way until I started doing this. In these seven hours, I am on my feet all day long, talking constantly, keeping twenty-six little bodies and minds motivated doing stuff that I want them to do, which usually isn't exactly what they want to do. Sure I can have summers off, but I need them. You have a short day, but at three-fifteen I am so tired. I don't have a desk and a phone. I can't put someone on hold. I can't close the door. I can't go to the bathroom when I want. I have to stay here and grin and bear it until it is time to go to lunch. I have people crying, sick, and with runny noses.

If you're in an office and you have twenty grown employees, you can say, "Okay, Bob, you do this and this and I can come back and get it." And everyone gets to close a door.

It is hard to show some of these kids a textbook full of pictures with children in suburbia. They don't live like that. They don't know anybody who does. That is not real to them. They don't care about that. Those sorts of things need to change.

Expecting children to sit still is ludicrous. Children cannot sit still. Sure it's easier if they're quiet, but they don't sit still. But that is not how kids are, or how they learn.

We're treating kids like little adults. They are not. Years ago, attitudes were different. There was more corporal punishment, in schools as well as at home. God forbid, you didn't want the teacher to call home, because after getting hit at school, you'd get hit at home. I think for some kids there are too many consequences — no matter what it is, you're going to be in trouble about something.

I think the whole curriculum should be changed. I think the expectations should be a little more realistic. They need to take into account when I have a child coming from a home where there has been no reading going on, no education of any kind going on.

Many of the standardized tests that children take are based upon a white, middle-class environment. If these kids have no idea what the test is talking about, how are they going to give the right answer? It doesn't mean they are any less intelligent, or mean that they can't perform. It means only that they don't know what this is. So there has got to be a way of testing knowledge without penalizing children for not having the same kinds of experiences.

There used to be this question that burned me up: "A buffalo: Is it a fish or a cow?" Many of the kids in this area will answer a fish, but they get it wrong on the test. They don't know it looks like a cow. They think it is the fish they can buy at the corner store. From this environment, the fish answer is right. They might not know that Indians used to kill buffalo. Or even if they do know it, their immediate response will be fish because that is what they see every day. Those sorts of questions penalize children.

Pat Maier is a teacher of French at Palos Verdes Peninsula High School outside Los Angeles:

My first year I taught in Ohio. I was nineteen. They needed a teacher. I needed a job. I had one of those special credentials to allow me to teach. It was the most interesting year I ever taught. I was supposed to teach Spanish, English literature, and run the library. I immediately closed the library because none of the books had ever been cataloged.

That was the year I had Phillip in my class. Phillip, who was older than I was. He came in and said, "I got to graduate and get out of this school, lady. I got to go to barber school. I want to be a barber."

I said, "Well, Phillip, you do your work and you'll graduate."

He said, "Yeah? But I got a problem: I can't read."

"You what?" I said.

I opened up the literature book and asked him to read a paragraph. The first word was "the" and he couldn't read it.

"Oh, shit," I thought. What am I going to do with this kid?

Anyway, I got to listening to him and he could tell me verbatim what I had said in class two weeks earlier, right down to crossing the *t*'s and dotting the *i*'s. So I went to the history teacher and asked him to give him his next test both written and orally. He got an A on the oral and flunked the written. He was telling the truth.

So I went down to the elementary school and I got this special reading program. He came in at lunchtime and we started learning the alphabet and sounds. The greatest moment in my life was when he came in to me and said, "Hey, lady, do you know what I was doing this morning?"

I said, "No, Phillip. What were you doing this morning?"

And he said, "Reading the words on the milk carton."

God, I had to leave the classroom and cry.

I think teachers have to be accountable, but I am not necessarily in favor of standardized tests for students. I don't think they take care of the issue. Instead, they create a minimum level of competency rather than a maximum level of competency. Standardized tests are generally multiple-guess, whereas they should be written tests. We need to change the testing situation in the United States 100 percent. Of course, I believe that we need some kind of national education standards in the United States desperately.

It's a touchy issue because you don't always have great students. You can get a bad class. By bad class I don't mean bad kids. I mean they might not be up to par. You could just have a bad year, when your best friend is dying or you're going through a divorce. Or there may be a chemistry that just doesn't work because each class has its own global personality.

Over the continuum, we still need to have standards, and I believe that pay has to be tied to accountability. I also believe that all kids can learn something.

Sherry McCarty left another school in Albuquerque, New Mexico, to teach at Van Buren Middle School because she admired its reform-minded principal, Gary Hocevar, and his efforts to involve teachers in running the school. She teaches language arts:

We are held accountable already, but it is a lousy way to do it. We are held accountable by tests like the SATs and ACTs. These things don't talk to you about what the child knows. They provide only an estimated guess at what the child might minimally know. We are working on something else.

I am cochair of a committee to study curriculum and evaluation, and we are looking at alternative assessments. One alternative is the portfolio, where the kids put samples of their best works — writings, videos, best speeches, best dances.

We are also looking at getting the kids out into the community, at taking them to elementary schools for tutoring elementary kids, getting them to the high schools to work with older students on the computers, and getting them into the business community to see how they work. We want critical thinkers, kids who can make decisions and react positively to lots of situations.

Personally, I would like to see us assess each individual student with a panel of teachers and other students so the kid's final performance is just a culmination of several smaller performances, each time getting it more perfect. They could be graduation performances. It would be verbal, visual, and written.

Kids have to do so much more. They have to read and write, think, measure, make their best guesses in a situation where there isn't enough information to make a real decision. They have to be able to ask questions and find information from lots of sources — people, books, and computers. They have to be able to persuade other people — to be able to return a dress to a store, to be able to convince the social worker that they will be a good mother.

I hope the mission of our public schools is changing. I hope we are beginning to meet the needs of the community. Our community doesn't need cookie-cutter kids. It doesn't need an assembly-line education. It needs us to address the individual child, based on exactly what his or her needs are.

Rita Gilbert teaches at South Pointe Elementary School in Miami Beach, Florida:

I am accountable for Rita. I can only do so much, and I have no control over what happened to my sixth graders in first through fifth grades. We have to draw lines of who is accountable for what.

If you really want to talk about accountability, you have to start in kindergarten and look at who passed them and who did not remediate. In Florida, you are discouraged from retaining kids, especially if they have already been retained once. Especially in sixth grade, there is this feeling that kids should stay with their classes. You don't want big kids in with the little ones.

It's frightening, but what do you do? They put so much pressure on teachers for performance when they should involve others, too. What about parents? If you know Johnny is not functioning on a fifth-grade level, why don't you spend some extra time with him? Or get some extra tutoring?

I had one parent tell me I just don't know what I am going to do about Johnny. "Well," I said, "can't you work with him? He isn't performing, he won't get serious."

The parent replied, "Well, why don't you do something?"

I said, "You can't expect me to do for your child what you haven't done in eleven years."

When parents throw their hands in the air like this, that's frightening. Then who is really accountable? Can the teacher really be a miracle worker?

Most of Mark Mattson's art students at Francis Parker School in Chicago come from backgrounds of far more privilege than those of Rita Gilbert, but he, too, bristles at the blame heaped on his profession:

"Accountability" is a big buzzword. We have always been held accountable. Always. We are always being evaluated, scrutinized, and tested. Back in the early 1980s, when there was a lot of criticism directed toward teachers, I was absolutely dumbfounded by the fact that nobody questioned principals or superintendents or boards of education. Nobody is criticizing the taxpayers for saying, "No, I don't want to put more money in the schools." The teacher is working with a shrinking budget and more kids in the classroom. But it is all the teacher's fault.

Marion Clermont teaches at Tilden High School in Brooklyn, New York City:

I resent parents and people in the community who have not been into a school lately putting all the blame on the teachers. That is a crock. Granted, there is some deadwood in the system, but I tell you from the heart, the majority of the teachers do their best. They dress well. They come to school prepared. They want to do their job — at least the teachers I have known throughout my career. There are a few, how they got into or through the system is beyond me. They are basket cases, just doing time, but that is not the majority.

I think the problem is a political thing. It is beyond a teacher's control. The paperwork, the red tape, the administration, the people in charge. What matters more to them is statistics, numbers, balancing out the quotas, and making sure the superintendent sees so many passing grades. I have been told in the past that I have to pass so many students. When I say, "But they can't do the work," they say, "Well, it's up to you."

Accountability has been a hot issue among teachers in Florida because of attempts by the state legislature in Tallahassee to adopt standards for evaluating teacher performance. Third-grade teacher Alice Golub was angered by the narrowness of the solution:

They've started in Tallahassee now. They want accountability. Yet they take no account of what's going on in their homes, no account of their background.

Accountability wants me to motivate a child who has no interest. Unless the child just has a love for learning, loves to read — and you know how many of those there are — he is not going to learn without support from the home. What am I supposed to do? You can't ignore the home.

Sanford Bearman, who also teaches in the Miami public schools, expressed similar complaints:

Accountability is something you have to live with. I can look at it from three different points of view. As a parent, I want to know the quality of education going on in my children's school. When they publish the testing scores, I want to see how my son's elementary school is doing. There has to be some form of accountability, but it has to be across the board.

Students have to be accountable. Teachers have to be accountable. Administrators have to be accountable, and let's not forget the parents. I am all for laws that say that if kids do damages, the parents are responsible for the costs of the damage. I am also for holding parents responsible for how their kids do in school and for making sure they are in school.

But I am not happy with the new accountability bill coming down from Tallahassee. I don't think the process will take into account all the variables: Do we measure a first-year teacher the same way as a sixth-year teacher or as a teacher with twenty years in? Do we measure a teacher teaching at the Highland Oaks Elementary School, which is an upper-middle-class, predominantly white school, the same way we would measure someone teaching at an inner-city school? How do you keep track of the variables and make it fair?

Then, what happens when the students don't progress? Do you punish the teacher? The plan coming from Tallahassee is punitive. We have found in Dade County that punitive measures do not make better teachers, just lower morale. I find that if you want to get a better product, you get more with honey than vinegar. A reward system works much better than a punitive system.

The state of Florida has one system for evaluating teachers, and Dade County has another. We have TASK — teacher assessment and development system. Teachers are observed and asked to perform at certain minimums. If they go beyond that, fine. If they don't, the system offers them opportunities to remediate. If they do not, then they begin the process of termination.

After twenty-three years, I have seen about half a dozen teachers dismissed. The process is there for removing a teacher if the principal is willing to pursue it. The union position is that the teachers are guaranteed due process the entire way and the opportunity to remediate themselves. If they refuse, eventually they will get dismissed. It is much easier to do with a first-year teacher. But you know, things happen, divorces, family changes, sometimes people just have a bad year. Does that mean they should be dismissed?

You can run education like a business, but not like a profit-making business. Business is not put under the constraints with its products as we are with teachers, such as you must keep these students in school until they are age sixteen. They are not put under the constraint that you have to teach them all the different subject areas, and that you have students coming and going — transients. You have students of different ability levels. Students who speak different languages. Students with different backgrounds at home. All these variables make it a lot different from running a business.

There is some merit to the businessman's comments about education. There should be a process to reward the best teachers, just like they give bonuses and better raises to those who do best in sales or the best in management. Everyone knows who the best teachers are. They just have the knack for getting the most out of their kids year in and year out. It doesn't have to be the top-level kids.

Artie Sinkfield is a tough disciplinarian with high expectations for her colleagues and her students. She is chairwoman of the Science Department and a teacher at Brownsville Middle School, which is in a low-income section of North-Central Miami:

The accountability law is unreal, because people — children and grown folk alike — operate at different levels. All people are not going to excel at the same level. I don't care how much effort the teachers put there, some of them are not going to excel, and I don't think it's fair to judge teachers this way.

The home environment has a lot to do with how well children do in school. The neighborhoods, health problems, there are so many factors. A lot of times a child's success is based on whether or not he is in the right program.

I think they need to look at the way they've structured education to the point where the question should be whether all children go on to the next level. Maybe some should go into vocational education at a certain level. Once they have reached a certain peak, if they show no interest in school, and you get them to a point where they are equipped to handle high school, if they can do nothing else, they will at least leave the school setting with a trade or something that they can survive with.

You have to look at it this way: There are parents with five or six children, and they do their best for all the children. Maybe three of them will excel and go beyond what is expected of them, and maybe one of them will do average, and the other will do nothing. It's the same way with school. They don't hold the parent accountable, and I don't think they should hold the teacher accountable for what didn't happen.

Besides, unless the state and government are willing to put the money there for smaller classes, they can forget about accountability.

When there is a widespread sense that a new reform has fixed the education system, pressure builds on teachers for quick results. Parents want to see test scores go up and dropout rates come down. These expectations are often unrealistic, particularly in the short run. Teachers at the Walt Disney School, a magnet school that draws elementary and middle-school students from throughout Chicago, have experienced some of those unrealistic expectations. Tom Starnicky, who is head of the Science Department at Disney, says:

I know a lot of teachers are frustrated. They're frustrated because they feel there is all kinds of pressure on them for the children to perform for these tests, and everything they do is relegated to a number as to how they're teaching or how they are doing with the children. I sense resentment.

As a teacher, you're looking at a year's effort with a child, and you're putting it down to a single number. This child is four months below grade level, and it is as if you have not done your job, and there are possibilities that this child is four months above what he would be without your efforts. That isn't seen, though.

The only thing that really bothers me with this whole accountability situation is the test interpretation. All of a sudden everybody should be scoring at or above normal. I can understand when 50 percent of the children would be above normal, but if they're using standardized tests, 50 percent will be below normal. But that is not acceptable. Everybody must be at norm or above. I don't think it's realistic.

Gail Davis teaches at Hilton Elementary School in Newport News, Virginia:

I would be willing to say you can pay me on how well my children perform in my class, provided I have 100 percent support from the parents and the principal. You can pay me on how good their test scores are, based, of course, also on their abilities. I can't be held accountable if I don't get the support I need.

But I have worked for principals who say you do it this way, you do it this way, you do it this way. So I do it that way when I am observed, but when the door is closed I do it the way I think is best. Teaching the same grade for years, I can use some of the same lessons, but also I have to change, add, delete, lower the level, increase the level, add enrichment activities.

Billy Sue Vogel teaches at Claude Pepper Elementary School in Miami:

Children learn at different rates. They all learn to walk at different times. They all learn to talk at different times. Yet we plunk them in school when they turn five by September 1 and we expect them all to do the same thing. Sometimes there is just a developmental lag there. It doesn't mean the child isn't bright. They may just not be ready.

You should be able to say to a parent, "This is where your child was when he entered in September and this is a sample of what he can do now." It is not an issue of whether it is A work or B work. It is how much the child has grown in the time, but this approach is going to take a lot of parent education.

I really don't have positive feelings about judging children by test scores because there is always going to be a bottom and a top. Just because you can score on the test doesn't mean you can go out and be successful. I don't think it is realistic.

Jeffrey Calkins recently left teaching after several years as a history teacher at Hampton Roads Academy, a private school in Newport News, Virginia:

I don't subscribe to the philosophy that if a kid doesn't learn, the teacher is a bad teacher. That is not necessarily true. I think some kids are not interested in learning. It's not like Lake Wobegon, where every kid is above average. There are some kids who are not good students. A teacher will not always succeed with everybody.

The teacher should be accountable for his material. He should have a certain amount of knowledge about the subject, and should be able to control his classroom and have the respect of his students and the faculty.

Alan Marks is a former New Mexico teacher of the year. Educated in law and business, he has a piercing intelligence that sometimes needles colleagues and administrators at Rio Grande High School in Albuquerque, New Mexico, where he teaches the unlikely combination of English and economics:

Here's my biggest criticism of the schools: There is zero accountability. I find nothing, and I went to the state school board when I got recognition and when I was named teacher of the year. What happened was that the people who chose teacher of the year had nothing to do with education. They were industry.

I am appalled by the accountability issue, that kids can go through and learn nothing. The kids are shunted aside. They are patronized.

Let me give you an example from our district. You've seen the film *Stand and Deliver.* You're familiar with the story, which is basically that, given enthusiasm and encouragement, kids from a background whose first language can be anything can certainly be taught to handle mathematics.

Would you agree with me, then, that the top twenty kids in any high school in an evenly distributed city would be roughly as intelligent as the top twenty kids in any other school? That doesn't mean they are going to do as well, or that they are exposed to the same kind of language at home or reading or anything else. Just that they have the same basic native intelligence.

But listen to this. Why is it then that just taking these twenty kids and no one else, why is it that their college entrance scores are hundreds of points and tens of percentile points below their peers' at another school? If these kids are as intelligent, if they're the top kids in the district, and if the school is doing any kind of an adequate job, you would expect that very small percentage of kids to be more or less comparable.

No way. No way. Kids in my school can't do any math. Kids in poor schools across the country can't do any math.

Teachers can get away with teaching almost nothing in areas where parents don't know any better. There is no one pushing them.

I think it's crazy not to have some evaluative instrument that teaches us, that lets us learn from what we're doing. I don't think it happens. I don't think we evaluate ourselves. I don't think our systems evaluate us. We can relieve teachers from the fear that the effort will be to punish teachers by making it bring everybody up, students and teachers alike.

But yes, we're going to have to do some weeding out. That's why I started out being one of the main union organizers in New Mexico and now I find myself being very antagonistic to that same union that tries to protect incompetent people.

Antonio Gil teaches Spanish at West Windsor-Plainsboro High School in Princeton Junction, New Jersey:

Teaching is like any other profession. When you get one hundred people, you are going to get ten people who are relatively inept, thirty people who are average, and hopefully, sixty people who are good to excellent. That's the nature of life. Schools strive to have as many of those sixty as possible join their individual staffs.

Many times you hear people say it is not fair for a teacher to be evaluated based on his student's performance, that it is really not an equitable way of measuring performance. Why not? Because many times the human factor is not taken into consideration. That is, that you can have an excellent teacher who is motivational and who knows the subject matter, is very concerned, prepares his classes, then has a group of students who, for whatever reasons, do not perform as well as the next-door teacher who has done less work, is less prepared, and is less motivational.

Margie Eriacho teaches Indian students at Dowa Yalanne Elementary School on the Zuni Indian reservation in western New Mexico:

I think testing for teacher accountability is good. When we did have testing here, I used to use it for my own purposes. Say there was a child who I thought was maybe top in the class, and then I saw his testing, and I would look and say, "I haven't taught this," or "I should have taught this," or "I just assumed I had taught this." That was a good measure for me.

A lot of us assume that our children are so verbal, that we've taught them or given them enough practice through stories we've read to them over and over again, that receptively they understand. One year, I said to my children, "Let's do some bulletin board decorations. Let's put up pictures of the Little Red Hen." So they were all excited about this. They all got busy. Everybody was through, and I collected the papers. On one of the papers, I got a picture of a little red hand. We had lost that little one to confusion for how long? I think I've become more aware that you need to do assessments. You need to do testing in many more different ways than just pen and paper.

Catie Bell was working as a researcher in Santa Fe, New Mexico, when she got to know some teenagers. She found them to be excited and enthusiastic, which made her wonder why people are so critical of today's young adolescents. Pursuing her curiosity, she became a teacher. It was an interim job, but Bell has found that she enjoys the work and the students in her history classes in the middle school at the University of Chicago Lab School:

I'm not sure that schools have ever been that good. I think that people have a tendency to romanticize their education over the years. So I don't know to what extent schools have ever been that good. The United States has a special problem in education because we are such a diverse population and we believe in democracy and equal opportunity. It's extraordinarily hard to deliver. On the one hand, we believe this, but on the other, we don't pay for it. We don't really make it happen.

Donna Madath teaches third grade at Wadsworth Avenue Elementary School in Los Angeles:

If you're held accountable, that's fine. If you're held accountable on test scores, that's ludicrous. I mean, I took my SATs and just scored through the roof, and then I wanted to score even higher, and I did worse the next time. I didn't know any less. I was just luckier the first time, probably. That's not fair.

But I think that teachers should be held accountable for teaching a curriculum. Most teachers are very, very good, but there are some lazy teachers who need to be held accountable, and I think that is the principal's job.

Dan Ruggaber teaches math at Menchville High School in Newport News, Virginia:

There is a lot of pressure on us to produce passing grades for these kids. The goal is that we are supposed to lower our D's and F's percentage rates. The theory is that we are to do that by bringing the kids up. You lower your standards, of course. I have been told by other teachers that they have been pressured by administration to reduce their numbers. It is handled as if it is a bad reflection on the teacher.

One teacher went back and looked up the past grades and said, "How do you expect me to teach them at this level in a math course, when they were getting D's and F's in the previous level?" If they got a D in Algebra 1, how can they do better than that in Algebra 2?

Marla Sculley teaches seventh grade at St. Isaac Jogues School in Hinsdale, Illinois:

We should be accountable. So should doctors. So should nurses. So should anybody who has the influence that we have. It is serious.

You know, I never pray that I'll be a success as a teacher. I pray that I'll be just, and that I will be fair, because if I am just and fair, everything else will fall into place. I will be a successful teacher.

Parents here are extremely supportive. We have 100 percent attendance at parent-teacher conferences. One hundred percent. I think that is crucial. I don't know if it is what makes a school good, but my heart goes out to those teachers who don't have the support of parents because I'm sure they want for their students what I want for these kids.

I know our parents care, and we're put on the carpet, so to speak. I think parents care more about the result than the process, but doesn't everybody? I think it's okay for parents to care about the end result. They're looking out for the future of their kids. In a lot of respects, what that says is that they trust me. It says to me, "Please, do it right."

Barbara Knowles teaches sixth grade at Hampton Roads Academy in Newport News, Virginia:

Some are quick to give accountability to one person. I think it has to be a combination. We have to have the school counselor help us out, we have to have a good team of teachers whom you trust and work well with, you've got to have the cooperation of the parents. Sometimes we need a psychologist, outside people, brothers, sisters, it's got to be a combination. But in the long run, the bottom line is, the kid has to be accountable.

We use that word a lot in the sixth grade. I told one of my sixth-grade classes this, and they were really surprised to hear it. I may have made a couple of them feel a little guilty. But I was talking about accountability and responsibility, and I said, "I've had conferences with parents in this school (and I'm not talking about any parents in this class), and you know, we sit down and Mrs. X says she doesn't know why her daughter is not doing what she's supposed to be doing, she has everything, the VCR, the TV, and the phone, and the skateboard.

Then I ask what responsibilities the daughter has in the home. Is there anything that she must do to earn these privileges? And Mrs. X says that they don't require her to do anything. And I said to these sixth-grade kids, "Where is the responsibility going to come?" I'm listening to this mother, and I'm saying, "That's it. That's the problem."

Accountability is a big thing, and I think some parents don't think beyond the next skiing trip. They want the child to go to an Ivy League college where he's going to be around people who are just like him. Teachers cannot by themselves instill accountability. They can require it but they have to have backup from the family. Sometimes parents get so caught up in things and their lives are so busy — I can understand that, I've been guilty of it. Face it: It's easier to fix your child's book report yourself than take the time to show him how to do it.

CHAPTER 13

ADVERSARIES

I T IS NOT just education officials and parents who do not listen to America's teachers. Their own principals and other administrators often turn deaf ears to their advice and expertise. Those who know best about how to improve education are too often treated like children — better seen than heard.

The roots of this strict top-to-bottom management go back at least a century to the model for American schools, the factory. American industrial management at the turn of the twentieth century was intent on breaking down as many jobs as possible into rote tasks that could be performed easily and repetitively. This system matched the low skills of the workers and made them little more than interchangeable parts.

The schools that were created to provide these workers were constructed around the same philosophy — that of a hierarchical management that stood as a bulwark against anarchy. It left principals with the decision-making power and relegated teachers to executing policies set by the administration. The emphasis was on uniformity and rigidity. The most extreme example of this philosophy was in Texas, where state law still dictates exactly how many minutes a teacher must spend each day teaching each subject.

As Edward B. Fiske points out in his book *Smart Schools, Smart Kids,* this model worked well enough when the basic task of American schools was turning out millions of workers to perform routine tasks in the country's factories. Students who could not fit into the program were removed from the system; until 1950, roughly half of the students did not graduate from high school. The consequences were not so great because it was possible to get a decent job without a high school diploma.

Times have changed. Schools now are called on to educate students to a much higher level. Students have to be able to think. However, just as American industry has been slow to respond structurally to the more complex demands of the modern world, so American schools have resisted efforts to adjust the management formula.

"The great American school is one of the most conservative, redundant places in America," says Chicago teacher Mark Mattson, who has spent a quarter of a century as a teacher. "Why is education, the place where we are pushing up against the limits of what man can be, full of people who want to maintain the status quo? Does that make any sense?"

Rehabilitating the nation's schools to cope with the demands of the times will require a change in the status quo, disrupting the existing forms of power and opening the way for teachers to become part of the solution. The ultimate task is building the institutional basis for education as a shared enterprise.

One of the first and most notable efforts to recognize the new demands on education and decentralize decision-making occurred in 1985 in Florida's Dade County, which encompasses Miami and is the nation's fourth-largest school system.

The plan centered on a two-step process. First, district administrators granted more autonomy to local schools, allowing them to define some of their own priorities for allocating resources. The concept is known in education circles as school-based or site-based management.

Second, schools were offered the opportunity to place some of the decision-making reserved for the principal in the hands of a governing team. The team could include teachers; clerical, maintenance, and cafeteria staff members; parents; and community representatives. Approval of the principal and a vote of two thirds of the faculty were required to implement the new program. Not every school signed on. Some teachers rejected the notion because they did not want the additional power and accompanying responsibilities.

"I don't think teaching attracts aggressive people," says Jeffrey Calkins, who spent two years as a banker before becoming a teacher in Newport News, Virginia. "I think some people go into teaching because they don't want to have to fight."

However, by 1993 more than half of Dade County's schools were being run under programs that granted more authority to teachers. Some of the results are dramatic. At Miami Springs Middle School, teachers used their new power to redesign the curriculum and, among other things, choose textbooks that they felt were more appropriate for the largely Hispanic student population. At an elementary school led by teachers, the faculty voted to offer Saturday classes, and two hundred students signed up. Another sign of success: The rate of job applications has risen from two to eight for every slot at teacher-led schools.

This is a radical overhaul of the education system, and one that has not been adopted widely. At most schools, teachers do not have the opportunity to decide anything more important than what books they will use in the classroom, and sometimes not even that. Determinations on curriculum and allocation of financial and teaching resources remain the exclusive province of principals, higher-level administrators, and school boards whose members often have no background in professional education.

The results are predictable. Teachers grow angry and restless as they struggle to cope with new demands in an old structure. They bicker with principals, and cooperative relationships deteriorate into adversarial ones. Rather than professionals working as part of a team, teachers are treated as, in the words used by so many of them, "second-class citizens."

Strange as it may seem in an arena where conflict appears to govern, the simplest and least threatening investment that educators can make is to begin talking to each other about their shared problems. Principals do not have to serve solely as commanders; teachers need not be reduced to soldiers. Most of all, there needs to be an end to hostilities, an elimination of the adversarial positions, and a beginning of mutual understanding.

Alan Marks is always pushing for his students at Rio Grande High School in Albuquerque, New Mexico. Sometimes that leads him into conflicts:

I have a bachelor of arts in English from Stanford University. I lived and worked in Latin America for a couple of years and then returned to the United States and went to law school. I was an attorney and then I studied economics for a few years. Then I became a teacher. After a few years, though, I went to Stanford Business School and then returned to teaching. Never once has the school asked my opinion on one thing. Never asked what I could do to help them, which is the most obvious thing that they should have done. It's a foolish style of management.

I think by and large the people who are excellent managers are the people who know you need to adapt, that you need to take advantage of whatever resources you may have, to be innovative. Those kinds of people are rewarded more in the private sector, and so that's where they go.

I'm excusing our system, saying that I understand why they are the way they are. I don't appreciate it one bit, but I understand that people who are here are people who try to be very careful and are always afraid of doing something wrong and losing their job or losing their chance to rise up their little career ladder. The kind of people who tend to go into administration and education are pretty insecure people. They're not the kind of people who are really very dynamic.

So it's this self-perpetuating system of administrators who are endlessly the same. They are terrified of anything that goes outside of the parameters. A bureaucratic system doesn't encourage risk-taking, basically. You're afraid to go beyond the bounds you've been given because that is how you are going to be judged. And your superior is going to have to answer for you, so he's going to keep you on a very tight leash, too.

Sherrill Neale is a reading teacher at Patrick Henry Elementary School in Alexandria, Virginia:

The administration is mostly male, teachers are mostly female. There is no hierarchy in teaching. You do the same thing the day you leave as the day you started. There is no striving to be better. You become so complacent. You do the same thing year after year after year, and no one lets you do something different or suggests and encourages you to do new things.

The system stymies teachers, stymies their thinking. You get stagnant. You get so you don't want to hear any new ideas. You don't want to change.

Pat Maier, a teacher of French at Palos Verdes High School in Palos Verdes, California, has seen what she calls "the old-boy network":

This is supposed to be the best school district in California. One of the reasons they say that, of course, is that we test very well in the state tests. Of course, our kids all come from middle-class or upper-middle-class families.

In this school, there is no way to effect change, to make a difference. In education, for people who care, there is no way to make a difference. That's why teachers burn out.

Administration is riddled with old-boy pockets. The person who was chosen for principal is a wonderful individual, and he's great dealing with kids, and he plays softball and basketball. He cannot speak correct English for five minutes.

He knows nothing about curriculum development. He is a good PR person, and he is gifted dealing with kids. A real good example of the Peter Principle. He played adult, male games with the superintendent of the district when he was just a physical education teacher, and that's how he got the job.

There are so many PE teachers in administration because they never intended to be teachers.

Gary Hocevar, a former state legislator and the fiery and controversial principal of Van Buren Middle School in Albuquerque, is trying to work himself out of a job:

We don't need principals. Schools of the twenty-first century are in absolutely no need of a twentieth-century principal. Schools of the twenty-first century, which need to begin today, need to be formulated so that there are community boards formed within the geographical location served by the school. Those boards should be composed of residents, parents, businesspeople, and maybe even the school staff. They should determine the future of that particular chain of schools within that geographical region.

The management council should be a cadre of individuals who are freely elected from the school population. When I say school population I mean parent, business leader, custodian, teacher, whatever they feel constitutes the community. All would have equal voting rights.

They should then select a chief executive officer of their management council. That CEO would be a person who, like any good leader in business, would be ultimately responsible for carrying out the management directives from the council. This would eliminate the need for principals.

The problem implementing this is not going to be with the communities. It's going to be with the principals across America. No one wants to give up his job. You'd be changing the whole focus. This CEO needs to be a leader-coach. He or she needs to be the Lee Iacocca of education. They need to be the guy who comes in there and says that his board of directors has given him this mandate, this is what they want him to do. I think the need for principals and assistant principals would be cut.

If there is going to be true systemic curricular change in American public education, then it needs to occur from the grass roots. The grass roots is the classroom and the home living room. You need to develop and offer curriculum based on the needs of the community; therefore it has to be customer-driven, with the experts who have been trained to do that, the teachers, developing it in concert and collaboration with the parents. You don't need a principal coming in and saying, "This is what we need." You need a CEO facilitating the process.

Serafin Padilla is a former administrator who returned to the classroom and teaches fifth grade at La Mesa Elementary School in Albuquerque, New Mexico:

The argument against site-based management is like the argument years ago when women wanted to have the same rights as men. What happened is men said, "Okay, use the same bathrooms we do, put up the telephone poles, et cetera." Now we're telling the teachers, "Okay, you want to make your decisions," then the principal exits the room and leaves the teacher making the decisions when he doesn't have the experience or understanding of what the budget is. You have to provide training so that people can make the decisions.

The teachers are the key. They are your work force; they provide the education for the children, not the principal or the superintendent. You're leaving your child with the teacher for seven hours a day. The principal should be there to serve the teachers, but the principals feel they are in charge and they're sitting there looking at those test scores. As soon as the scores come up, they pat themselves on the back. They had nothing to do with them.

I have been the superintendent, the principal, the director, so I've tangled with the system. What the principals really need is a good workshop with good counseling to realize that it would enhance and bring a positiveness to the job, sharing management responsibilities with teachers. I think a good principal who is not insecure about himself would realize that this is neat because you've got your work force out here, you're the captain of the team. The captain of the team also carries the ball.

Karen Lagemann is a young first-grade teacher at Glenn Elementary School in Durham County, North Carolina. Rather than perceiving administrators as team captains, she finds too many plays being called from the sidelines:

In North Carolina, we have something called the Basic Education Plan, or BEP. I'm not sure how long they've had it, but it's caused a lot of anxiety. The BEP states goals for each grade and each subject for what children basically need to know. It is so imposing, a huge notebook for each grade, for each curriculum area — math, social studies, science, language arts, music, art, physical education.

I'd really like to be able to go through the BEP and sit down and plan out everything according to what it says, but I think it really stifles the teaching process. I know that by signing my contract, I have agreed to do this, and I will. But it really takes the excitement out of learning.

And it really puts a lot of pressure on some teachers. They are like, "Oh, my God, I've got to get to addition of two-digit numbers this week or I'll be off schedule." I say, "Please, are your children happy? Are they learning something? Are you comfortable with what they are doing?"

My goals are to have these children leave my classroom knowing more than they knew when they came in, knowing how to work in groups, reading or with the basic framework for knowing how to read, knowing not to solve problems by hitting or stealing. I feel that if you give them that foundation, then they will be able to get the rest. I have children who are adding two-digit numbers, but I have others who just go through everyone else's book bags and eat.

The BEP tends to focus more on results than the kids. It doesn't teach kids to think. They are not getting problem-solving skills. I take out the BEP notebook, use what I need, then put it away. Many teachers do what I do, but others stick to it regardless, right down the line.

I write down what I want to accomplish every single day, but things happen. If we find a bug in the classroom, or a kid wants to talk about something, we do it. I honestly don't know how people come to work and stick to something like the BEP. I'd go to work in day care if that were the way a public school had to be. You might as well be in an office answering a telephone.

John Scott teaches English at Hampton High School in Hampton, Virginia:

That is a hole in the system today. Administrators lose touch with the bottom line, and the bottom line is the kid. You are out of the trenches. You no longer understand what is going on.

A lot of good ideas just flounder in education. Sometimes it is the politics. Sometimes it is the credentials of the presenter.

When we are brought into the decision process now, it is almost as an afterthought. It is not part of the process. They create an artificially structured basis for bringing in teachers. They say, "We have this plan, and we'd like you to come in and give us your input." You go in and you see that it is already laid out. Teachers don't exercise a lot of power. We don't demand a great deal.

There are some interesting experiments in some school systems, where they are bringing in business management people to serve on the administrative level. Nobody understands that education is a whole different animal, because it keeps changing. Our product — the kids — keep changing. And they are people. They are not widgets.

Mary Bicouvaris teaches at a private school in Newport News, Virginia:

A few schools have made experiments and they have expanded the role of teachers. They have made the structure more horizontal. But most schools operate on a very, very vertical structure. If people understood what teaching is all about, it would be exactly the opposite.

The system is self-preserving. It is preserving occupational securities. It is advancing aspirations of people who learn very early in their careers to play a game. It is with no regard to true ability.

If you stay a teacher and do a dynamite job and next door is somebody who has the same number of years on the job as you and does nothing, you get the same pay. Although research will show that teachers do not do what they do for money, it is demoralizing to be in that kind of situation. There is nothing that can happen to a teacher to elevate her position, and the obstacles are not only administrative obstacles. They are from the teachers themselves.

Billy Sue Vogel, a Miami teacher, has taken advantage of Dade County's program to give teachers decision-making powers. She spends part of her time as an administrator and teamed up with a school principal to win a grant to design a new school:

One reason for wanting to do this project is that I have a little more say in how the school is run. We have school-based management and all of our groups of teachers have people they have elected to represent them. This management approach is important because it gives teachers a lot more voice in what is going on in the school. Teachers are what makes the schools work.

Even on little things, like dictionaries. I call three or four teachers and get different opinions about the different publishers. I don't have all the answers, but I involve other people.

Ruby Wanland, a teacher at Miami Beach Senior High School, likes seeing teachers involved in making decisions:

We've had examples here in Dade County where they have Saturday classes, and they have been quite successful with it. The teachers did that. They had insight and input and they said, "This is what our kids need." And sure enough, their kids scored off the test. They did beautifully. That's teacher input.

Darlene McCampbell teaches high school English at the University of Chicago Lab School:

At another school, I had a friend who was a passionate, wonderful teacher. She taught the journalism classes. She loved teaching.

I still get chills remembering this. You had to sign in in the morning. Classes started at eight-fifty and you had to sign in by eight-thirty. If you got in at eight thirty-one, the sign-in sheet was moved from the front desk in the office to the dean of students, the disciplinarian. You'd write down 8:32 and he'd look at you and he'd circle it in red.

One day my friend sent to the principal's office a kid who was brutal and violent. In the meeting with the principal, the teacher, and the student, the principal said to the teacher, "In five years, this kid will be able to buy out you and me. He is going to own it all. Look where you will be — doing nothing but teaching your class. Get back there." The teacher was humiliated. The kid was defended. Mediocrity was rewarded.

Joyce Byrd teaches business at Woodrow Wilson High School in Camden, New Jersey:

I have a horrid time understanding why it takes longer for supplies and equipment to reach areas of this district than it took for us to get our troops and supplies to Desert Storm. I have a hard time understanding that, particularly since our product needs immediate reinforcement.

Well, if you're going to observe us and criticize us and hold us accountable, then, doggone it, give us what we're supposed to have when we're supposed to have it. Don't give us a lot of rhetoric about how this has to go here and there and whatever.

If we did the same thing we'd be called incompetent. Administrators do the same thing and it's called a bureaucracy.

Dale Kenney, who says she is counting the days until she qualifies for her pension, has little respect for the principal at the middle school where she teaches in Washington, D.C.:

I've been with the same principal for eighteen years, and I know that he isn't going to change anything. The assistant principal has been assistant principal all those years.

The administration is almost an enemy. When the principal comes up in the mornings and makes sure that every teacher is on his or her way to duty, he greets you with snide remarks, always says something nasty. It's degrading. It's insulting. I walk in the door and the principal insults me.

We have two copying machines in this building paid for by teacher money, so we've got this thing going. The principal wants one in his office and lets us use one. He always had the big machine in the office and we had the smaller machine. It got to be a contest with the union.

He said, "Okay, you want your Xerox machine? I'll give it to you." He moved the big machine into the library and moved the other machine back into an office where we will never see it or touch it. Then he walks around saying, "You're going to be sorry for this."

Now, why do we want to use this machine? We want to teach these children. We are jumping through hoops trying to come up with creative things to keep these kids interested, to individualize instruction, and we've got a principal saying we can't use his Xerox machine.

Wayne Scheutter found himself and other teachers forced to undertake larger responsibilities to save South Putnam High School in rural Indiana:

The state of Indiana four years ago put in a program called performance-based accreditation. To meet that you have to meet certain criteria. One of the things the state did was start a program called Indiana Standard Testing for Education Performance. ISTEP we call it in Indiana.

A few years ago, our ISTEP scores dropped in math and English. They dropped considerably all across the grades. Mainly here at the high school, scores were dropping. Every five years schools are up for reevaluation, and when our scores dropped, they came in and took a look and they noticed that we had certain deficiencies and they decided to put us on probation.

The state sent a five-person team in to take a look. First, they felt that we did not have any written curricula that coordinated K through twelve. Second, we needed to improve our communication with people within the community about what we were doing. Third, over the years our school board had not really had the money to set up a program for staff development. The fourth thing was that they felt our ISTEP scores were too low and we had to work to bring them up.

They then gave us the grant of about forty thousand dollars to pay teachers to write the curriculum, to bring people in to provide workshops for our staff, to develop our school newsletter to send parents and other means of communication, and to apply toward improving our ISTEP scores.

At first we were very angry. Being put on probation is a dramatic step. It indicates to a lot of the people that we have been doing something wrong. We didn't feel that we had done anything wrong. Our students had graduated and gone on to do well. We recognized that we had some weaknesses, but we didn't feel that we were that bad.

We had some families move out of the school district because they felt their sons' and daughters' education was not going to be adequate. We had a realtor tell us that he had a family looking at real estate in the area and he asked about the schools and found out we were on probation and he canceled. It had a negative effect on students. We told the state that we felt the program was good, but some of the side effects were not.

Our students were ridiculed. At one of the local basketball games, one of our rival schools held up a big banner that said, "Can You Spell Probation?"

But one of the reasons they put us on probation was they felt our staff and our community needed that jolt. I think also it was intended to show our school board that the status quo is not going to work.

They did put their money where their mouth was. Teachers dug in and we developed a curriculum showing what is being taught in each class and seeing how it flows in a current of education. If I do something in second grade, I want to make sure it means something down the road. We have had staff development meetings all year and people going to workshops elsewhere. Teachers are involved in making decisions that have an impact on the whole school. And our newsletter goes out monthly to every parent.

The examination team came back in December and looked at what we had done, and in February they lifted our probation and gave us full accreditation.

The community here centers around the school, and the probation was a blow to the whole community. When my principal and I went to the state Board of Education and made our presentation and they voted to give us full accreditation, we came back as heroes to the whole community.

CHAPTER 14

SOLUTIONS

THERE IS no ideal school. There is no perfect way to structure a biology class or teach a first grader how to read, any more than there is a perfect way to bring up a child. There are many right ways. Sometimes all a teacher needs is permission to do it her way. In other situations, entire schools need to be turned upside down and given a good shake. That is not a bad idea for the whole educational system. Give it a good shake. Then, when the pieces are being assembled anew, listen to the teachers. They have a lot of good ideas about what needs to be done.

Fixing America's schools will take more than just the teachers. It will take involved parents and competent administrators and enlightened school boards and government officials. It will take money to pay teachers more and reduce the size of classrooms. It will take elevating the education of America's children to the highest priority. Otherwise there is no hope for the future.

The path to solving the nation's education problems is not smooth or easy to follow. There are bone-rattling bumps, hazardous detours, hairpin turns. There will be times when you have to stop, back up, and start again in a new direction. And the road will be different in New York from Florida. Along the way, however, teachers are putting up signposts that point in the right direction. If we follow them, the performance of America's schools will be improved dramatically.

Trust the teachers. There are bad ones. They should be fired. But most of America's teachers are dedicated, intelligent professionals. They work at demanding jobs with little reward. Given half a chance, they can steer the right course.

They don't all say the same thing. For some teachers, the solution is as simple as providing a good breakfast so every child can arrive at school ready and eager to learn. For others, it is as complex as integrating housing in the country's large cities to remove the barriers that have trapped generations in a welfare-dependent cycle of poverty and hopelessness.

Most teachers say today's parents are not involved enough in the education of their children. Too many social responsibilities have rolled downhill to the schools. Other teachers avocate something more radical, removing children from the influence of parents. The point was underlined a few days before Christmas in 1992.

Cabrini-Green is one of the largest and most depressing housing projects in Chicago. To brighten Christmas for students at the middle school that serves the project, community merchants donated presents. Parents were invited in to wrap them for the children. Instead, they stole the presents.

Most surveys find that the top priority for a majority of teachers is higher pay. It will attract brighter people and keep those who leave the profession for better-paying jobs. It will send the right signal, too: Teachers are as valuable as lawyers, doctors, and plumbers. And pay them differently. The current pay structure is geared to reward longevity, regardless of the quality of the teaching. Adopt a concept from outside of education: Use merit pay.

Some teachers are demanding bold efforts. Fundamental flaws must be attacked, not just tinkered with, they say. Dade County's site-based management has empowered teachers, with positive results after only a few years. Teachers are happier, students are scoring better and staying in school.

Teachers say reduce the bureaucracy. In 1992, the Cincinnati public school system followed the recommendation of a panel of Ohio business leaders and slashed sixty-five positions in the administration. The sixteen million dollars in savings was used, among other things, to create a new social studies curriculum.

Radical reforms lead to conflict and divisions. School choice means allowing students to choose the schools they attend, rather than requiring them to go to neighborhood schools. The form proposed by the administration of former president George Bush was rejected by most public school teachers. His plan was to provide parents with education vouchers that would enable them to move their children and their tax dollars to private schools if wanted. While backers argued that the concept would introduce needed competition into the education system, most teachers feared it would have been a death knell for many public schools.

A version of choice that allows students to move among different public schools offers a more valuable reform. It is more popular among teachers, and it is working already in some cities. This is a form of competition that increases the responsibilities for teachers and students alike. There is an incentive to create a special program, such as computer training, to attract more and brighter students. The courses that are weak and fail to draw students will not survive. But the money remains within the public school system.

Among the backers of choice within the public schools is President Bill Clinton. The Clinton message of change must encompass not only the economy and defense spending. Ready or not, education must change, too. And teachers must have a say in its new direction.

Devising the perfect school is not important. There is no such institution. What is important is beginning the conversation, opening the debate. The answers to revitalizing America's educational system lie in many places. Important solutions are being identified by America's teachers.

Mary Bicouvaris, a former national teacher of the year, teaches senior social studies at Hampton Roads Academy, a private school in Newport News, Virginia, after a twenty-year career in public schools:

Begin with parents, custodial adult, grandmother, sister, whoever takes care of the child. If I were a principal, I would say, "You cannot send your child to school until you come to school for two days." That child cannot come to school without you. Then go ahead and tell adults what teachers are telling each other in those highfalutin conferences: We are worried sick about your child, and about everybody's child, and about the future of this country, and we think that you are the key to the solution, and we will ask you to help us do this and that. Do you want your children drug-addicted? Do you want them casualties? Do you want them statistics? Do you want them to fail? I have never met a parent who would want that.

Then I would have business tell parents, "Go to school. We will give you time to go for this important meeting." And then we'd start the school, not by issuing books to children, but by drilling in their heads the things that are important, not in any threatening way, but in a conspiratorial way where the students and the teachers and the principal and parents are conspirators to success, not to failure.

We are talking behind the parents' backs, behind the students' backs. I have gone to conferences and I have heard so many times, "What is wrong with education?" But the people who need to hear it never hear it.

When I came back to Bethel [a previous public school], after the year that I was absent for teacher of the year activities, they invited me to go one day to speak to students about how to be a writer. I spent five minutes. I said, "To be a writer, be a reader. The more you read, the better you write."

I said, "Now let me tell you what I have heard from going around the country." So I told them how much everybody is worried about education, how they cannot compete with the Japanese and the Europeans. I never expected the reaction I got. Six periods I said the same thing. Six times I got the same reaction. "Miss B, who says that? We don't want to be bad."

They would stay after class, at the risk of being late for the next class, twenty, fifteen of them, and they say, "Who says we're bad?" These kids don't know they're bad. They have no idea. They don't read the paper. They didn't read statistics. They don't go to conferences. They don't know that this country is worried sick about them. And their reaction to me was, at least the ones who stayed after class and they were just run-of-the-mill kids, nothing special: "I don't want to be bad. I don't want to be worse than the Japanese. I don't want to polish the shoes of the Japanese."

So it's my idea that we leave the most important people out of the most important decisions. We must tell them how much we worry about them because of how much we love them and how much we like for them to accept the responsibility to go on.

Of course, that doesn't answer the question of the inner city. It doesn't answer the question of the pregnant teenager who has two children at home. It does not answer the question of AIDS. It does not answer these questions. But there's got to be a beginning, and the beginning is at school, because at least we can rescue the next generation.

Bill Walters's years of experience and dedication have made him a mentor for other teachers at Camden High School in Camden, New Jersey:

We are on the right road to reform, with all the new programs coming out. The idea of teachers being involved in the decision-making process, in site-based management, is interesting. The more people involved in a school or process from the very beginning, they are going to work harder to see it succeed. They are going to buy into it. No one wants to be a failure.

Students also have to have a say and representatives in that process. Teachers have to be listened to and not punished. Often they aren't now because everybody wants to keep the boat even. Schools are in the public eye. Administrators say, "Don't rock the boat because you will have everyone on my back." The state, the public, parents.

Teachers are punished by lack of promotions. If teachers question an administrative judgment or a move, they are treated as if they are not a team player, and if you can't be a team player we will put you someplace where it won't matter. Or you may have five classes, all in a row.

I am studying to be an administrator. I am thinking, "Where could I go where I could be the kind of principal I want to be?" I think the only way to improve is to get teacher input and criticism and use that as a basis for making decisions and enriching the school. A good administrator shouldn't be threatened by criticism. What happens a lot in education is that teachers are told, "Here's a program, put it in operation." They are given no training and they are told to make it successful in one year. At the end of the year it comes down to saying it didn't work, and saying it was because of a poor teacher.

Everyone is eager to jump on the bandwagon for site-based management, but there are going to be a lot of problems with it, and there will be some failures. It is going to need a lot of planning. But we will learn. Don't judge us so quickly. Business takes years to make a development successful sometimes. Then they practice it and improve it each year. Education has to have the same opportunity.

You have to give schools an opportunity to succeed. And when the American education system begins to involve teachers more in the process, it is like anything else: If the teachers own it, they will work to make it the very best.

Alfredo Lujan teaches writing at Pojoaque Middle School in Pojoaque, New Mexico:

How do you give teachers more support? The most obvious, and the biggest, controversy is through paying them better. You pay them more so that they're happier doing their job, so they don't take another job.

There are things that I would like to be involved in, though, like hiring the chairman of the English Department. When a person gets hired into that English Department, I would like to be involved in the hiring of that person, which we don't have right now. I don't think that would take away from my instructional time. In fact, it would benefit it. To get someone who agrees philosophically with what is going on in that department, to be able to look at their credentials and so on is important. As it is, sometimes you come to school in the fall, you have one or two new teachers in your department. Where did they come from?

Donna Madath teaches third grade at Wadsworth Avenue Elementary School in Los Angeles:

If I could do one thing, it would be to limit my class to seventeen kids. If you could guarantee me no more than that in my class, not eighteen or nineteen, but between fifteen and seventeen, it would work.

There are days now when I don't even talk to all my kids, because there are so many kids to be dealt with. So the quiet, well-behaved ones who do their homework every day, there's probably a day a week when one of them doesn't get the personal attention from me that he deserves.

You could do away even with the textbooks. Kids can share textbooks. That's fine. If there is pencil and paper, you can make up for anything. There are millions of libraries, but if you were to reduce the class size to seventeen there would not be a problem.

You don't have to raise teachers' salaries. You do not have to make them work more days. Nothing. You do not have the discipline either, because the child who wants attention isn't acting up to get it. You can spot a bully and nip it in the bud. That's what I think.

I think class size is the answer to public education. Not having to go to school on Saturdays, not giving them five hours of homework a night.

Year-round school is good for nonnative speakers, really good. If you were to tell me that every school in the country is going to year-round, and multitrack systems where you share classrooms and they were going to have seventeen children, I'd say fine. It's the answer, especially in the inner city. Those children need about one teacher to every twelve kids. Their vocabulary is so much more limited than a middle-class child.

You know, I think the Republican party has a lot of good ideas, but this voucher system. Whew. What will it do to the schools? For every twenty-five students who leave the public school, you'll lose a teacher, and that portion of a custodian, and that portion of a librarian. What will be left in the public schools will be the children with a great deal of learning disabilities and the very poor children.

Michelle Kaufman is a teacher at the Anna Howard Shaw Elementary School (Public School 61) on the Lower East Side of New York City:

I wish that we could have an ungraded primary education, from first to third. No grades. That children could flow from one competency level to the next. And that they wouldn't be allowed to leave the ungraded primary situation until they mastered certain competencies. For the children who couldn't, there would be diagnostic help. This is what the child needs. Let's take care of it.

Grades make too much pressure. By getting rid of the grades you're teaching them to succeed, and there's no stigma attached to needing more time.

Alan Marks is a teacher at Rio Grande High School in Albuquerque, New Mexico:

I think the solution is radical. I think it's raising standards, not lowering them. I think that's the solution. I think kids respond beautifully to expectations. If you don't have high standards, they're going to look for the path of least resistance.

I tend to think that you need democratization, too. You need people who are willing to throw out the book and sit down with a bunch of bright people, as they did in the Harlem schools, and say, "What do we want to do? What do we think is going to work?" And it has precisely to do with your notion of having high expectations for everyone. You had white parents standing in line to get into these Harlem schools.

Eve Stark teaches advanced fifth graders at Tzouanakis Intermediate School in Greencastle, Indiana:

The American public underestimates what children can do. All children are very bright students. We just don't ask enough of them. I never talk down to my students, whether I teach this gifted class or a regular class. I throw out what I think is important to them. If I see them running with it and understanding it, we go with it. If I see that I have to back up, we do. But I never talk down to them. Children are too intelligent to do that and I think it is a big mistake of American education when it happens as frequently as it does. Backing up and repeating some material is a lot better than not giving them the kind of stretch that they should have.

Art Murnan is a religion teacher and guidance counselor at Chicago's Providence-St. Mel:

I've been an athletic coach all my teaching career. If you are a coach, and all you are concerned about is winning, you're missing the point. I look at coaching as a vehicle to other ends.

I have a boy, Clarence Brown, on the cross-country team who has the highest grade-point average in the school. I asked him to speak to the whole team. He told them, "You know, when I first started at Providence my grades were okay, but when I started indoor track practice and we had to go from the basement to the fifth floor on those stairs, up and down, up and down, I couldn't believe it. It just wore me out.

"I decided the first day it just kicked my butt, but I was going to come back and do this. So the second day I came back to try again. It was hard, but each day I finished it. I worked. I told myself I have to do this. I thought this coach was crazy and insane. You know, pretty soon it was ingrained in my brain, that I have to complete, I have to do this. So I went home and did homework. It clicked in. I have to finish. I have to work hard. I have to succeed."

And suddenly Clarence has a 4.17 on a 4.0 grade-point average. He tells everyone that track is what turns him on. I explain this to my kids on the team all the time. "You know most of you will not make money off of athletics, but athletics might pay for your education. So you have to make athletics work for you." And I said to them that athletics is also something that fifteen years from now you can look back on. You accomplished this. You succeeded.

Coaches can teach more life skills than classroom teachers can. How to set realistic goals for yourself. How to motivate yourself. How to deal with success or lack of success.

I have a kid on my cross-country team who has run for three years. He is big. He shouldn't be on track. The other day he took tenth place in the novice race and got a little trophy. Everybody cheered him, even coaches from other teams went over and shook his hand. They've seen him for years. He might come in ten minutes behind everyone else, but he always finishes. Always. He has never quit. People spot that and respect it.

I keep telling my athletes. I work on the mind-set. If you get a mind-set, it carries over into other aspects of your life. In the classroom, washing the kitchen floor, whatever. If your mind-set is for excellence, then you're going to scrub that kitchen floor like no one else has ever scrubbed it. So what you try to do is develop a mind-set in kids and get them to incorporate it. It's ownership. You might plant the seeds, but you turn it over to them as soon as possible and let it become them. Once you get them in the mind-set, you don't have to worry about them ever again. When they mess up, they'll get right back in line, because they know they messed up.

Barbara Ruggles and Gordon Kridner teach third grade at Black Hawk Elementary School in Park Forest, Illinois. Ruggles:

If I had a magic wand, I'd have home-cooked breakfasts every day, for everyone at school, where kids could sit down, where they could have enough and they didn't have to fight about it. It would be for all kids so there wasn't the stigma of the free meal. That way you avoid the aspect of "You eat free, but I can afford this real cool lunch box."

You can't believe how much time these kids take just trying to maintain their dignity as a person. You might need free lunches, but it's much more cool to take the food and throw it away, saying, "I don't need this, I can eat at home," to maintain your dignity. So we have kids who are hungry throwing food away. Rather than getting put down, they just throw it away.

Kridner:

What made it better for the children on the free lunch program was when, a few years ago, we went to a school board meeting and asked them to put the free lunches in paper sacks. You see, the free lunches used to come in cardboard boxes. No one brings lunch in a cardboard box. Because a lot of kids bring their lunches in paper sacks, no one knows who gets the free lunch and who brings his own.

Also, I never thought that I would say this, but I'm almost at a time that I think we should have everyone wear a uniform, just blue jeans and a white shirt, or something like that. Years ago, I used to fight that whole idea, but I've changed my mind, especially in urban areas. Just a pair of blue canvas tennis shoes. No brand names.

Marion Clermont is an English teacher at Tilden High School in Brooklyn, New York City:

If I could I would make the school environment nice to let the kids know that we care about them, that we want to put them in a nice place so they will have the sense they are being taken care of, not just corralled and kept off the street for the protection of the taxpayer. I know I sound like an anarchist.

Then I would have the best books and supplies and computers and audiovisual stuff, the state of the art. I would have a dress code. Absolutely. I was in the forefront in the sixties of getting rid of uniforms. I went through twelve years of strict Catholic training, plaid skirt, white blouse, black beret. I really thought I knew what I was doing back then, freedom, express yourself. Once that dress code was removed from the New York City school system, you saw problems right from the start. When they had their blue pants on, white shirt, and a tie, they weren't going to roll around on the floor. Also, a uniform is a great equalizing factor. They won't steal each other's jackets and sneakers. You won't have that horrible, horrible peer pressure to get those seventy-five-dollar sneakers.

The poor young teenager down the hall here just stopped going to school. His mother said, "Why?"

"I don't have the clothes," he said.

She opens up his closet and she has already gone out and bought every possible Gitano this and that. Still something is lacking.

Peer pressure sounds so trite. I don't remember having any peer pressure when I was in high school. But it is phenomenal now. It is a major problem. Just things like clothing. If they don't have something, they'll go out and steal. Knock you down, beat you over the head, grab those sneakers, rip the jewelry right off your ear.

Rita Logan teaches at the Juvenile Justice Center School in Miami:

What would I do to make it all better? Maybe integrated housing. I hate to break up the black neighborhood because it is a very powerful community, a very exciting community, but as my husband said the other night as we were walking around where we live, "There's a sense of sadness here. No one steps outside to speak to anyone." At eight o'clock the town is silent. We have a low crime rate. Anyone who doesn't belong there is hustled right out. You see TVs blinking.

Let those who want to get out have some kind of extra support to get out, some kind of supplemental mortgage. I feel that has to be done, to break up that inner city, and get the kids into integrated schools, heavily integrated, not where they're going to be one of three black kids and four thousand white kids. Mix it more.

Pat Maier is a teacher of French at Palos Verdes Peninsula High School in Palos Verdes, California:

We have to encourage all communities to get behind their schools and support them financially, beyond the financing they get through the state. There are some states where communities fund their own schools.

We cannot create a nation of just barely educated. But there will always be an educational elite, because they chose to work harder, or because their parents have chosen to make education a priority. Not every parent is willing to do that. Not every community is willing to.

But you have to give those people the opportunity to do that, just as you give other people the opportunity not to do that. That is a choice that parents must make. The government's responsibility is to give a minimum level across the board and that has to be more equitably divided, particularly in states other than California, where it hasn't been done that way.

At our school, we have a parent-run educational foundation that funds thousands and thousands of dollars each year. We couldn't survive without it. But education is a priority in this community. It is not necessarily a priority elsewhere.

But if the parents in South-Central Los Angeles had the opportunity to send their kids to Palos Verdes schools and education was enough of a priority to them to see that their kids got here in the morning, I think they should be allowed to do that.

The ones who don't care to do that should be allowed to keep their kids in South-Central Los Angeles High. That's the reason I like the idea of vouchers in public education. You will always have inequities in schools.

Marion Hamilton is a fifth-grade teacher at Wadsworth Avenue Elementary School in Los Angeles:

A few nights ago, a friend of mine called me up. He's got four kids in private school. He said, "Marion, this voucher initiative is going to help me."

I said, "You are a public school teacher, are you not?"

"Yes, I am," he said.

I said, "It's like robbing Peter to pay Paul. Listen here: That is going to take money from the public schools. We know where we are now. It will just take the upper 5 percent of the children, the ones the private schools will accept. That is what it is going to do. Then you will be sitting in your classroom thinking that you have no kids in your class who can do this, and none who can do that. It is not going to provide choice at all."

Dwight Brown is a fifth-grade teacher at Moton Elementary School in New Orleans:

The old Moton, where I went to elementary school, was a dilapidated old building. It was a school that was always overcrowded. It was located directly in the center of the Desire housing project, which is one of the largest housing projects in the United States. The new school is outside the project. Now, outside the project there is some violence, but inside the project there is consistent violence all day long, twenty-four hours of the day. The new school gives the kids a chance to escape that. Even though it is not too far away, it is not within the confines of the project. This means that kids don't have to spend their entire life within the project.

The new school is the jewel of the whole community, believe it or not. It gives the community a sense of oneness. The children come here for school and the people and community agencies come in and use the school at night. The Head Start program has its graduation here.

Desire got its name because of the streetcar. The streets here have names such as Abundance, Hope, Benefit, Pleasure, Industry. Now, I don't know where those names came from for the streets. You think that we have hope here? No. You think we have abundance? No. Pleasure? Oh, it's happy here. No. We got nothing at all. Except this school. It is something new.

We have an extended school year here at Moton, with kids in class for eleven months out of the year. In our community, there is nothing to do all summer, and, you know, idle minds are the devil's workshop. So here we have the year-round school and we try to incorporate some of the things that other kids would normally do during the summer vacation. We take trips to Jellystone Park a little bit out of town or visit museums. By having the kids come in early I have time to reteach skills from the end of the previous year and there is not much of a gap either. The kids' retention level is much higher by coming right back.

Our test scores did not go up dramatically. But in Head Start they did not see any gains until after ten years. So I think it is going to take a while to see any real gains in tests in our school. You have to be realistic. Your gains may not be in test scores. Your gains may be in developing self-images by having a child involved with something.

———————————————

Alice Golub teaches fifth grade at F. S. Tucker Elementary School in Miami:

I know what the answer is. Take all these kids all away from their parents, like they do in Israel. Put them in a kibbutz for about ten years. Just take them out of this environment, have somebody love them and kiss them and tell them how cute they are. When my kids were little, I'd tell my son he was the most wonderful child in the world. He believed that he could do anything because his mother told him he was wonderful, he could do everything, and damned if he didn't.

Jim Hosney is head of the Film and Video Department at Crossroads Arts Academy in Los Angeles:

You can't compare turning out educated kids with turning out automobiles. Kids are human beings. So to tell people that a school is an assembly line is a completely wrong way to address the problems in education. You have to look at these students as people.

If I could wave a magic wand, I'd decrease class size and bring in teachers who really cared about their subject matter and their students. I find, in hiring people for my program, I don't really care about what degrees they have. What is important is their passion for the material.

Kaye Furlong is a third-grade teacher at Vista Grande Elementary School in Rancho Palos Verdes, California:

They can do a hundred studies saying that paying teachers more doesn't make a difference, but eventually it will have an impact because it discourages people from going into education.

I've got two sons who are now just out of college. Both would have been good teachers, but neither would go into teaching. One is an artist at a big aerospace company, and his raises are huge, while our teachers are fighting over 1½ percent. The other is in banking. He said he'd much rather be a teacher, but he doesn't want his wife to feel she has to work for the rest of her life so they could have children. How many families are going to pay the kind of tuition to send their people to these good colleges to have them come out and work for twenty-two thousand dollars?

Joel Kaplan teaches chemistry at Alexandria, Virginia's, T. C. Williams High School:

To get quality in the schools, you need to pay for it. The salaries are lower than they should be. They probably should be 50 percent higher. If you were to make salaries up in the eighty-thousand-dollar range, you'd get hordes of people coming from law and engineering and medicine. People love to teach. This is a really exciting job when you do see children turning on. I'd love to have them here as colleagues. But the starting salary is only twenty-five thousand dollars. It takes about eighteen years to get into the fifty-thousand-dollar category.

Now, more demands are made, partly because they are trying to mainstream kids and you get kids at such different developmental abilities, all in the same class. We are supposed to wave magic wands and make it work. But the school board is blind to what is going on in the classroom. What the kids are not doing is terrible. If you see how they write, if you hear how they think, it is really terrible. We need to do something to change this. Just pouring more money in is not going to do it. We need a lot of money, but we need something before that.

We are in trouble. This whole country is in trouble. It didn't start with the kids. It started with our generation. It's our generation that has fallen behind Japan. It's our own selfishness. To demand more of these kids when we act the way we do is ridiculous. They are not stupid. They see the hypocrisy. Where is our will to do a good job and produce good products? It is not here. Let me do the least and pay me the most. This is the American ethic. So what we do is to lower our standards.

The educational system, this was always a grandiose baby-sitting service. I knew that when I went into it. This is a very cheap way of baby-sitting. Where are your kids if they are not in school? They will get into trouble. So we have schools. I mean, the public school did arise so we could incorporate all the immigrants and have them adapt to our values, learn the language. But just as important was the baby-sitting service. And it still functions as that.

We have kids who shouldn't be in school. They aren't students. But if we kick them out they will be in jail. It's cheaper to take care of them in school than in jail. Think about it. Keeping someone in jail is very costly.

You need a revolution in the schools.

What I would like to have is what we call "minischool." They are schools within schools, and teams of teachers. We need to engage the kids and get info out of them. How do you relate to this? Get them to work on projects in groups, with other kids. At the same time as you have these teams, you have to set aside a certain percentage of time to deal with the values that kids have to deal with.

Have the kids relating to each other as human beings. That way John can see that Jamaal is the same person, underneath that skin of a different color. They have the same fears, which is what drives us anyway. It's just that they come from different backgrounds.

Artie Sinkfield is chairwoman of the Science Department and a teacher at Brownsville Middle School in Miami:

We bite into too many programs that are not educationally sound. People present things for money. They're not really educationally tested, or they're educationally tested with one set of people and they don't fit the mold for all of the people. And we buy them and I think a lot of times we do our children a disservice.

If you will notice, the Japanese keep basically one standard of learning, and they learn by that same standard. I would like to see some standards coming out of Washington, not all the standards, but some.

I would not favor having so many new programs all the time. If you find a good program that works statewide, nationwide, keep it. If it works and if it can be funded, and if they have found it to be fair, I don't see any need to change.

Sanford Bearman is a math teacher at North Miami Beach Senior High School in North Miami Beach, Florida:

We need standards of excellence for teachers, not a standard of minimum perfomance. The medical and legal professions have standards. Why not teachers?

If we want to be recognized as a profession, then we need professional standards. I know minorities might have a problem with that because of a concern that any test will be biased. You have to make sure that the instrument and the process are not. It must be cleansed of bias.

I think there should be differentiated diplomas, too. If you want to go to college, you should get a college-prep diploma. If you want to go to a vocation immediately after high school, you get that. So you have different standards for different courses you want to take. I hope that doesn't sound prejudiced against certain groups.

Lyn Smith teaches third grade at Hilton Elementary School in Newport News, Virginia:

I would like to require some sort of relationship between parents and schools, like Hampton Roads [a nearby private school] and their parents. They have a demerit system. I'd like to be able to give demerits and one day a week have detentions for children who need to stay, and the parents would have to come to get them after.

The kids would have to do labor. It shouldn't be up to teachers to come up with extra busywork for them, which would just add to their load. I think kids should have to wash floors, pull weeds, scrape gum. But parents work and they say they can't come to get them. It works for the private and independent schools. If the parents don't come to get them, then we could call a cab or the police and have the court system charge the parents a fee. In this way we could impose consequences on the parents, too. I think then the discipline problems we have would get better.

Kids have to know that there are consequences for their actions. And the consequences are not that we get to go see the guidance counselor for hugs, or that we draw pictures, or get extra help in math. It is really cruel to send them out in the world without that knowledge of consequences. But then I am pretty much an old-school type. I don't see that the ways we did things thirty or forty years ago were all that bad. Kids came out of school reading. They came out of school being able to think, solve problems.

Richard Garcia teaches science at MAST Academy, the Marine and Science Technology High School in Miami:

I would prefer that our curriculum be more defined than what it is now. I would be inclined to want somebody to define what we should teach and how much time, et cetera. It is one of the ways you can develop standards for students. You can't very well give people an examination on what they have learned in biology if their teachers haven't been required to teach a certain curriculum and cover a certain number of subjects in a certain amount of time.

I am inclined to want more standardization. Also I am inclined to want more central authority as opposed to more local authority. I think the school system should be run out of Washington and not out of Tallahassee. By taking it out of the hands of local authorities, we would be able to upgrade the quality of the system.

Ricki Weyhe, a language arts teacher at Miami Beach Senior High School in Miami Beach, was sitting in the same conference room as Garcia. She disagreed with him:

This is a real paradox. We said earlier that there are a lot of teachers who we don't think are competent, yet they are the very people demanding a voice in the decision-making process, as to how the school operates.

I am not a proponent of school-based management for the very reason that I don't think the judgments of teachers in making decisions about budget and personnel are all that wise. I don't like putting my future in the hands of people I don't always think know enough about what they may have to deal with.

Ray Devenney teaches English as a Second Language to students at Bell Multicultural School, part of the public school system in Washington, D.C.:

Our students are wonderful students. They could be brilliant students. They could be great. But the reality of the situation is that the pressure on people to live is so great, so overwhelming, that it becomes a battle to convince them that education will pay off.

There's always someone with a bad job for you. There's always somebody who will exploit you. There's always a huge building to be cleaned, and if something falls on you, there's always someone else who wants that job. These are the realities, I think, of life for a lot of people.

I think that separating the kind of system that we live in from educational goals is preposterous. My goals when I come to school every day are to get involved and make a difference and try to show the students that in the long run the things that I'm saying are beneficial, that it does give them control, and that it does give them power. What they get now is not power. They get powerlessness. They get to be exploited. They get to be used.

Day care is a fundamental priority. Sweden says it is. We don't. That's why Swedes do better in school than we do. We have never adopted a fundamental commitment to education.

If you come from a family whose members are marginally literate, the kind of role language and literacy will play in your family is very different from the role that language and literacy may play in my children's family. The only way to break this cycle is to provide that child with ten thousand interactions with text as fast as possible. It's not just Head Start. It's recognizing that these kinds of things are critical, critical. To me, you're not always going to be able to get those parents to do it.

That is what public education is about. It's that commitment of a society to produce a generation of literate people who are then able to give their children a basis for developing literacy as well. Schools are already five years behind by the time they get the kid. What we need to do is move to providing those kinds of meaningful opportunities to interact with text and to learn.

———————————————————

AFTERWORD

THE MAJORITY of the teachers we've heard are possessed by their jobs long after quitting time. They recognize the problems besetting their profession and their schools. They carry those anxieties with them long after the day's final school bell.

Their insights were darker than we expected, reflecting the gravity of the plight of the schools. We didn't expect to hear about discipline so out of control that no learning can go on, about public school classrooms with forty and more children even in wealthy communities, or about children packing guns as well as peanut butter sandwiches before heading off each morning for school. But even teachers whose students face the most insurmountable obstacles, people such as Carolyn Epps Jackson, Dren Geer, and Alan Marks, have refused to give up hope.

In speaking out, these teachers offer lessons to all of us. Although not delivered in a single voice, it is a singular message: Education's troubles are far too deep-seated and important to leave in the hands of the politicians and the administrators. Teachers are asking for a place at the table when the plan to revitalize the educational system is written. And they are telling parents that they had better be there, too.

The people making decisions for our schools — the administrators, school boards, and elected officials at both the state and federal levels — are prone to make mistakes because often they are too isolated from the debate. And because their visits are too often celebratory, rather than routine, they see only the happy faces put on by teachers and their students.

"It used to be that principals had to spend a day a month in the classroom, but they don't anymore," said Mary Horton, an outspoken history teacher at Richmond Heights Middle School in Miami. "If they spent at least a week every year, then they might know enough to make good decisions. School board members also should go into the classroom. State legislators should see the classrooms, the jails, the foster homes. But they don't. When they come, we make the mistake of painting this school and putting on plays instead of letting them see how it really is."

The teachers have shown how it really is inside their classrooms. It is not a pretty picture. Many of the stories they have told about what goes on there are alarming. They are warnings, attempts to convey the grim picture of the forces that are hobbling the educational system today. For too long, teachers have been relegated to silence, and the effect of that silence has been their own powerlessness. The road to improving education is long and complex. By raising their voices, teachers can empower themselves and start the dialogue that represents the first necessary steps along that difficult road.

Teachers are right when they insist that more money is a key to revitalizing the schools. If the gap is to be closed between the performance of poor students and middle-class students, states must equalize funding levels between rich and poor districts.

In a society where so many values seem to have a price tag, teacher pay needs to increase, too. There is no other way to attract the numbers of bright new people to the profession and to retain the topflight educators who are there already.

In addition, excellent teachers should be rewarded. Not all teachers with twenty years' experience are equally effective. Unions must no longer be allowed to dictate that teacher pay be linked solely to college credits and years on the job. Those factors too often ignore the quality of what is going on in class. Incentives need to be created for good teaching. Pay scales should be tied to other factors, such as peer reviews, professional training, and the progress of students.

The pay gap between administrators and teachers should be eliminated to reflect the primary importance of the teacher. This will keep more good teachers in the classroom. It should be part of a broader overhaul of the way schools are run. While some teachers are reluctant to transfer power from administrators to their peers, a stronger voice for teachers in running schools is essential. There is nothing new to this idea of ownership. If teachers feel more vested in their schools, they will work harder to make them succeed.

At the same time, these incentives must be paired with programs that hold teachers accountable for their performance. In Kentucky, for instance, teachers in schools that improve student performance are eligible for additional money. This incentive system is similar to the way that most businesses reward superior employees. Those who do not measure up risk mandatory state supervision and even the loss of tenure. The program was adopted as part of a mandatory education reform package approved by the Kentucky legislature in 1990. As part of the changes, money for teacher salaries was reallocated to set up the bonus pool.

The concept of site-based management is working well in Dade County, Florida, where more than half the schools are now using it in one form or another. But even districts unwilling to go that far should provide teachers with a say in hiring and promotion and curriculum development. The current hierarchical structure should be scrapped in favor of a collegial decision-sharing process. Teachers should be treated like adults.

Just as important as higher pay and a reorganized school is the need for money elsewhere. Students who must share books and desks have trouble learning. Children who are not allowed to take textbooks home because there are not enough to go around are missing out on a big part of education. In this age of computers, many children have little access to technology in the classroom. Science labs are often ill equipped. Teachers bemoan the dilapidated condition of their schools, worrying about the message imparted to children by the broken windows and crumbling ceilings.

Class size needs to be reduced. What parent would invite thirty or more children to a birthday party? It should be no surprise to discover that teachers cannot cope with thirty or more children in the classroom. The magic number for class size varies, from fifteen to twenty, depending on the needs of the children and the subject matter. The national average of twenty-four is too high, and classes approaching forty and fifty students are formulas for failure.

Many of these are steps that will require more money for education and reallocating existing education funds. Some solutions, however, do not cost anything.

Greater involvement by parents is cost-free; the price of absentee parenting is high. It is the responsibility of all parents to make sure that their children understand the value of education and are prepared to take advantage of the opportunities offered by the schools.

This is difficult to enforce, but educating children requires a full partnership between teachers and parents. Getting to teacher conferences and PTA meetings can be a financial hardship on poor parents and conflict with the busy schedules of working ones. Making sure homework gets done requires real involvement, not just a bullying tone. Sending children off each morning with a good night's sleep and breakfast demands time and discipline from parents. But what can be more important than ensuring that a child is receiving an education?

The business community could help parents by giving them the time to attend teacher conferences, school field trips, and special events. It could help by forming partnerships with local schools in which adults are given time to volunteer to tutor in the schools.

There is an alarming trend toward lowering school standards. Under such euphemisms as "democratic education" and "anti-elitism," attacks have been launched on advanced-placement classes and efforts have been made to reduce academic demands across the board. For instance, in Alexandria, Virginia, school board members branded a ninth-grade honors program as "elitist" and "racist" because the academic entrance requirements had the unintended effect of restricting minority enrollment. The solution is not to eliminate the program. It is to improve the performance of minorities so that they, too, can take advantage of tougher classes.

The problems of education are visible at both ends of the spectrum. A huge number of students leave school either as dropouts or graduates with very low skill levels. At the other end of the range, American schools produce among the smallest percentage of high-achieving graduates in the industrial world. Each of these groups presents different challenges to teachers and the education system, and these challenges must be met in different ways.

Yet, in the guise of providing a "democratic education," there is a movement afoot to provide the same education to all children. Gifted programs are being eliminated. Children in special-education classes are being mainstreamed. Tracking, in which students are grouped according to their ability, is being curtailed. The result is classes in which the range of skills is too broad for anyone to receive proper attention.

Nothing could be less democratic, less true to the historic ideals of this country, than treating all children the same. Instead, while providing equal opportunities to all children, individual needs also must be addressed. A good system of tracking offers a challenging curriculum to students at every level — top, middle, and bottom. Celeste Lenzini, the Alexandria kindergarten teacher who advocates blending children in younger grades, sees benefits in providing courses and curricula that offer challenges to students at every academic level in the upper grades.

The best teachers, the best programs, and the most effort must be allocated to the students who are farthest behind. The skills of those students need to be improved through enriched programs, such as the one at work at the Ninety-ninth Street Accelerated School in Watts, in Los Angeles.

"The basic notion is to accelerate the input, the whole process, because these at-risk children need to catch up, rather than to have their learning process remediated and slowed down, the way most schools handle them," says Anthony Jackson, who teaches at the school. "Give them more, not less."

Not every special program should be aimed at the collegebound. Failure to stress the real value of vocational classes and basic literacy dooms many students. European-style apprenticeship programs, in combination with the last two years of high school and two years of postsecondary education, would provide training for skilled workers among the 50 percent of high school graduates who do not choose college. This type of program could provide a way out of the economic morass of unemployment, poverty wages, and part-time jobs in which many young people are mired.

At the same time, a means must be developed to deal with students who leave school. More than 20 percent of America's students drop out of high school — almost 50 percent in many inner cities. As the National Center on Education and the Economy, a nonprofit organization created to improve educational standards, says, "Turning our back on those dropouts, as we do now, is tantamount to turning our backs on our future work force."

States should assume responsibility for developing and funding alternative learning environments for students who cannot master basic skills in a regular school setting. Youth centers, working in conjunction with local and federal job-training programs, should be created to recover those who have already left school.

We should heed another warning from teachers about adding so many nonacademic matters to the curriculum. Because of the increased demand on schools to fill the void left by the collapse of the family and other institutions, students are devoting more of their time to learning about sex, AIDS, and drugs. These are vital matters, but teachers despair about the time they eat up each day.

In the same vein, a multicultural approach to education should be blended into the traditional curriculum for two overriding reasons. First, there is a need to rewrite history to reflect the fuller story of the experiences of women and people of color. Second, when that is done, all students will benefit by gaining a sense of their place in the history of this country, a sense of belonging, and a sense of pride and self-esteem. Critics are correct when they worry that multicultural or Afrocentric curricula that exclude large portions of history are repeating the mistakes of the antiquated Eurocentric course structure. The need is for balance and depth.

Equality of opportunity starts well before a child enters kindergarten. How can children whose homes do not contain a single book and whose parents place no value on education ever catch up to those children whose families nourish their minds? Teachers whose students come largely from disadvantaged families worry that these youngsters are lost before they leave elementary school, left so far behind that school becomes a bitter, failure-ridden experience.

Early childhood programs, such as the highly successful Head Start, must be guaranteed for all children. Society cannot force parents to prepare their children to learn, but it is incumbent on society to offer this opportunity to all its children. In families earning at least thirty-five thousand dollars a year, two of every three four-year-olds are in some type of preschool program. In families where the income level is less than ten thousand dollars a year, only one in three four-year-olds is enrolled in such a program. As a result, children from poorer families enter kindergarten at a disadvantage. The federally funded Head Start program and similar state programs in early childhood education can reduce the gap, but their low funding levels allow them to serve only a fraction of the eligible children.

It is a simple equation: Pay now, or pay later. Children from poor families often start school ill prepared, and they are far more likely to fail. Poor teens are more than three times as likely as nonpoor teens to drop out of school, resulting in fewer job opportunities and a lower standard of living. The solution to the low achievement levels of many poor students lies not in abolishing a ninth-grade honors program but in expanding the programs, especially early childhood educational programs, that promote educational equality.

Once students get to school, they deserve a safe, clean environment in which to learn. If students are to learn to value education and to respect the society they are preparing to enter, they have a right to know that society values them enough to provide a clean, decent place for their education. This is a particularly pressing problem in the poorest inner-city school districts, where a clean, safe school, such as Moton Elementary in New Orleans or the Ninety-ninth Street Accelerated School in Los Angeles, offers an oasis for an entire community.

Teachers, too, deserve nothing less than the freedom to pursue their difficult jobs free of fear and violence. With three million crimes a year committed on school grounds, the need for safer schools is no longer in doubt. The question is how to make schools more secure.

First, public school teachers must have the ability to discipline disruptive students. It is the most effective means of preventing violence, and it is essential to fostering a learning environment. Here the lesson can come from private schools, where teachers and administrators can expel unruly students. Public school teachers, who usually face far worse disciplinary problems, should have access to the same solution as a last resort. Short of that drastic step, numerous schools have adopted workable systems of in-house suspension and after-school detention. Unfortunately, many districts have stripped teachers of these tools, often in response to demands from parents who don't want to be inconvenienced by picking up a child kept after school or taking time off from work for a school conference.

Second, other steps can help reduce discipline problems and prevent violence. Problem-solving should involve students, teachers, and administrators whenever possible. It promotes respect and a sense of ownership. Codes of conduct, discipline procedures, and student responsibilities should be written, so everyone knows what is expected. Teachers should receive training for dealing with discipline problems and averting violence.

Finally, with a system of preventive measures in place, a policy of "zero tolerance" must be adopted by teachers and supported by administrators. Teachers deserve to know which of their students has a serious criminal or mental-health record that could pose a threat to themselves and others in the class. There must be alternative schools to handle violence-prone, severely disruptive students. In addition, teachers deserve fast backup support in the event of an emergency and the type of victim-support services provided in places such as New York City. Counseling must be available in schools to support teachers and help them deal with the special needs of their students.

Teachers' unions serve an essential function in maintaining and improving conditions for their members, and students also benefit from their efforts. However, the unions must acknowledge the necessity of getting rid of bad teachers. The overall assessment of their colleagues by teachers interviewed for this book was alarming: As many as a third of today's teachers are viewed as unqualified by their peers. Yet removing ineffective teachers is far too difficult.

It is one of the most contentious issues in education today. There have always been bad teachers, just as there are bad lawyers, accountants, mechanics, and doctors. No longer, however, can society afford to have teachers who don't care about teaching, who have lost the ability to help a child learn. The stakes are too high.

Programs must be instituted to provide additional training for weak teachers. Teachers, like their students, sometimes need remedial help. Some schools have adopted mentor programs in which teachers who are recognized for their outstanding ability help new teachers and those who are struggling in the classroom. It is a cost-effective program; mentor teachers receive a small stipend, which also serves as a reward for their excellence. Weak teachers who refuse to participate in training exercises or who do not improve after receiving help should be replaced.

The nation's schools need bold efforts to revitalize and reform the education of our children. There is no more pressing national priority.

Marian Wright Edelman, founder of the Children's Defense Fund, has written about consequences for a society that does not recognize the importance of its children. "The greatest threat to our national security and future comes from no external enemy but from the enemy within — in our loss of strong, moral, family, and community values and support," writes Edelman.

If the United States is to rebuild its economic strength, the new foundation will be a strengthened education system. If the gulf between rich and poor is to be narrowed and class and racial divisions alleviated, the starting place will be schools that work with teachers and parents to provide equal access to excellence. Our children and our teachers deserve no less.

ACKNOWLEDGMENTS

We would like to thank the more than 150 teachers whose generosity, intelligence, and spirit made this book possible; Dominick Abel, Ruth Ann Collins, Catherine Crawford, and Fredrica Friedman for invaluable assistance; and, for their time and help in many ways, Paul Cummins, Carolyn Damron, J. R. Damron, Jack Davis, Mimi Davis, Carol Finery, June Feder, Liz Frantz, Jack Gallagher, Patricia Guthrie, Gary Hocevar, Annette Katz, Steve Kuykendall, Lee Liss, Kathy Price, David Reiss, Debbie Berger Reiss, Ronald D. Stephens, Georgine Tomasi, Scott Treibitz, Ruby Wanland, and Patrick Welsh. Also, Alfredo Lujan's powerful story about the influence of his two favorite teachers was first published in *Breadloaf* magazine, and we tracked down Helen Mrosla after reading her marvelous story about Mark Ecklund in *Proteus* magazine.